DATA ANALYTICS 2021

The Tenth International Conference on Data Analytics

October 3 - 7, 2021

Barcelona, Spain

DATA ANALYTICS 2021 Editors

Sandjai Bhulai, Vrije Universiteit Amsterdam, The Netherlands

Ivana Semanjski, Ghent University, Belgium

Les Sztandera, Thomas Jefferson University, USA

Printed from e-media with permission by:

Curran Associates, Inc.
57 Morehouse Lane
Red Hook, NY 12571

Some format issues inherent in the e-media version may also appear in this print version.

Printed with permission by Curran Associates, Inc. (2023)

International Academy, Research, and Industry Association (IARIA)
412 Derby Way
Wilmington, DE 19810

Phone: (408) 893-6407
Fax: (408) 527-6351

petre@iaria.org

Additional copies of this publication are available from:

Curran Associates, Inc.
57 Morehouse Lane
Red Hook, NY 12571 USA
Phone: 845-758-0400
Fax: 845-758-2633
Email: curran@proceedings.com
Web: www.proceedings.com

Table of Contents

DATA ANALYTICS 2021

Forward

The Tenth International Conference on Data Analytics (DATA ANALYTICS 2021) continued a series of events on fundamentals in supporting data analytics, special mechanisms and features of applying principles of data analytics, application-oriented analytics, and target-area analytics.

Processing of terabytes to petabytes of data or incorporating non-structural data and multi-structured data sources and types require advanced analytics and data science mechanisms for both raw and partially processed information. Despite considerable advancements on high performance, large storage, and high computation power, there are challenges in identifying, clustering, classifying, and interpreting of a large spectrum of information.

We take here the opportunity to warmly thank all the members of the DATA ANALYTICS 2021 technical program committee, as well as all the reviewers. The creation of such a high-quality conference program would not have been possible without their involvement. We also kindly thank all the authors who dedicated much of their time and effort to contribute to DATA ANALYTICS 2021. We truly believe that, thanks to all these efforts, the final conference program consisted of top-quality contributions. We also thank the members of the DATA ANALYTICS 2021 organizing committee for their help in handling the logistics of this event.

DATA ANALYTICS 2021 Chairs

DATA ANALYTICS 2021 Steering Committee
Wolfram Wöß, Institute for Application Oriented Knowledge Processing | Johannes Kepler University, Linz, Austria
Kerstin Lemke-Rust, Hochschule Bonn-Rhein-Sieg, Germany
George Tambouratzis, Institute for Language and Speech Processing, Athena R.C., Greece
Les Sztandera, Thomas Jefferson University, USA
Ivana Semanjski, Ghent University, Belgium
Sandjai Bhulai, Vrije Universiteit Amsterdam, The Netherlands

DATA ANALYTICS 2021 Publicity Chairs
Lorena Parra, Universitat Politecnica de Valencia, Spain
José Miguel Jiménez, Universitat Politecnica de Valencia, Spain

DATA ANALYTICS 2021
Committee

DATA ANALYTICS 2021 Steering Committee

Wolfram Wöß, Institute for Application Oriented Knowledge Processing | Johannes Kepler University, Linz, Austria
Kerstin Lemke-Rust, Hochschule Bonn-Rhein-Sieg, Germany
George Tambouratzis, Institute for Language and Speech Processing, Athena R.C., Greece
Les Sztandera, Thomas Jefferson University, USA
Ivana Semanjski, Ghent University, Belgium
Sandjai Bhulai, Vrije Universiteit Amsterdam, The Netherlands

DATA ANALYTICS 2021 Publicity Chairs

Lorena Parra, Universitat Politecnica de Valencia, Spain
José Miguel Jiménez, Universitat Politecnica de Valencia, Spain

DATA ANALYTICS 2021 Technical Program Committee

Arianna Agosto, University of Pavia, Italy
Madyan Alsenwi, Kyung Hee University, Global Campus, South Korea
Najet Arous, University of Tunis Manar, Tunisia
Abderazek Ben Abdallah, The University of Aizu, Japan
Rudolf Berrendorf, Bonn-Rhein-Sieg University, Germany
Flavio Bertini, University of Bologna, Italy
Nik Bessis, Edge Hill University, UK
Sandjai Bhulai, Vrije Universiteit Amsterdam, Netherlands
Jean-Yves Blaise, UMR CNRS/MC 3495 MAP, Marseille, France
Jan Bohacik, University of Zilina, Slovakia
Ozgu Can, Ege University, Turkey
Julio Cesar Duarte, Instituto Militar de Engenharia, Rio de Janeiro, Brazil
Richard Chbeir, Université de Pau et des Pays de l'Adour (UPPA), France
Daniel B.-W. Chen, Monash University, Australia
Giovanni Costa, ICAR-CNR, Italy
Mirela Danubianu, University "Stefan cel Mare" Suceava, Romania
Monica De Martino, National Research Council - Institute for Applied Mathematics and Information Technologies (CNR-IMATI), Italy
Corné de Ruijt, Vrije Universiteit Amsterdam, Netherlands
Konstantinos Demertzis, Democritus University of Thrace, Greece
Paolino Di Felice, University of L'Aquila, Italy
Marianna Di Gregorio, University of Salerno, Italy
Ivanna Dronyuk, Lviv Polytechnic National University, Ukraine
Magdalini Eirinaki, San Jose State University, USA
Nadia Essoussi, University of Tunis - LARODEC Laboratory, Tunisia
Panorea Gaitanou, Greek Ministry of Justice, Athens, Greece
Raji Ghawi, Technical University of Munich, Germany
Boris Goldengorin, Moscow Institute of Physics and Technology, Russia
Ana González-Marcos, Universidad de La Rioja, Spain
Geraldine Gray, Technological University Dublin, Ireland

Luca Grilli, Università degli Studi di Foggia, Italy
Riccardo Guidotti, ISTI - CNR, Italy
Samuel Gustavo Huamán Bustamante, Instituto Nacional de Investigación y Capacitación en Telecomunicaciones – Universidad Nacional de Ingenieria (INICTEL-UNI), Peru
Tiziana Guzzo, National Research Council/Institute for Research on Population and Social Policies, Rome, Italy
Rihan Hai. Delft University of Technology, Netherlands
Jeff Hajewski, University of Iowa, USA
Qiwei Han, Nova SBE, Portugal
Felix Heine, Hochschule Hannover, Germany
Mohd Helmy Abd Wahab, Universiti Tun Hussein Onn Malaysia, Malaysia
Jean Hennebert, iCoSys Institute | University of Applied Sciences HES-SO, Fribourg, Switzerland
Béat Hirsbrunner, University of Fribourg, Switzerland
Tzung-Pei Hong, National University of Kaohsiung, Taiwan
LiGuo Huang, Southern Methodist University, USA
Sergio Ilarri, University of Zaragoza, Spain
Jam Jahanzeb Khan Behan, Université Libre de Bruxelles (ULB), Belgium / Universidad Politécnica de Cataluña (UPC), Spain
Mahdi Jammal, The International University of Beirut BIU, Lebanon
Zahra Jandaghi, University of Georgia, USA
Wolfgang Jentner, University of Konstanz, Germany
Md Johirul Islam, Iowa State University, USA
Ashutosh Karna, HP Inc. / Universitat Politecnica de Catalunya, Barcelona, Spain
Alina Lazar, Youngstown State University, USA
Kerstin Lemke-Rust, Hochschule Bonn-Rhein-Sieg, Germany
Yuening Li, Texas A&M University, USA
Ninghao Liu, Texas A&M University, USA
Weimo Liu, Google, USA
Fenglong Ma, Pennsylvania State University, USA
Mamoun Mardini, College of Medicine | University of Florida, USA
Miguel A. Martínez-Prieto, University of Valladolid, Spain
Archil Maysuradze, Lomonosov Moscow State University, Russia
Gideon Mbiydzenyuy, Borås University, Sweden
Letizia Milli, University of Pisa, Italy
Yasser Mohammad, NEC | AIST | RIKEN, Japan / Assiut University, Egypt
Thomas Morgenstern, University of Applied Sciences in Karlsruhe (H-KA), Germany
Lorenzo Musarella,University Mediterranea of Reggio Calabria, Italy
Azad Naik, Microsoft, USA
Roberto Nardone, University Mediterranea of Reggio Calabria, Italy
Alberto Nogales, Universidad Francisco de Victoria | CEIEC research center, Spain
Panagiotis Oikonomou, University of Thessaly, Greece
Ana Oliveira Alves, Polytechnic Institute of Coimbra & Centre of Informatics and Systems of the University of Coimbra, Portugal
Riccardo Ortale, Institute for High Performance Computing and Networking (ICAR) - National Research Council of Italy (CNR), Italy
Moein Owhadi-Kareshk, University of Alberta, Canada
Massimiliano Petri, University of Pisa, Italy
Hai Phan, New Jersey Institute of Technology, USA

Gianvito Pio, University of Bari Aldo Moro, Italy
Antonio Pratelli, University of Pisa, Italy
Michela Quadrini, University of Camerino, Italy
Christoph Raab, FHWS - University of Applied Science Würzburg-Schweinfurt, Germany
Andrew Rau-Chaplin, Dalhousie University, Canada
Ivan Rodero, Rutgers University, USA
Sebastian Rojas Gonzalez, Hasselt University / Ghent University, Belgium
Antonia Russo,University Mediterranea of Reggio Calabria, Italy
Gunter Saake, Otto-von-Guericke University, Germany
Bilal Abu Salih, Curtin University, Australia
Burcu Sayin, University of Trento, Italy
Andreas Schmidt, Karlsruher Institut für Technologie (KIT), Germany
Ivana Semanjski, Ghent University, Belgium
Patrick Siarry, Université Paris-Est Créteil, France
Angelo Sifaleras, University of Macedonia, Greece
Josep Silva Galiana, Universitat Politècnica de València, Spain
Malika Smaïl-Tabbone, LORIA | Université de Lorraine, France
Christos Spandonidis, Prisma Electronics R&D, Greece
Les Sztandera, Thomas Jefferson University, USA
George Tambouratzis, Institute for Language and Speech Processing, Athena R.C., Greece
Tatiana Tambouratzis, University of Piraeus, Greece
Ioannis G. Tollis, University of Crete, Greece / Tom Sawyer Software Inc., USA
Juan-Manuel Torres, LIA/UAPV, France
Chrisa Tsinaraki, EU Joint Research Center - Ispra, Italy
Torsten Ullrich, Fraunhofer Austria Research GmbH, Graz, Austria
Inneke Van Nieuwenhuyse, Universiteit Hasselt, Belgium
Ravi Vatrapu, Ted Rogers School of Management, Ryerson University, Denmark
T. Velmurugan, D.G.Vaishnav College, India
Juan Vicente Capella Hernández, Universitat Politècnica de València, Spain
Sirje Virkus, Tallinn University, Estonia
Marco Viviani, University of Milano-Bicocca, Italy
Maria Vlasiou, University of Twente / Eindhoven University of Technology, Netherlands
Zbigniew W. Ras, University of North Carolina, Charlotte, USA / Warsaw University of Technology, Poland / Polish-Japanese Academy of IT, Poland
Pengyue Wang, University of Minnesota - Twin Cities, USA
Shaohua Wang, New Jersey Institute of Technology, USA
Wolfram Wöß, Institute for Application Oriented Knowledge Processing | Johannes Kepler University, Linz, Austria
Shibo Yao, New Jersey Institute of Technology, USA
Ming Zeng, Facebook, USA
Xiang Zhang, University of New South Wales, Australia
Yichuan Zhao, Georgia State University, USA
Qiang Zhu, University of Michigan - Dearborn, USA
Marc Zöller, USU Software AG / University of Stuttgart, Germany

Copyright Information

A Comparison of Machine-Learned Survival Models for Predicting Tenure from Unstructured Résumés

Corné de Ruijt
Faculty of Science
Vrije Universiteit Amsterdam
Amsterdam, the Netherlands
Email: c.a.m.de.ruijt@vu.nl

Vladimer Kobayashi
Faculty of Economics and Business
University of Amsterdam
Amsterdam, the Netherlands
Email: v.kobayashi@uva.nl

Sandjai Bhulai
Faculty of Science
Vrije Universiteit Amsterdam
Amsterdam, the Netherlands
Email: s.bhulai@vu.nl

***Abstract*—This paper explores to what extent job seekers' future job tenures can be predicted using only the information contained in their own résumés. Here, job tenure is interpreted as the time spent in a single job occupation. To do so, we compare the performance of several machine-learned survival models in terms of multiple error measures, including the Brier score and the C-index. The results suggest that ensemble methods, such as random survival forest and Cox boosting, work well for this purpose. We further find that in particular time-related features, such as the time a person has already worked in a particular field, are predictive when predicting the person's future tenure. However, the results also show that this prediction task is difficult. There is substantial subjectivity in both how job seekers define their jobs, and at what level of granularity they indicate their job tenures. As a result, the best performing models (survival ensemble methods) only perform marginally better than the used benchmark (a Kaplan-Meier estimate).**

Keywords*—*Human resource management; turnover prediction; résumé mining; machine-learned survival models; job churn.

I. INTRODUCTION

Given the high Internet penetration of job seekers, one could expect it to become easier for recruiters to find and select potential candidates. The reality, however, sometimes turns out to be different. Early studies on online recruitment (also known as e-recruitment) reported profitable benefits for recruiters, including an increased speed of hiring, or an improved quality applicants. However, they also reported the problem of having to sift through a (sometimes) overwhelming number of candidates [1].

Many of the methods proposed in the literature that assist in matching job seekers and vacancies online, use the semantic overlap between the résumé and the vacancy as a proxy for the quality of this match [2]. This, however, neglects other types of information contained in résumés that could provide information about the quality of the match. In this paper, we will instead use the temporal data often contained in résumés. Most job seekers indicate their job history in their résumé, in which their previous occupations are listed, along with a start and end date for each job. Our aim is to predict job tenures, defined as the time difference between these start and end dates, using other data that is contained in the résumé. This data includes features such as the type of job, education history, and the number of years of experience.

Predicting future job tenure from résumés is not a new problem. In fact, it has been the subject of many studies in personnel psychology in the last few decades [3, Ch. 12]. The problem we consider, however, differs from these studies in two ways: 1) we automatize the processes of extracting features from the résumé, both using a pre-trained résumé parser, and by using word2vec. 2) We focus on methods that emphasize on making accurate predictions, mostly by incorporating a large number of second or larger order interaction terms, rather than models that emphasize on explanations.

This paper has the following structure. Section II discusses related work. Sections III-A and III-B discuss properties of the résumé dataset, with a focus on properties of such unstructured datasets that may lead to biased results, and it considers how to avoid such bias. Section III-C introduces the survival models used in this study, and discusses how to measure the error of these models. Section IV presents the outcomes of the survival model comparison from different perspectives. Section V draws a final conclusion and provides directions for further research.

II. RELATED WORK

With the digitization of résumés, the automatic extraction of features from (manually written) résumés has become more common practice (e.g., [4], [5]). Apart from its application in job or candidate search engines, such features can also be used in job or candidate recommender systems. In both applications, the semantic overlap between the résumé and vacancy is often used as a proxy to evaluate how well the job seeker and vacancy match [2]. We will refer to the problem of matching job seekers and vacancies as *job seeker - vacancy matching*. Hence, since most literature considers the problem from a semantic perspective, we deliberately focused on non-semantic methods. In particular, we consider the potential of predicting how long someone will stay in a new job position, given that the candidate would be hired for the position, as a measure for the quality of the match.

Few studies consider the sequential and time-based elements in a résumé, which in particular present themselves in the job history section. In résumés, it is common to write down one's previous jobs in chronological order, and indicate the start and end date of each job. This information could be used to infer a job seeker's most likely next job, given a sequence of previous jobs. Such perspective to job seeker - vacancy matching has been considered by various contributions in the literature [6]–[9]. Li et al. [9] compared several sequential models for this task, where in particular a Long Short-Term Memory (LSTM) recurrent neural network worked well, especially when additional contextual data was included in the model.

From the start and end dates, one could also infer how long job seekers will be likely to remain in their jobs. For this problem, survival analysis has been a frequently used method in personnel psychology, in particular in the form of Cox regression [10]. Survival models often allow for censored data, making these models attractive for studying turnover. I.e., job seekers included in a study might still be "alive", or in other words still occupying the job under study, at the end of the study. Even though there has been a substantial increase in the number of studies applying machine learning methods for predicting employee turnover, only a few consider combining machine learning methods with survival analysis [11].

Wang et al. [12] propose a survival model that is fitted using a Bayesian model. The Bayesian model was chosen to cope with the high dispersion in the number of observations for a job transition from some job a to job b. I.e., most transitions have little to no observations, whereas some self-transitions may be very frequent. The authors show that if one is indifferent about to which job the job seeker switches, and only considers how long the job was occupied, the Bayesian model outperforms a model ignoring covariates in terms of perplexity. Though, this difference between the with/without covariates models evaporated when considering more passive job seekers.

Li et al. [8] discretize time and predict a value proportional to the survival function using a squared loss function. As the predicted values are only proportional to the probability of remaining in a job, the study considers the correct order of turnover events, rather than predicting tenure. The method outperformed typical parametric or semi-parametric survival methods such as a Cox regression or the log-logistic model.

III. Methods

A. Feature extraction from résumés

The data used in this study was extracted from résumés, which were uploaded to the Dutch job board Gus [13] between 2005-01-01 and 2016-10-17. The jobs to which these applicants applied were temporary jobs. In total, the dataset contains 50,000 unique job seekers, which we split into a training, validation and test set according to a 70/10/20 split. I.e., all jobs from one job seeker are either completely in the training, test, or validation set.

In total, the dataset encompasses 131,059 unique jobs. Note that the start and end dates of these jobs may be outside of the 2005-2016 range. E.g., if the job seeker applied in 2005, he/she will be likely to have jobs in his/her resume before 2005. To avoid data dredging, all statistics presented in this section are based on the training set.

Since the résumés are plain text documents, we used technology from Textkernel [14] to extract information from the text. Here, we make use of a common convention in résumés to include job history in a table, where each record includes a (textual) description of the job, and the start and end date of the job. From this data, we extracted the variables *transition lustrum* (the year in which job seeker j started job h, grouped into clusters of 5 years), *order* (the number of previous jobs job seeker j had occupied just after starting job h), and *expdays* (the total observed work experience of candidate j, just before the start of job h, in days).

We also extracted the *edu_lvl* (the candidate's highest education level, mapped to the Dutch education system), *age* (candidate's age at the start of the job), *gender*, and the *job description* given by the candidate. The job description was mapped to a vector space in two ways. The first approach used a classification model from Textkernel, which maps the job to a three-layer hierarchical classification (of which the upper two were used as covariates) and classifies the *industry* of the job.

We also trained a *word2vec* model on the candidates' previous job description. Before training the *word2vec* model, we removed (Dutch) stop words and stemmed the words using the *Snowball* stemmer [15]. We used a vocabulary of 20,000 unique words having the largest *tf-idf* values. We used negative sampling with a sampling factor of 10^{-5}, from which word pairs were constructed using skip grams with a window size of 3, as larger window sizes did not improve the results.

The *word2vec* model was trained using Keras with a Tensorflow backend [16], [17]. We used an embedding size of 64; 100 training epochs; a batch size of 65,536; an initial learning rate of 0.1; and we used *rmsprop* [18] to update the learning rate in subsequent epochs. To obtain document vectors from word vectors, we computed a weighted average over the word vectors for each job description. As weights we used the *tf-idf* value of each word. We did experiment with different epochs, batch sizes, and initial learning rates; these did not improve the results.

B. Computing tenure from parsed résumé data

From analyzing the job seekers' start and end dates, one can readily observe that job seekers tend to indicate the start and end date of each job at different levels of granularity. Some indicate the start and end dates on a monthly level, whereas the majority indicate these dates on a yearly level. In case candidates indicate their start and end dates on a yearly level, we considered this a case of interval-censored data. Besides the interval censoring, the start and end dates also may incorporate other types of censoring.

The survival models we will introduce in Section III-C only cope with right censoring. Hence, to cope with other types of censoring in the tenures, the following procedure was applied.

All observations with *Complete* (no start and end date; 1.62%) and *Left FJ* (no start date, and the job is the First Job of the candidate; 0.03%) censoring were removed. The former were removed because they are non-informative. The latter were removed because these only encompass a small number of jobs. *Year interval* (44.18%) indicates jobs with rounded start and/or end dates to entire years. If this was the case, a random number of months were added (subtracted) to the start (end) date, following the monthly turnover distribution. Since the observed turnover in the months January and December was inflated, due to the interval censoring, we did not use the observed turnover frequencies in these months to estimate the monthly turnover distribution. Instead, we estimated the turnover probability in these months by interpolation, using a cubic spline over the remaining months.

Right censoring, Not Last Job (*Right NLJ*; 10.3%), and Right censoring Last Job (*Right LJ*; 5.87%) indicate cases of right censoring. In case of *Right NLJ*, the start date of the next job was taken as end date of the job. In case this start date was again year interval-censored, the job was relabeled as year interval-censored and processed accordingly. *Right LJ* were treated as normal cases of right censoring, using the date of application as the date of censoring. 38% of all jobs did not have any type of censoring, hence remained in the dataset as-is. Although theoretically other types of censoring could have occurred (e.g., *Left NFJ*), these did not occur in the dataset.

Besides removing and correcting censored data, we also removed observations having occupations with tenures lasting longer than 50 years, occupations that started before the candidate's 18th birthday, occupations that started after the candidate's 67th birthday, and observations with negative tenures. To reduce the number of unique values for categorical attributes, we reassigned categorical values with fewer than 30 observations to a category "other". Missing data was imputed using adoptive tree imputation, as described by Ishwaran et al. [19], and which is implemented in the `RandomForestSRC` R package [20]. To fit this random forest model, the package's default parameters were used.

C. Survival estimation methods

1) Notation: Before discussing the survival models, we require some notation. Let T_i be the observed job tenure of job $i = 1, \ldots, I$, which is computed following the procedure described in Section III-B. Although we corrected for different types of censoring, T_i may still be right-censored. Whether this is the case, is indicated by δ_i (1 if not censored, 0 otherwise).

Furthermore, let $\tilde{T}_i$ be the full job tenure. That is, the job tenure we would have observed if no censoring had occurred. We are interested in estimating the survival function $S_i(t) = \mathbb{P}(\tilde{T}_i > t|\mathbf{x}_i)$. Here, $\mathbf{x}_i \in \mathbb{R}^P$ is some covariate vector. We assume independence between $\tilde{T}_i$ and $\tilde{T}_j$, given covariate vectors $\mathbf{x}_i$ and $\mathbf{x}_j$. I.e., $\mathbb{P}(\tilde{T}_i, \tilde{T}_j|\mathbf{x}_i, \mathbf{x}_j) = \mathbb{P}(\tilde{T}_i|\mathbf{x}_i)\mathbb{P}(\tilde{T}_j|\mathbf{x}_j)$, for all pairs (i, j): $i \neq j$. Furthermore, we assume $\tilde{T}_i$ to be independent of the censoring time. Note that, due to right censoring, $\tilde{T}_i$ may not be completely observed. Hence, survival estimation methods use the (possibly right-censored) job tenure T_i, and censoring indicator δ_i, to estimate the uncensored survival distribution.

To estimate the survival function, we will frequently use the cumulative hazard function $\Lambda_i(t) = \int_{\tau=0}^{t} \lambda_i(\tau)d\tau$ with $\lambda_i(t) = \lim_{\Delta t \to 0} \mathbb{P}(t \leq \tilde{T}_i \leq t + \Delta t|\tilde{T}_i > t, \mathbf{x}_i)$ being the hazard rate. From the cumulative hazard rate, the survival function can directly be derived [21, p. 16].

Some of the models that we consider assume discrete time. To discretize time, we bin time intervals into bins $r = 1, \ldots, R$, each having equal length ρ. Since the number of jobs having tenures longer than 5 years was sparse, we took $R = 5$. The time interval of period r is denoted by $u_r = [(1 - r)\rho, r\rho)$. To balance between sparsity within the bins (which happens for small ρ), and the precision of the estimate, we selected $\rho = 3$ months.

2) Benchmark models: All machine-learned survival models presented in this paper were benchmarked against three benchmark methods: 1) a Kaplan-Meier (*KM*) estimate [21, Ch. 4], 2) a Cox proportional hazard model with an elastic net penalty [22] (we named this *Cox Lasso*, since using a Lasso penalty produced the best results). The baseline hazard was estimated using the Brewlow estimator [23]. 3) A binary survival tree (*Surv. tree*), using the log-rank splitting rule [19].

3) Ensemble survival models: A common approach to improve the quality of predictions from weak learners is by using model ensembles. In this study, we considered two approaches: the Random Survival Forest (*RSF*) introduced by [19], and a Cox boosting approach (*GBM*) [24].

A Random Survival Forest [19] for the most part employs the same procedure as the original random forest algorithm by Breiman [25]. Though, since we wish to predict a survival function, there are two main differences. First, as with the binary survival tree, the log-rank splitting rule is used to recursively branch the observations in the tree. Second, for each leaf node, the cumulative hazard rate is estimated using the Nelson-Aalen estimator, based on the observations in the leaf node. An estimate of the cumulative hazard rate for some time t and covariate vector $\mathbf{x}$ is then obtained by computing the unweighted average over all cumulative hazard rates at time t, for leaf nodes subject to $\mathbf{x}$.

To employ boosting, we used the boosting procedure by Friedman [26]. As the method employs Cox's partial likelihood, the method does not provide an estimate of the baseline hazard. To find the baseline hazard, the same procedure as for the Cox model was applied. That is, we use the Breslow estimator to estimate the baseline hazard, though we now used the output from the boosting model instead of the linear link function.

4) Neural survival models:

a) Feedforward neural survival models: To model neural survival models, we used a similar approach as Gensheimer & Narasimhan [27]. This study models the neural survival model as a feedforward neural network, only adjusting the output layer to produce a survival curve. To rewrite the problem, let $\gamma_{i,r} = 1$ if $T_i \in u_r, \delta_i = 1$ (zero otherwise), and $v_{i,r} = 1$ if $T_i < (r - 1)\rho$ (zero otherwise). The output layer of the neural network is modeled in two ways. In the flexible variant (*NN-Flex*), a simple feedforward neural network is used with one or multiple hidden layers, applying a sigmoid activation to each output $r \in \{1, \dots, R\}$ to end up with estimates of the hazard rate.

The proportional hazard (*NN-PH*) variant uses the proportional hazard assumption. I.e., it assumes the hazard rate has the form $\lambda_i(t) = \lambda_0(t)\exp(\mathbf{x}_i^T\boldsymbol{\beta})$, $\boldsymbol{\beta} \in \mathbb{R}^P$ being a weight vector. Following [21, p. 43], when assuming intrinsically discrete time, the (now also discrete) estimated hazard rate $\hat{\lambda}_i(r)$ can be written as

$$\hat{\lambda}_i(r) = \frac{1}{1 + \exp(\alpha_i(r) + z_i)}, \tag{1}$$

with z_i and $\alpha(r)$ being outputs of different feedforward neural networks. Here, $\alpha_i(r)$ has as input the covariate vector $\mathbf{x}_i$, followed by one or multiple hidden layers. The variable z_i is obtained by a weighted average over the elements in the last hidden layer. Note that (1) is a sigmoid activation function, which simplifies the implementation in, for example, Keras.

For both the NN-PH and NN-Flex approach, we find a loss function in the form of the binary cross-entropy

$$\mathcal{L} = \sum_{i=1}^{I}\sum_{r=1}^{R}[\gamma_{i,r}\log(\hat{\lambda}_i(r)) + (1-\gamma_{i,r})\log(1-\hat{\lambda}_i(r)v_{i,r})]. \tag{2}$$

Note that when $r\rho > T_i$ and $\delta_i = 0$, we have $y_{i,r} = 0$ and $\hat{\lambda}_i(r) = 0$. Therefore, these predictions do not contribute to the log-likelihood.

b) Recurrent neural networks: In addition to the two feedforward models, we also considered recurrent neural networks. Here, each output corresponds with one of the time periods $r = 1, \dots, R$. We considered a standard recurrent neural network with either a Gated Recurrent Unit (*NN-GRU*) [28] or a Long Short-Term Memory (*NN-LSTM*) unit [29]. As we do not include time-varying covariates, only at $r = 1$ an input vector is inserted, whereas at the other time periods a vector containing only zeros is fed to the network. Also here we multiply (element-wise) the output vector $(\hat{\lambda}_i(1), \dots, \hat{\lambda}_i(R))$ by the censoring vector $(v_{i,1}, \dots, v_{i,R})$ to exclude observations after censoring.

D. Model evaluation

To evaluate the survival models, we used the Brier score to assess the accuracy of the survival curve [30], and the C-index [31] to assess the accuracy in correctly predicting the order of turnover. Since the number of observations at some time points was quite sparse, we decided not to use IPCW weights [32].

Since the C-index assesses the correct order of job churn at the start of both jobs, and it considers any job pair, even those unrelated, we also considered a somewhat altered C-index. This altered C-index, which we will refer to as the Integrated Conditional Concordance Index (ICCI), has two adjustments compared to the C-index. First, instead of assessing the correct order of survival estimates at some time t, it assesses the correct order of the expected remaining survival times, conditioned on survival up until times t_i, t_j for jobs i and j respectively. Second, we only sample over pairs in the same (*function_group, transitionlustrum*) bin. Since the number of observations in each bin differs, we use three types of sampling: 1) stratified sampling, 2) sampling the same number of observations from each bin, 3) sampling random pairs, ignoring the bins. As the name ICCI suggest, we integrate the conditional concordance indices over time.

TABLE I. HYPERPARAMETER GRID SEARCH

Model	Hyperparameters	Best param.
Cox-PH with elasticnet penalty	$\alpha \in \{0$ (Ridge), $0.5, 1$ (Lasso)$\}$ penalty weight as in [33]	$\alpha^* = 1$ (Lasso), penalty$^* = 0.0107$
Survival tree	term. node size $= 6$	NA
Random survival forest	trees $\in \{100, 500, 1000\}$, term. node size $= 6$, depth $\in \{6, 12\}$, random split points $= 5$, tree feature sample size $= \sqrt{P}$	trees$^* = 500$, depth$^* = 12$
Cox boosting	trees $\in \{1000, 2500, 5000\}$, shrinkage $\in \{0.001, 0.05, 0.01, 0.1\}$ depth $\in \{3, 6\}$	trees$^* = 2,500$, shrinkage$^* = 0.01$ depth$^* = 3$
Neural survival non-sequential	hidden units $\in \{64, 128\}$, hidden layers $= 2$, epochs $= 100$, batch size $= 65,536$, learning rate $\in \{0.001, 0.01, 0.1\}$	hidden units Flex$^* = 128$ hidden units PH$^* = 64$ learning rate Flex$^* = 0.01$ learning rate PH$^* = 0.001$
Neural survival sequential	time periods $= 21$, hidden layers $\in \{1, 4, 16\}$, epochs $= 100$, batch size $= 9,292$, learning rate $\in \{0.001, 0.01, 0.1\}$, drop out $= 0.1$	hidden layers GRU$^* = 16$ hidden layers LSTM$^* = 16$ learning rate GRU$^* = 0.001$ learning rate LSTM$^* = 0.001$

IV. Results

A. Overall performance

Table I gives an overview of the grid search we applied to the validation set to find appropriate values for the models' hyperparameters. The obtained best parameter values are given in the last column of Table I. Our dataset contains some variables that could introduce unwanted discrimination in terms of *gender* and *age*. Instead of removing these attributes upfront, we included them while training the model, but imputed them by their overall average value (in case of categorical values, we imputed after dummification) during validation. However, it should be noted that this procedure was only partially effective, due to the many missing values for both *year_of_birthlustrum* and *gender*.

Figure 1 shows the resulting Brier and C-index on the test set, whereas Table II shows the integrated and normalized scores. Since the Kaplan-Meier estimate is the model with the least complexity (i.e., it does not take into account any covariates), the results of the KM model are emphasized in Figure 1. Gradient boosted trees and a random survival forest produce the best results, with a slight preference for GBM. Interestingly, the neural models and the Cox model barely outperform the Kaplan-Meier estimate both in terms of the Brier score and C-index. The single survival tree shows a trade-off between the Brier score and C-index. For $t < 3$ it shows reasonable performance in terms of the C-index, but the results are poor in terms of the Brier score.

The good performance of random survival forest and GBM seems to diminish when we include conditional survival times, as shown in Table II. Although in absolute terms the ICCI for

GBM and random survival forest are somewhat comparable to their C-index, the values are also closer to the results of a KM-estimator. Furthermore, taking different kinds of samples only had a marginal impact on the ICCI. Hence, when predicting the correct order, the advantage of using more complex models seems to diminish.

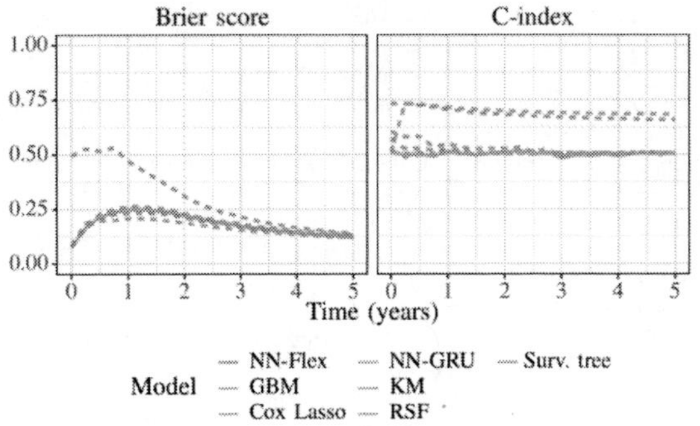

Figure 1. Brier score and C-index over time.

TABLE II. INTEGRATED BRIER SCORE, C-INDEX AND ICCI

Model	Integrated Brier	Integrated C-index	ICCI stratified	ICCI eq. per group	ICCI random
GBM	**0.16**	**0.69**	**0.66**	**0.66**	**0.67**
RSF	0.17	0.68	0.65	0.65	0.66
NN-Flex	0.19	0.51	0.64	0.64	0.63
NN-PH	0.18	0.51	0.64	0.65	0.63
NN-LSTM	0.18	0.51	0.63	0.64	0.64
NN-GRU	0.18	0.50	0.63	0.62	0.63
KM	0.18	0.50	0.64	0.64	0.64
Cox Lasso	0.19	0.50	0.64	0.65	0.63
Surv. tree	0.30	0.53	0.56	0.55	0.54

B. Performance on sub-datasets

Next, we split the results per *function_group* in order to study differences in predictive ability for different job types. As GBM had the best overall score (Table II), we used this model for further inference. The results over the five largest job types in the dataset are shown in Figure 2. As we may have expected from the Brier scores in Figure 1, which are somewhat similar to those of a Kaplan-Meier estimate, the fitted survival curves for the different job types are also rather similar.

We also considered the effect of excluding certain attributes from the model. To do so, we construct four sub-datasets: 1) a dataset in which age and gender were not imputed, 2) a dataset without the *word2vec* word embedding, 3) a dataset in which we exclude attributes derived from the job classifier (i.e., excluding *function_class*, *function_group*, *sector*, *expdaysfunctiongroup*, and *orderperfunctiongroup*), and 4) a dataset including only features related to time-dependent variables (i.e., including *transitionlustrum*, *order*, *expdays*, *month_of_startdate*, *orderperfunctiongroup*, and *expdaysfunctiongroup*). A comparison between the performance of GBM on these datasets and the full dataset is shown in Figure

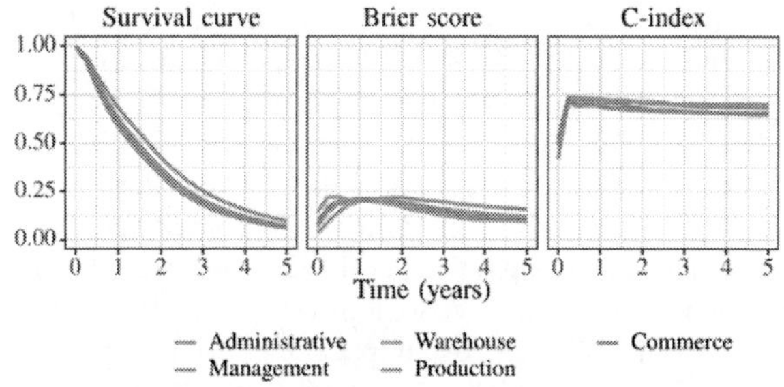

Figure 2. Results over the 5 most common job types.

3. Especially inclusion of the time variables caused a substantial improvement in both the Brier sore and C-index. Inclusion/exclusion of other types of attributes had a negligible effect.

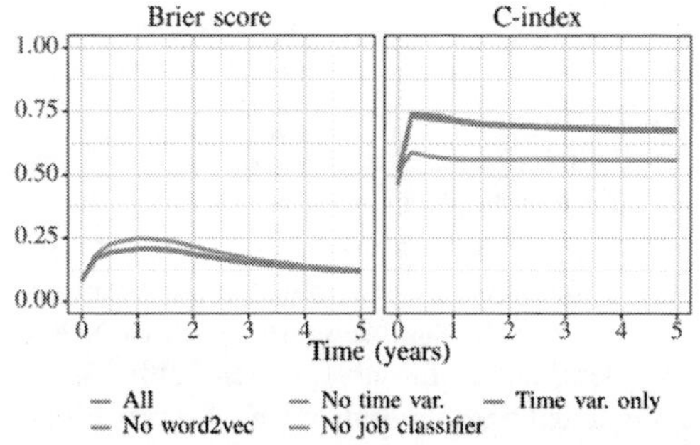

Figure 3. Scores on other datasets.

V. Conclusion and Future Work

From our comparison of machine-learned survival models, we find that especially tree-based ensembles, such as a random survival forest and Gradient Boosting Machines, work well to predict job tenure from unstructured résumés. They outperformed benchmark models in terms of the Brier score and C-index. These benchmarks included a Kaplan-Meier estimator and Cox regression, but also more complex models such as neural survival models and recurrent neural networks. Especially the importance of time-related variables in these models is interesting. Job - vacancy matching is often done using semantic overlap, e.g., comparing skill overlap between the vacancy and job. Our results suggest that including time-related variables in these matching algorithms may improve their performance.

Although tree-based ensembles outperformed benchmark models, still the prediction problem remains difficult. The difference with benchmark models are relatively small, and if one takes into account conditional survival times, and compares more similar job pairs, the error scores between the tree-based ensembles and benchmark models become more similar.

This limited performance may be explained in several ways. First, it should be acknowledged that predicting job tenure from résumés is a difficult prediction problem. Previous work (using mostly Cox-PH models [10]) finds only weak correlations between predictors and tenure, (r^2 between 0.33 and 0.37) [3, p. 261]. Second, as illustrated in this study, résumés come with considerable fuzziness. Turnover itself may be indicated at different levels of granularity. Missing data is a considerable problem, as the résumé parser has to deal with a variety of formats. Also, job seekers may have different definitions of a job. E.g., one might define two positions at the same employer as one job, whereas another will consider these as two jobs. Naturally, such fuzziness complicates interpreting models derived from résumés.

Given these results, we are in particular interested in two directions for further work. Given the fuzziness of résumé data, an interesting direction would be to study whether survival analysis on résumés could benefit from models trained in different contexts, i.e., transfer learning. One could think of applying language models trained on larger corpora. But also training survival models on corporate turnover data, for which we expect to have more precise measurements, would be an interesting direction.

A second direction is with regards to the practical implications of predicting tenure from résumés for candidate recommendation. It would be interesting to consider how these models compare with semantic matching methods, using more application-directed error scores, such as NDCG. From a practical perspective, further research could also consider whether the model benefits from asking the user for additional data when uploading one's résumé.

VI. ACKNOWLEDGEMENTS

We would like to thank Ton Sluiter and USG People for their collaboration and guidance during the course of this work.

REFERENCES

[1] F. Suvankulov, "Job search on the internet, e-recruitment, and labor market outcomes," Ph.D. dissertation, Pardee RAND Graduate School, 2010.

[2] M. N. Freire and L. N. de Castro, "e-recruitment recommender systems: a systematic review," *Knowledge and Information Systems*, pp. 1–20, 2020.

[3] W. F. Cascio, *Applied psychology in human resource management*. Prentice-Hall, 1998.

[4] K. Yu, G. Guan, and M. Zhou, "Resume information extraction with cascaded hybrid model," in *Proceedings of the 43rd Annual Meeting on Association for Computational Linguistics*. Association for Computational Linguistics, 2005, pp. 499–506.

[5] S. K. Kopparapu, "Automatic extraction of usable information from unstructured resumes to aid search," in *2010 IEEE International Conference on Progress in Informatics and Computing*, vol. 1. IEEE, 2010, pp. 99–103.

[6] I. Paparrizos, B. B. Cambazoglu, and A. Gionis, "Machine learned job recommendation," in *Proceedings of the fifth ACM conference on Recommender systems*. ACM, 2011, pp. 325–328.

[7] M. Jiang, Y. Fang, H. Xie, J. Chong, and M. Meng, "User click prediction for personalized job recommendation," *World Wide Web*, vol. 22, no. 1, pp. 325–345, 2019.

[8] H. Li, Y. Ge, H. Zhu, H. Xiong, and H. Zhao, "Prospecting the career development of talents: A survival analysis perspective," in *Proceedings of the 23rd ACM SIGKDD International Conference on Knowledge Discovery and Data Mining*. ACM, 2017, pp. 917–925.

[9] L. Li, H. Jing, H. Tong, J. Yang, Q. He, and B.-C. Chen, "NEMO: Next career move prediction with contextual embedding," in *Proceedings of the 26th International Conference on World Wide Web Companion*. International World Wide Web Conferences Steering Committee, 2017, pp. 505–513.

[10] P. W. Hom, T. W. Lee, J. D. Shaw, and J. P. Hausknecht, "One hundred years of employee turnover theory and research." *Journal of Applied Psychology*, vol. 102, no. 3, pp. 530–545, 2017.

[11] S. Strohmeier and F. Piazza, "Domain driven data mining in human resource management: A review of current research," *Expert Systems with Applications*, vol. 40, no. 7, pp. 2410–2420, 2013.

[12] J. Wang, Y. Zhang, C. Posse, and A. Bhasin, "Is it time for a career switch?" in *Proceedings of the 22nd international conference on World Wide Web*. ACM, 2013, pp. 1377–1388.

[13] Gus, *Website Gus*, 2017, https://www.gus.nl, retrieved: September 2021.

[14] Textkernel, *Website Textkernel*, 2017, https://www.textkernel.com/, retrieved: September 2021.

[15] M. Bouchet-Valat, "Package 'SnowballC'," R package version 0.6.0, https://cran.r-project.org/web/packages/SnowballC/index.html, 2019, retrieved: September 2021.

[16] F. Chollet *et al.*, "Keras," https://github.com/fchollet/keras, 2015, retrieved: September 2021.

[17] M. Abadi *et al.*, "Tensorflow: A system for large-scale machine learning," in *12th USENIX Symposium on Operating Systems Design and Implementation*, 2016, pp. 265–283.

[18] T. Tieleman and G. Hinton, "Divide the gradient by a running average of its recent magnitude," *COURSERA: Neural Networks for Machine Learning*, 2012.

[19] H. Ishwaran, U. B. Kogalur, E. H. Blackstone, and M. S. Lauer, "Random survival forests," *The Annals of Applied Statistics*, pp. 841–860, 2008.

[20] H. Ishwaran and U. B. Kogalur, "Random Forests for Survival, Regression, and Classification (RF-SRC)," 2018, R package version 2.6.0, https://cran.r-project.org/web/packages/randomForestSRC/index.html, retrieved: September 2021.

[21] S. P. Jenkins, *Survival analysis*, 2005, unpublished, https://citeseerx.ist.psu.edu/viewdoc/download?doi=10.1.1.176.7572&rep=rep1&type=pdf, retrieved: September 9, 2021.

[22] J. Friedman, T. Hastie, and R. Tibshirani, "Regularization paths for generalized linear models via coordinate descent," *Journal of Statistical Software*, vol. 39, no. 5, pp. 1–13, 2011.

[23] D. Lin, "On the Breslow estimator," *Lifetime data analysis*, vol. 13, no. 4, pp. 471–480, 2007.

[24] B. Greenwell, B. Boehmke, and J. Cunningham, "Package 'gbm'," 2019, R package version 2.1.5, https://github.com/gbm-developers/gbm, retrieved: September 2021.

[25] L. Breiman, "Random forests," *Machine learning*, vol. 45, no. 1, pp. 5–32, 2001.

[26] J. H. Friedman, "Stochastic gradient boosting," *Computational statistics & data analysis*, vol. 38, no. 4, pp. 367–378, 2002.

[27] M. F. Gensheimer and B. Narasimhan, "A scalable discrete-time survival model for neural networks," *PeerJ*, vol. 7:e6257, 2019.

[28] K. Cho, B. Van Merriënboer, D. Bahdanau, and Y. Bengio, "On the properties of neural machine translation: Encoder-decoder approaches," *arXiv preprint arXiv:1409.1259*, 2014.

[29] S. Hochreiter and J. Schmidhuber, "Long short-term memory," *Neural Computation*, vol. 9, no. 8, pp. 1735–1780, 1997.

[30] U. B. Mogensen, H. Ishwaran, and T. A. Gerds, "Evaluating random forests for survival analysis using prediction error curves," *Journal of Statistical Software*, vol. 50, no. 11, pp. 1–23, 2012.

[31] P. Wang, Y. Li, and C. K. Reddy, "Machine learning for survival analysis: A survey," *arXiv preprint arXiv:1708.04649*, 2017.

[32] M. Wolbers, P. Blanche, M. T. Koller, J. C. Witteman, and T. A. Gerds, "Concordance for prognostic models with competing risks," *Biostatistics*, vol. 15, no. 3, pp. 526–539, 2014.

[33] N. Simon, J. Friedman, T. Hastie, and R. Tibshirani, "Regularization paths for Cox's proportional hazards model via coordinate descent," *Journal of Statistical Software*, vol. 39, no. 5, pp. 1–13, 2011.

Electric Vehicle Charging Locations for Uber in New York City

Victor Salazar Ramos, Andreea Mateescu, Elisabeth Fokker, Jacky P.K. Li, and Sandjai Bhulai

Faculty of Science
Vrije Universiteit Amsterdam
Amsterdam, The Netherlands
Email: vss920@vu.nl, mmu680@vu.nl, efr330@vu.nl, jacky.li@vu.nl, s.bhulai@vu.nl

***Abstract*—Electrification is widely considered an attractive solution for reducing the oil dependency and environmental impact of road transportation. This paper examines the viability of the current charging stations with the assistance of taxi service strategy optimization. We study charging station data along with ride pickup data. Our methodology is to model the pickup location data and the charging station data by K-means clustering and to determine the optimized distance between the pickup locations and the charging stations. Consequently, we shed light on the number of charging stations that can improve the efficiency of using electric taxis.**

***Index Terms*—Electrification; K-means clustering; electric taxis; charging stations.**

I. Introduction

Transportation accounts for nearly 70 percent of U.S. oil consumption and 28 percent of the country's greenhouse gas emissions, according to U.S. Energy Information Administration [1]. This makes it a prime target for technological improvements that can reduce emissions and combat climate change. Electrification of transportation represents one of the highest impact strategies to help achieve that goal. In particular, public vehicles (e.g., taxis) provide a crucial opportunity for electrification. Despite the benefits of eco-friendliness and energy efficiency, the adoption of electric taxis faces several obstacles. This includes constrained driving range, long recharging duration, limited charging stations, and low gas prices, all of which impede taxi drivers' decisions to switch to electric taxis. To contribute to a sustainable future, Uber Technologies Inc. has recently released the 'Uber Green' option, which connects potential customer(s) with electric or hybrid-electric vehicles [2]. However, the 'Uber Green' option can be an alternative to fuel-based driving only in the presence of an optimally distributed web of charging stations.

Previous studies have focused on developing electric taxi strategy optimization compared to conventional taxis with an internal combustion engine. Tseng et al. [3] studied empirically under various battery capacities and charging conditions to conquer the long charging period and optimize the number of taxis needed to satisfy the demands.

Raboaca et al. [4] propose a new operational model for the mobile charging station through temporally stationing it at different places for certain amounts of time. Their model is built by a queuing process. The goal is to place a minimum number of temporary service centers to minimize operating costs. Jung et al. [5] compare the revenue differences between electric and non-electric taxis. The research concentrates on individual versus whole-fleet policies. This concludes the advantage of non-electric taxis over electric taxis due to the long charging periods.

Wang et al. [6] investigate the effectiveness of the charging stations over the taxi demand. Their research contains five years of taxi transaction data, charging station data, and the distance traveled after each charge. This research provides the evolving patterns of electric taxi networks and also charging stations. Wang et al. [7] also research Large-Scale Electric Bus Fleets. Their research invents a real-time charging scheduling system to optimize the charging time and usage for the electric bus fleet.

Scorrano et al. [8] investigate the taxi data of Florence, Italy. The city of Florence and many European cities have lower vehicle tax in order to encourage taxis to switch from a combustion engine to fully electric. Their research evaluates the impact of the annual distance traveled, purchase subsidy, and new revenue loss.

In terms of using K-means clustering research in electric taxi fleeting, Zhang et al. [9] create two stages of charging stations for electric taxis and electric vehicles to solve the long charging period. Dong et al. [10] concentrate on the optimal location model in the service region to calculate the optimal sites of the charging stations to maximize the operational efficiency and charging convenience. Jia et al. [11] investigate the large-scale Cellular Signaling Data and illustrate the method to generate the 24-hour travel demand for each electric vehicle.

This paper examines the viability of the current charging stations with the assistance of taxi service strategy optimization. We investigate the distribution of the charging station data along with the Uber pickup trip data. Our methodology is to model the pickup location data and the charging station data by K-means clustering and to determine the optimized distance between the data. Consequently, we shed light on the number of charging stations that can improve the efficiency of using electric taxis.

The paper is structured as follows. In Section II, we analyze

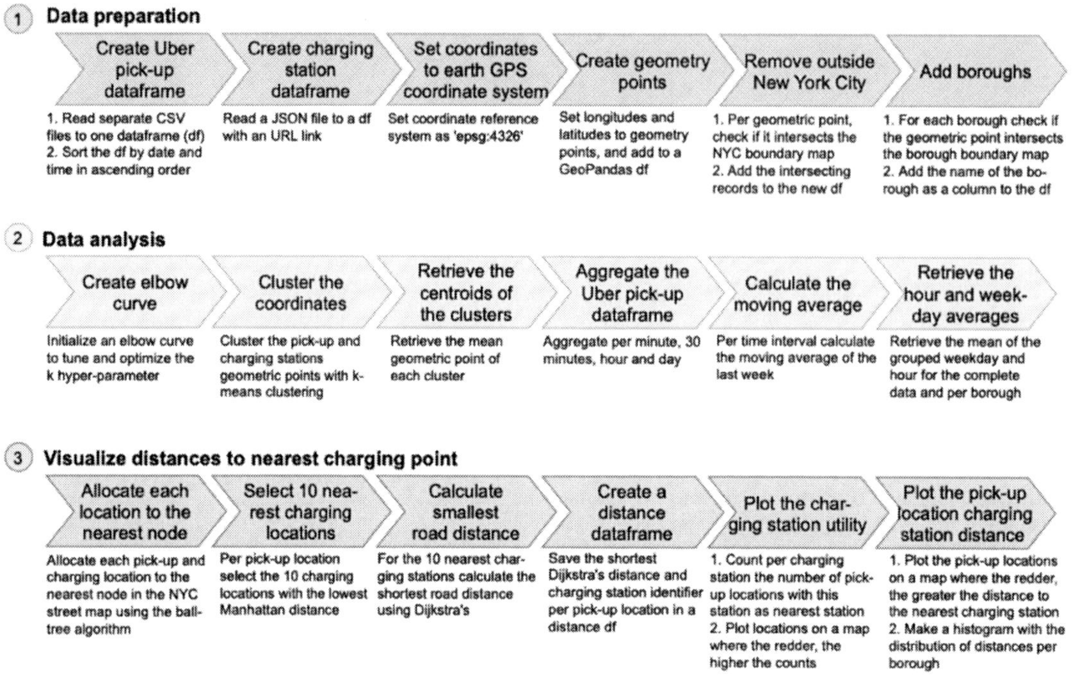

Figure. 1. Data wrangling methods.

the Uber dataset from April 2014 to May 2015 and the charging station data of New York City of 2021. This provides the input for our analysis and visualizations, which are explained in Section III. Finally, the paper is concluded in Section IV.

II. Dataset

In our research, we are investigating the ride-hailing service and the charging stations in New York State. The first data source consists of Uber trip data from April of 2014 to September of 2014. The data are separated by month for New York State. The data consist of 4.5 million ride demand records which contain the date, time, and detailed location with the latitude and longitude of each pickup. This dataset is retrieved from Kaggle [12]. The second data source consists of the electric vehicle charging station records in New York State. The data contains 2,347 registered stations as such and various location information, including the zip code, the borough, latitude, and longitude. It can be found on the government website of the New York State [13] dated 29th of January 2021. In order to answer the research question, we assume all Uber vehicles were operated by electric vehicles in 2014, and multiple data wrangling techniques were engaged. Figure 1 summarizes these techniques.

A. Data preparation

To prepare the data, the Uber pickup data was initially separated by month. Hence, we concatenated the monthly data into one data frame and ranked the date by the index, the date, and the time of the pickup location. The charging station data was read as a JSON file.

In order to work with spatial data, we converted all the dataframes in GeoDataFrames. This was done by creating a GeoSeries column that is referred to as the GeoDataFrame's geometry and indicates the latitude and longitude of a GPS coordinate using the geopandas library [14]. Next, we removed all the coordinates outside New York City. We only added the five boroughs of New York City: Bronx, Brooklyn, Manhattan, Queens, and Staten Island. To visualize the map of New York City with both the pickup points and the charging stations, the OSmnx package [15] for spatial visualizations was used. The background for this visualization was the street map of New York City, which can be interpreted as follows: the nodes represent intersections, and the edges represent street segments.

B. Data analysis

To have a better understanding of the hot spots for the time-dependent pickup locations and charging stations, the K-means clustering algorithm [16] is employed. The objective is to build a clustering model of the pickup data and the charging stations, by which we generated elbow curves to estimate and optimize the hyperparameter K. Based on the results, we assign five different clusters for the pickup data, which we display in Figures 2 and 3. There are four different clusters for the charging station data, which we display in Figures 4 and 5. The similarity of the centroids of the K-means clustering analysis suggests a high concentration of

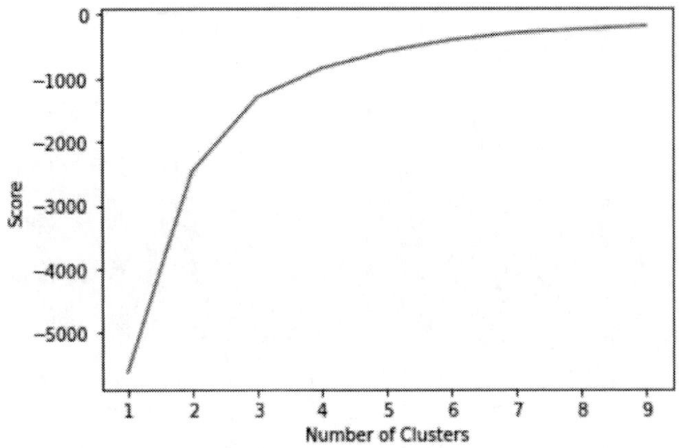

Figure. 2. Elbow curve for the Uber pickup location data.

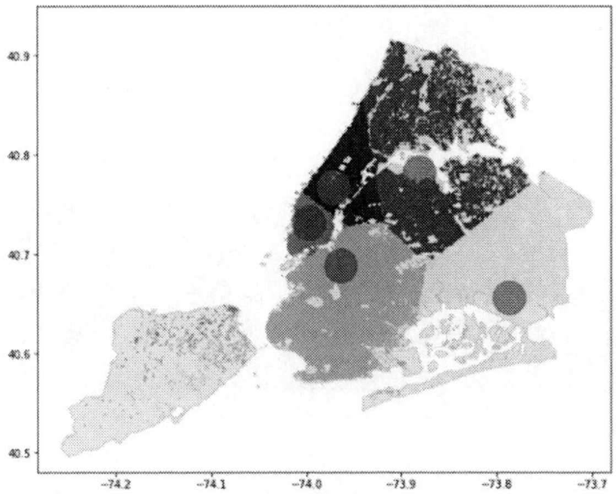

Figure. 3. Clusters for the Uber pickup location data.

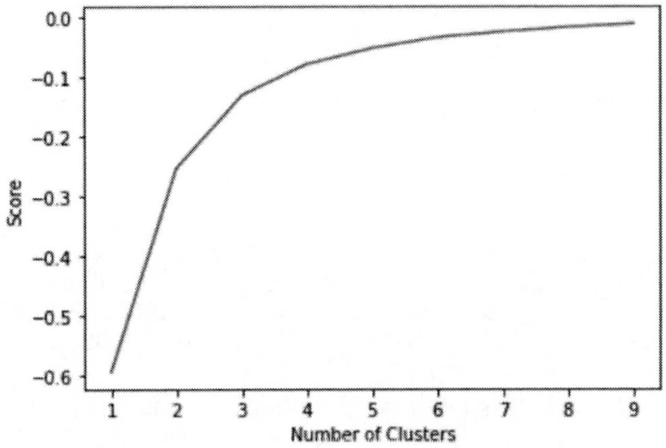

Figure. 4. Elbow curve for the charging station location data.

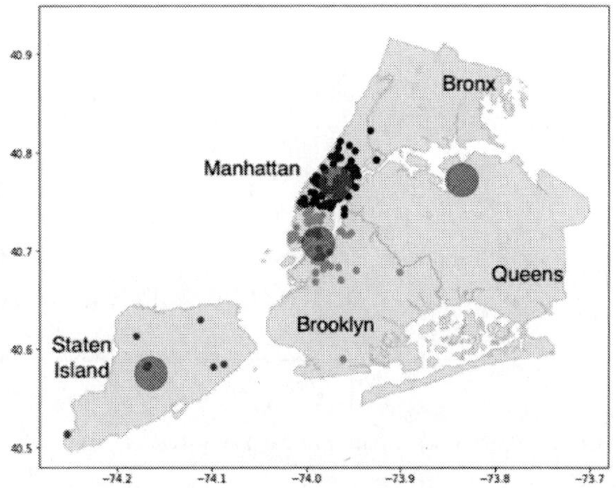

Figure. 5. Clusters for the charging station location data.

both pickups and charging stations in Manhattan and the west of Brooklyn.

When analyzing the distribution of the minutely arrivals of Uber, the data present substantial noise and could not depict a solid trend of the moving average [17]. However, the trend becomes strongly positive when moving to hourly and daily distributions of arrivals, suggesting the increasing popularity of Uber services in Figures 6, 7, and 8.

Next, we analyze the average number of Uber pickups per weekday in Figure 9. We notice the presence of two peaks: the morning rush hour and the leaving-work in the afternoon rush hour. We observe a clear distinction for Fridays and Saturdays. There is a distinct peak during the night, probably caused by the happy hour on Friday and stay out later in the evening. When comparing averages for the five boroughs, there is a distinguishable indication that the majority of trips take place in Manhattan, followed by Brooklyn, Queens, and ultimately the Bronx and Staten Island.

III. VISUALIZE DISTANCES TO NEAREST CHARGING POINT

In order to assess the improvements that can be made at the charging station level, we must investigate the distances between pickups and the charging stations. To calculate the nearest charging point from each pickup location, we allocate each coordinate to the nearest node in the graph. We then minimize the travel times between the pickup and the charging locations using Dijkstra's algorithm [18]. However, due to the large number of calculations required, this approach would take approximately 13 years of run time, which is not feasible for a research as such. Therefore, we used a good enough approximation method with the help of the ball tree algorithm [19].

We approximated the ten nearest charging stations with the Manhattan distance [20]. We managed to reduce the running time from 13 years to 3.5 days when running Dijkstra's algorithm on the ten nearest stations. The data consists of 4.4 million pickup locations and 266 charging stations. The results are somewhat intuitive, as suggested by the hot spot analysis. As expected, Manhattan has by far the shortest travel distances,

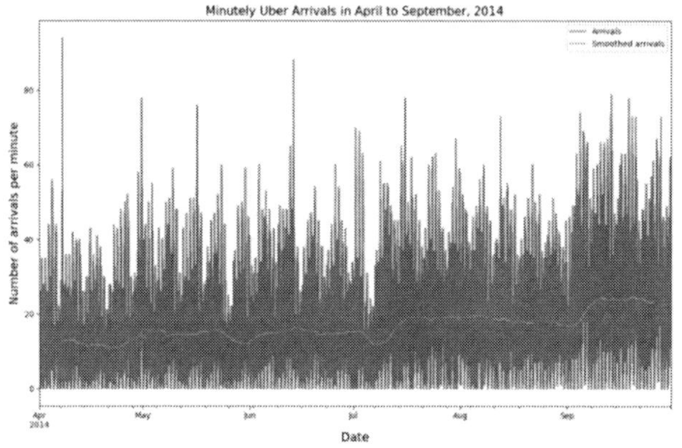

Figure. 6. Minutely Uber arrivals from April to September, 2014.

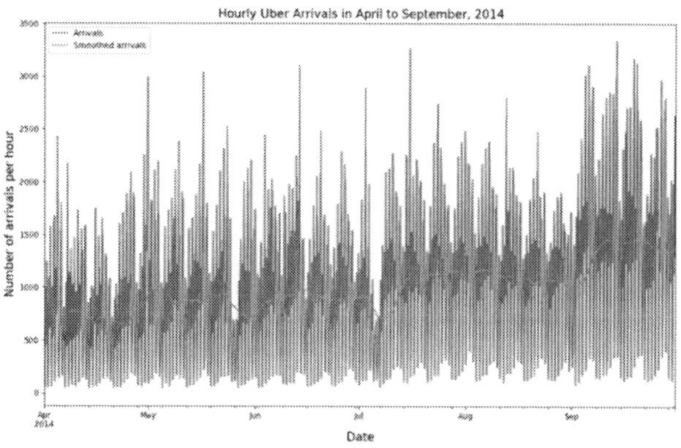

Figure. 7. Hourly Uber arrivals from April to September, 2014.

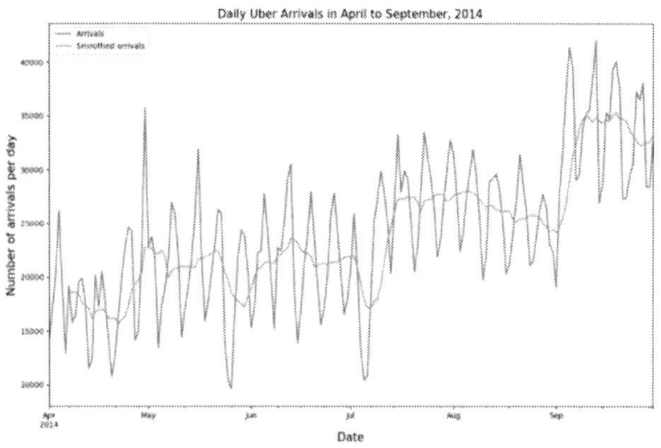

Figure. 8. Daily Uber arrivals from April to September, 2014.

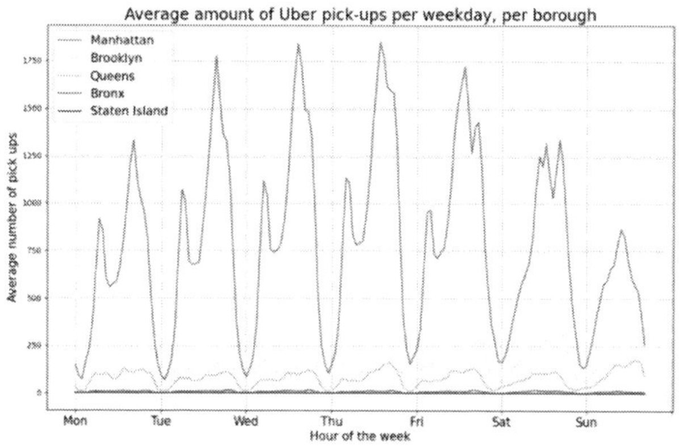

Figure. 9. Average number of Uber pickups per weekday per borough.

hinted by the fact that it had the most pickup locations and a high concentration of charging stations. Table I presents the number of times the rank of the stations with the smallest Manhattan distance have the smallest Dijkstra's distance. The charging station with the 10th smallest distance according to the Manhattan distance covers only 0.07% of the smallest Dijkstra's distance, indicating that ten nearest charging stations is a good cut-off point.

Next, we investigate which charging stations are the most utilized and in which places there is a need for more charging stations. In Figure 10, a visual utility analysis plots four categories of charging stations, ranging from highly utilized indicated by dark red toward a light cream color to indicate slightly used charging stations. A conclusion drawn from the utility analysis suggests that more charging locations are needed at the Southside of Manhattan, the Westside of Brooklyn, and the center of Queens.

In Figure 11, a complementary visual analysis plots the distances from the pickups to the nearest charging stations. The dark green color of the figure represents short distances between pickup points and charging locations. Furthermore, the red color represents longer distances between the pickup points and the charging locations. From this analysis, we depict that overall, Manhattan has small distances from pickup points and charging stations which makes common sense as Manhattan has the highest density in North American Cities. The predominantly yellow coloring in the Southeast of Queens and the North of Staten Island, culminating with intense red coloring in the Southeast of Queens, clearly suggests that more charging stations are needed. To provide a better understanding of the pickup locations versus the charging stations, we separated each Borough and created 5 histograms that represent the cumulative amount of the distance between pickup location and charging station at each Borough.

Figures 12, 13, and 14 provide the shortest distance to the nearest charging stations in Staten Island, Bronx, and Queens, respectively. These three figures provide insufficient evidence about the distance due to the insufficient number of pickup locations for one year in those areas. On the other hand, Figures 15 and 16 indicate that the majority of the pickup locations of Uber in 2014 are in Brooklyn and Manhattan. The majority distance between the pickup location and the charging stations is less than 2,000m. In order to investigate further, Figure 17 displays a complementary visual analysis from the pickups to the nearest charging stations in Manhattan. The figure indicates the further distance in upper Manhattan

TABLE I
PERCENTAGE OF OCCURRENCES WHERE THE TEN NEAREST MANHATTAN DISTANCES EQUAL THE SHORTEST PATH DISTANCE BASED ON DIJKSTRA'S ALGORITHM.

Rank station smallest Manhattan distance	1	2	3	4	5	6	7	8	9	10
% station smallest Dijkstra's distance	61.64%	19.28%	8.50%	6.67%	1.98%	0.99%	0.48%	0.22%	0.16%	0.07%

Figure. 10. Charging station utility map.

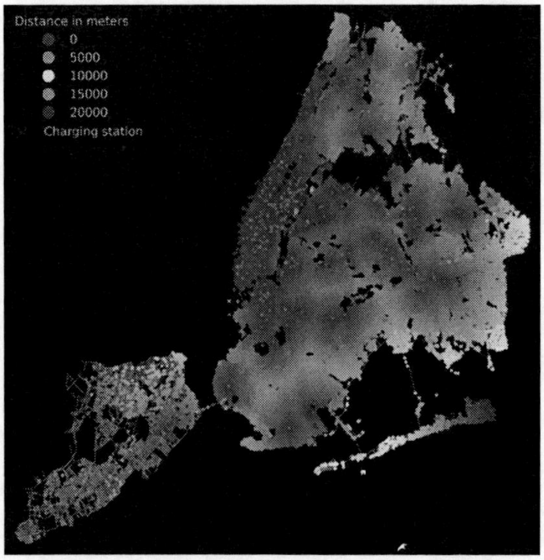

Figure. 11. Distance to nearest charging station map.

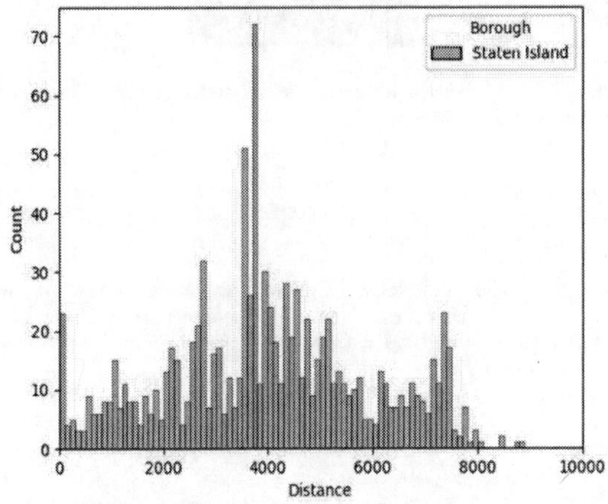

Figure. 12. Shortest distance to nearest charging station in Staten Island.

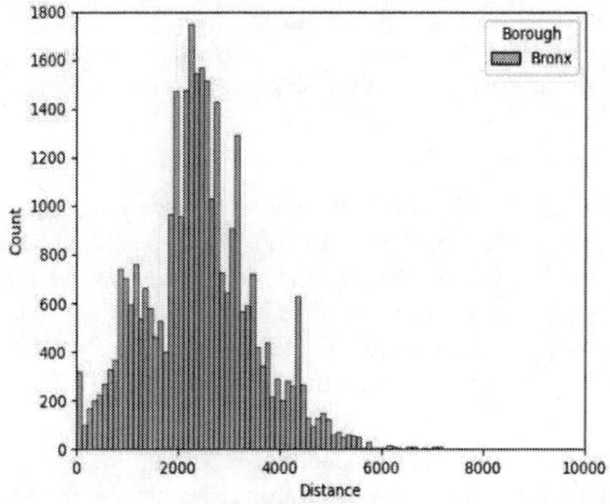

Figure. 13. Shortest distance to nearest charging station in the Bronx.

and east of Manhattan (East Harlem area).

IV. CONCLUSION

This research examines the viability of the current charging stations with the ride-hailing service of Uber by addressing (1) the distributions of charging and Uber pickup locations and (2) the distances between the pickup locations and their nearest charging station. According to cluster centroids, the pickup locations and charging locations are mostly distributed in Manhattan and the West of Brooklyn. Manhattan has the smallest charging station distances, while the distances from pickup locations in the East of Queens, the South of Queens, and the North of Staten Island to the nearest charging station is further away.

In conclusion, we performed multiple visual and hot spot

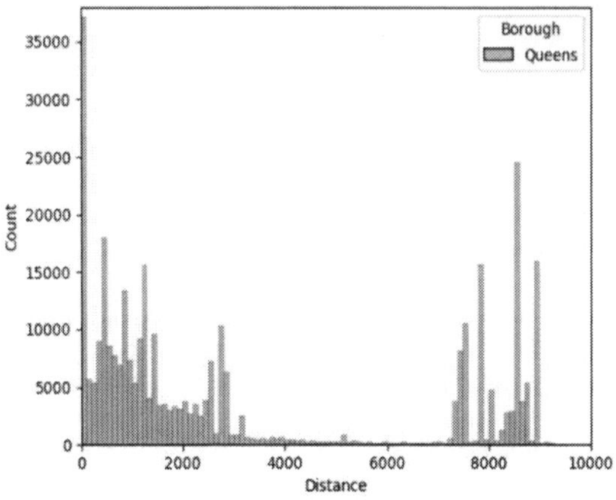

Figure. 14. Shortest distance to nearest charging station in Queens.

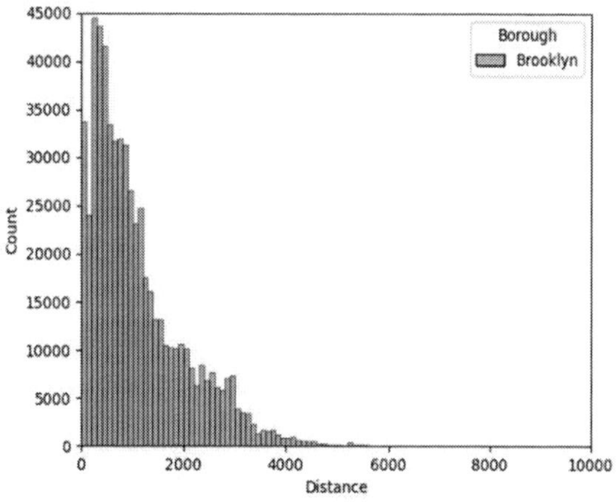

Figure. 15. Shortest distance to nearest charging station in Brooklyn.

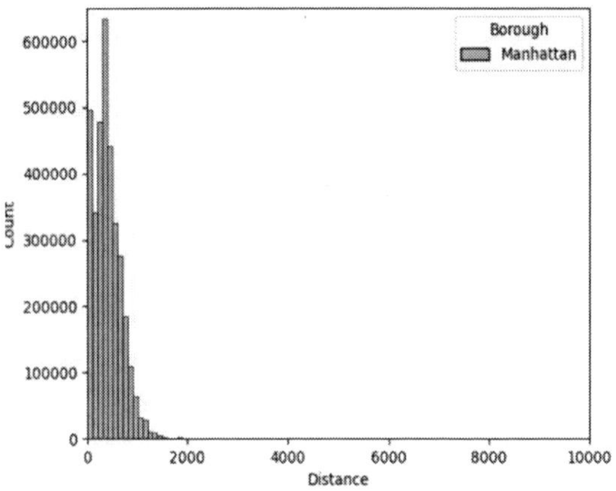

Figure. 16. Shortest distance to nearest charging station in Manhattan.

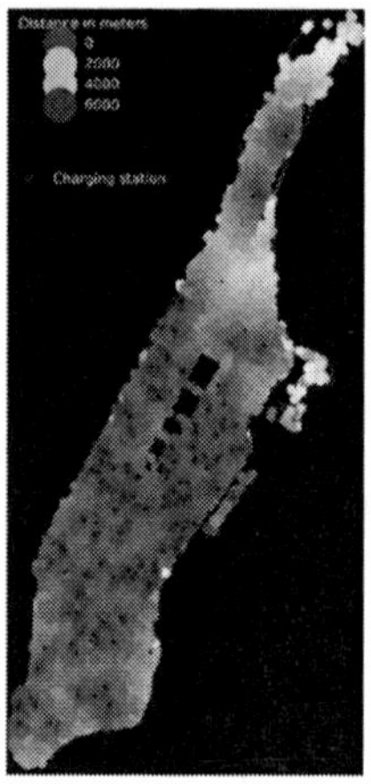

Figure. 17. A visual analysis of the shortest distance to the nearest charging station in Manhattan.

analyses, which conclude that more charging stations are needed in the Northwest of Brooklyn, upper Manhattan, middle of the Bronx, the Southwest of Queens, and the North of Staten Island. The favorable behavior of middle Manhattan shows that there are enough charging stations for Uber Inc. to be fully electric based on the 2014 data.

As for future discussion, Uber pickup data consists of 4.4 million data points measuring the closest distance with 10 nearest charging stations out of 266 charging stations using Dijkstra's algorithm. This creates the first glance of electrification with ride-hailing in New York City. With 4.4 million ride-hailing data points which only counters 15% of total New York City pickups in 2014 [21]. To fully understand the significance of the charging stations and the movement of the New Yorkers, a future study can combine the New York taxi data with Uber data to analyze and optimize the driving distance and charging period of each vehicle. This study attempts to present an image of the electric driving scene for Uber, and the granularity of data serves the purpose well.

REFERENCES

[1] EIA, "Oil and petroleum products explained: Use of oil," Jan 2021, Last access date: 30 September 2021. [Online]. Available: http://www.eia.gov/energyexplained/oil-and-petroleum-products/use-of-oil.php

[2] K. Korosec, "Uber expands green rides option to 1,400 cities – Techcrunch," Jan 2021, Last access date: 30 September 2021. [Online]. Available: https://techcrunch.com/2021/01/12/uber-expands-green-rides-option-to-1400-cities/

[3] C.-M. Tseng, S. C.-K. Chau, and X. Liu, "Improving viability of electric taxis by taxi service strategy optimization: A big data study of New York city," *IEEE Transactions on Intelligent Transportation Systems*, vol. 20, no. 3, pp. 817–829, 2018.

[4] M.-S. Răboacă, I. Băncescu, V. Preda, and N. Bizon, "An optimization model for the temporary locations of mobile charging stations," *Mathematics*, vol. 8, no. 3, p. 453, 2020.

[5] J. Jung and J. Y. Chow, "Effects of charging infrastructure and non-electric taxi competition on electric taxi adoption incentives in New York city," *Transportation Research Record*, vol. 2673, no. 4, pp. 262–274, 2019.

[6] G. Wang, X. Chen, F. Zhang, Y. Wang, and D. Zhang, "Experience: Understanding long-term evolving patterns of shared electric vehicle networks," in *The 25th Annual International Conference on Mobile Computing and Networking*, 2019, pp. 1–12.

[7] G. Wang, X. Xie, F. Zhang, Y. Liu, and D. Zhang, "bcharge: Data-driven real-time charging scheduling for large-scale electric bus fleets," in *2018 IEEE Real-Time Systems Symposium (RTSS)*. IEEE, 2018, pp. 45–55.

[8] M. Scorrano, R. Danielis, and M. Giansoldati, "Mandating the use of the electric taxis: The case of florence," *Transportation Research Part A: Policy and Practice*, vol. 132, pp. 402–414, 2020.

[9] S. Zhang, H. Wang, Y.-f. Zhang, and Y.-Z. Li, "A novel two-stage location model of charging station considering dynamic distribution of electric taxis," *Sustainable Cities and Society*, vol. 51, p. 101752, 2019.

[10] Y. Dong, S. Qian, J. Liu, L. Zhang, and K. Zhang, "Optimal placement of charging stations for electric taxis in urban area with profit maximization," in *2016 17th IEEE/ACIS International Conference on Software Engineering, Artificial Intelligence, Networking and Parallel/Distributed Computing (SNPD)*. IEEE, 2016, pp. 177–182.

[11] J. Jia, C. Liu, and T. Wan, "Planning of the charging station for electric vehicles utilizing cellular signaling data," *Sustainability*, vol. 11, no. 3, p. 643, 2019.

[12] Kaggle, "Uber pickups in New York city – Kaggle," Feb 2018, Last access date: 30 September 2021. [Online]. Available: https://www.kaggle.com/fivethirtyeight/uber -pickups-in-new-york-city?select=uber-raw-data- apr14.csv

[13] N. Y. State, "Electric vehicle charging stations in New York — state of New York," Feb 2018, Last access date: 30 September 2021. [Online]. Available: https://data.ny.gov/Energy-Environment /Electric-Vehicle-Charging-Stations-in-New-York /7rrd-248n

[14] T. Russell and M. Fleis, "Geopandas:," Jan 2021, Last access date: 30 September 2021. [Online]. Available: https://github.com/geopandas/geopandas

[15] G. Boeing, "OSMnx: A Python package to work with graph-theoretic OpenStreetMap street networks," *Journal of Open Source Software*, vol. 2, no. 12, 2017.

[16] P. S. Bradley and U. M. Fayyad, "Refining initial points for k-means clustering." in *ICML*, vol. 98. Citeseer, 1998, pp. 91–99.

[17] J. Durbin, "Efficient estimation of parameters in moving-average models," *Biometrika*, vol. 46, no. 3/4, pp. 306–316, 1959.

[18] E. W. Dijkstra, "A note on two problems in connexion with graphs," *Numerische Mathematik*, vol. 1, pp. 269–271, 1959.

[19] S. M. Omohundro, *Five balltree construction algorithms*. International Computer Science Institute Berkeley, 1989.

[20] E. F. Krause, "Taxicab geometry," *The Mathematics Teacher*, vol. 66, no. 8, pp. 695–706, 1973.

[21] T. W. Schneider, "Analyzing 1.1 Billion NYC Taxi and Uber Trips, with a Vengeance," Jan 2015, Last access date: 30 September 2021. [Online]. Available: http://toddwschneider.com/posts/analyzing-1-1-billion-nyc-taxi-and-uber-trips-with-a- vengeance/

Feature Engineering and Machine Learning Modelling for Predictive Maintenance Based on Production and Stop Events

Ariel Cedola, Rosaria Rossini, Ilaria Bosi, Davide Conzon
IoT and Robotics Research Area
LINKS Foundation
Turin, Italy
email: {ariel.cedola, rosaria.rossini, ilaria.bosi, davide.conzon}@linksfoundation.com

***Abstract*—Manufacturing systems suffer from progressive degradation due to wear, fatigue, cracking, corrosion, with respect to both age and usage. Reduced performance of system components and even catastrophic failure could be the main consequences of not being able to detect such faults at early times. Fault diagnosis and predictive maintenance aim at showing the machine working conditions, indicating current and possible future abnormal states, and allowing to take appropriate actions in advance in order to avoid damages, minimize downtime, improve the safety of the whole system and reduce manufacturing and repairing costs. In this paper, we successfully apply a data driven modelling approach designed for log data to a new scenario. The methodology proposed transforms the production and stops data of an industrial machine into a thoughtfully elaborated series of timestamped events, and applies a set of feature engineering techniques that enables to exploit the pipelines typically implemented in log-based predictive maintenance modelling. The transformed data is used to train a binary classificator that predicts with high accuracy (96.2%) the occurrence of a machine failure in the short-medium term.**

***Index Terms*—predictive maintenance, machine learning, feature engineering, manufacturing**

I. Introduction

The term 'Industry 4.0' refers to the Fourth Industrial Revolution, the recent trend of automation and data exchange in manufacturing technologies. The key fundamental principles of Industry 4.0 include data integration, flexible adaptation, cloud intranet, intelligent self-organizing, manufacturing process, optimization, interoperability, secure communication, and service orientation [1]. These innovative technologies are used to create a "smart factory" where machines, systems and humans communicate with each other to cooperate, monitor progress and connect sensors to provide data concerning the quality and the quantity of the goods, along the assembly line [2]. Apart from the evaluation of the quality of the final products, Predictive Health Management (PHM) systems use real-time and historical state information of machines, subsystems and components to provide actionable information, enabling intelligent decision-making for improved performance, safety, reliability, and maintainability in the manufacturing sector. The focus of health management is to minimize operational loss and to maximize the objectives established by the facility [3]. PHM of components or systems involves both diagnostics and prognostics: diagnostics is the process of detection and isolation of failures or faults, while prognostics is the process of prediction of the future state or Remaining Useful Life (RUL) based on current and historic conditions [4], [5]. The RUL is the prediction of the cycle-time before the performance of a component, system or process reaches an unacceptable low threshold [6]. Prognostics is based on the understanding that machines fail after a period of degradation, which if measured and thoughtfully analyzed, can be exploited to prevent system breakdown and minimize operation costs. These are in fact the goals of the predictive maintenance methodologies [7].

Data are at the core of diagnostics and prognostics operations. Manufacturers that envision the importance of data as an asset and manage to implement effective strategies to leverage data in multiple ways, gain measurable advantage over competitors. All players at a small- or large-scale produce data, but an aspect that distinguishes each other is the harnessing and management of the data that they conduct [8]. Data have different types and formats and can be collected from numerous sources using a variety of technological approaches, processed accordingly, and saved in an extensive catalogue of data stores and databases both locally and on the cloud. Data typically applied to condition monitoring and hopefully to predictive maintenance of machines are sensor and log data. In the present work, based on the lack of these kind of information, we propose the combined use of production and stops records of machines to construct artificial intelligence tools able to anticipate machine failures, and satisfactory apply this approach to predict the RUL of a machine operating in the textile sector.

The remainder of this paper is organized as follows. Section II describes the data-driven techniques commonly applied in predictive maintenance. Section III presents the scenario and the data utilized in the work. In Section IV we introduce the proposed approach and explain its three main steps: data preprocessing, feature engineering and machine learning modelling. The application of the method and the obtained results are presented in Section V. Finally, in Section VI, we draw some concluding remarks and suggest important work to address in the future.

II. Background

Model-based and data-driven approaches are two main techniques for diagnosis, monitoring and predictive maintenance of machines [9]. Model-based approaches exploit mathematical and physical models to provide insights into the failure mechanism of systems [10]. Faults are diagnosed by monitoring discrepancies between model calculations and the actual measurements. Data-driven approaches, on the other hand, are featured by building machine learning models based on large volumes of data without using the knowledge of the physical mechanisms behind the failures, and can provide excellent diagnosis results and RUL estimation [11], [12].

Data-driven predictive maintenance can be classified as sensor-based or log-based, depending on the type of data able to be generated and extracted from the machinery system and used for model training. The most frequently implemented is the sensor-based methodology, in which the streams of sensor measurements describing the working conditions of the machine are stored, aggregated, processed and applied to train a machine learning model, and subsequently to monitor and score the algorithm in order to predict future failure events [13]–[15]. Machine sensor data consist essentially in a set of time series signals, collected in general at regular time periods, and device identifiers formatted according to a hierarchical structure like machine/subsystem/component/channel. Typical machine parameters monitored by sensors are temperature, pressure, rotation speed, vibration, electrical consumption, acoustic emissions, among others. Sensor data are usually complemented with environmental, production, alerts, failures and maintenance data in this kind of approaches, enabling through a feature engineering process the generation of more solid datasets from which machine learning models with a higher prediction power can be constructed. Modern machines incorporate sensors and data processing modules from factory, but in older equipment these devices must be installed with the machine already in production. IoT devices and technologies facilitate enormously the conditioning of machines into a predictive maintenance ready status, although in some cases the high cost, the intensive use or the presence of mechanical or even regulatory constraints can turn this process unfeasible.

Log-based approaches, conversely, use event-log data for machine diagnostics, and prevent the need of implementation or monitoring of sensor data to train machine learning models for prognostics and predictive maintenance [16]–[20]. Programmable Logic Controllers (PLC) and software applications running on machine controllers continuously produce logs containing valuable information about internal events, tasks carried out, warnings, errors, components state, dialogues between modules, etc. Logs are generated automatically at a very high rate, reaching typically volumes of hundreds of thousand records per hour. Every log is timestamped and appended into a plain text or Extensible Markup Language (XML) file. Many log files can be generated daily by machines, each one containing a limited amount of records in order to avoid complicating the reading process and the storage of very large sized files. The management of these files is in fact an important aspect to consider when preservation of log data of a machine is contemplated. Most data recorded in log files are unstructured text data, and the extraction of the small subset of data embedded into the logs, that might be useful for predictive maintenance purposes, requires a heavy preprocessing work. There is no data in the logs providing explicit information about the machine condition that can be directly applied to predict failures. This means that a careful feature extraction process must be performed in log-based approaches to obtain successful prediction results through appropriate machine learning modelling.

In both approaches depicted above, the integration of the data with machine failure records is mandatory for RUL prediction using supervised machine learning algorithms. Each instance of the dataset is composed by a vector of features and a label. Features are constructed from collected sensor or log data, whereas failure records are exploited for data labeling. Binary or multiclass classification are the most frequently applied model types in data-driven predictive maintenance scenarios, rather than regression models. In binary problems, particularly, the label usually expresses the occurrence (positive class) or not (negative class) of a failure within a prediction window ahead in time from a specific prediction point, to which the data instance is associated. These two classes define the RUL to be predicted by the model. Both sensor and log data are time-series data, and the construction of the features for every prediction point is not based only on the data at that single point in time but on the aggregation of data within a specific time window set before the prediction point. For log-based approaches, it has been also reported in the literature the use of Multiple Instance Learning (MIL), in which instances are bagged and bags are labeled positive or negative according to the labels of the instances within them [19], [21]. Typical classification models applied to predictive maintenance include XGBoost, Random Forest, Gradient Boosting Machines (GBM), Support Vector Machines (SVM), Neural Networks, among others [22]–[24].

III. Scenario and data description

A. Scenario

The equipment under study is a bleaching machine, utilized in textile industries to remove the natural yellowish-brown coloring of fabric fibers, in order to confer to the material a white appearance. The equipment owner is a big international textile manufacturer with headquarters in Turkey. The bleaching machine is a long production line that operates in continuous mode in a 24/7 regime, processing an average of 80 km of fabric per day and performing four different processes: Bleaching, Bleaching + Emulsion, Repairment and Washing. The machine operation and architecture are subdivided in four steps: pre-washing, bleaching, washing and drying of the fabric.

In the bleaching step, the fabric is subject to a chemical bath and a steamer, with controlled times, temperatures and

	Process	BatchNumber	FabricCode	Length	Production	StartTime	EndTime	Duration	InletTrolleyNumber	OutletTrolleyNumber
OrderID										
2000	BLEACHING	27377	IHB154	8535	13144	2020-06-01 07:55:30	2020-06-01 10:01:47	126.28	283	917
2001	BLEACHING	28431	FRF158	3666	5756	2020-06-01 10:04:57	2020-06-01 10:57:16	52.32	301	3038
2002	BLEACHING	28216	FRF208	5731	11978	2020-06-01 10:58:52	2020-06-01 12:31:49	92.95	301	3038
2003	BLEACHING	200001	FRF178	1509	2686	2020-06-01 12:36:06	2020-06-01 13:00:55	24.82	352	564
2004	BLEACHING	25409	FRF178	1652	2941	2020-06-01 13:01:05	2020-06-01 13:25:34	24.48	352	564

(a) Production data

	StartTime	EndTime	Duration	StopReason
StopID				
10000	2020-06-01 09:38:00	2020-06-01 09:41:00	153	Recipe change
10001	2020-06-01 10:01:00	2020-06-01 10:04:00	131	Unreasoned stops
10002	2020-06-01 10:04:00	2020-06-01 10:04:00	43	Unreasoned stops
10003	2020-06-01 10:04:00	2020-06-01 10:04:00	1	Unreasoned stops
10004	2020-06-01 10:04:00	2020-06-01 10:05:00	12	Unreasoned stops

(b) Stops data

Fig. 1: Samples of the tables containing production (a) and stops (b) data.

proportion of chemical bath components, which depend on the type and whiteness level of the inlet fabric. An excessive time of exposure of the material to the chemicals can produce irreversible damages, resulting in the loss of up to kilometers of textile. The long exposures to the chemicals are caused by different types of stops that the machine suffers during its operation. One of the most frequent stops are due to mechanical failures, specifically to failures of cylindrical roller bearings, which progressively deteriorate due to abrasion. The whole machine structure includes a total of 1259 roller bearings of 54 different types. Despite the intensive preventive maintenance activities, an average of 1 mechanical failure per day is reported by the machine owner. Other failure types affect the normal operation of the machine, i.e., electrical, electronic and power failures, depending on the root cause and the component or subsystem in which the issue is originated. Failures with a repairing duration exceeding 10 minutes are classified by the maintenance department as critical, based on Total Productive Maintenance (TPM) principles, and generally meet 10% of the total failures. Half of the total critical failures time is due exclusively to mechanical failures, which reach an average duration of 27 minutes. These statistics extracted from data provided by the manufacturer reveal the importance of targeting the prediction of mechanical failures to enable the predictive maintenance of the equipment. In addition to the huge quantity of roller bearings, this complex machine is composed also by 50 motors, 30 inverters, 5 chemical dosing pumps, and many other components. The machine is not equipped with a network of sensors for condition monitoring, and a collection of log files reporting a reasonable period of historical log events was not available at the moment of conducting this study. The lack of data questioned initially the possibility of executing a data-driven analysis for RUL prediction. Data provided by the manufacturer consist of four months of production and stop events in structured format, with complete information about the type of production process performed or stop undergone, and the corresponding starting and final timestamps.

B. Data description

Data about production processes and stop events were provided by the machine owner in two separate files, exported from the production management software and the PLC, respectively. The tables in the source files contain 1883 production records and 7663 stop events registered from June to October 2020. The structure of these tables and some example data are shown in Figure 1. The production table includes data about the performed process (Process), the ID of the order (BatchNumber), the code of the processed fabric (FabricCode), the input length (Length, in meters) and area (Production, in squared maters) of the material, the initial and final timestamps (StartTime, EndTime), and the order duration (Duration, in minutes). This duration includes the times of all eventual stops and failures undergone by the machine during the processing of the order. The stops table simply shows the type of stop experienced by the machine (StopReason), the initial and final timestamps (StartTime, EndTime), and

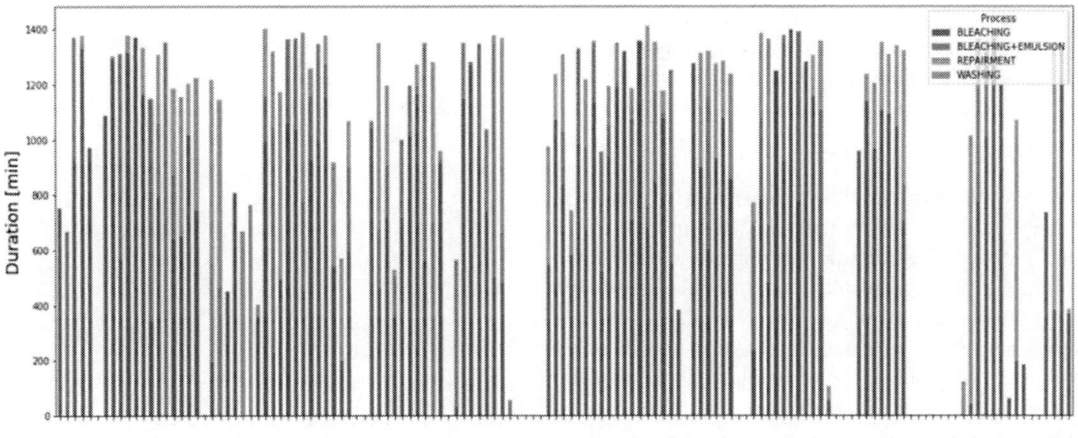

(a) Production processes

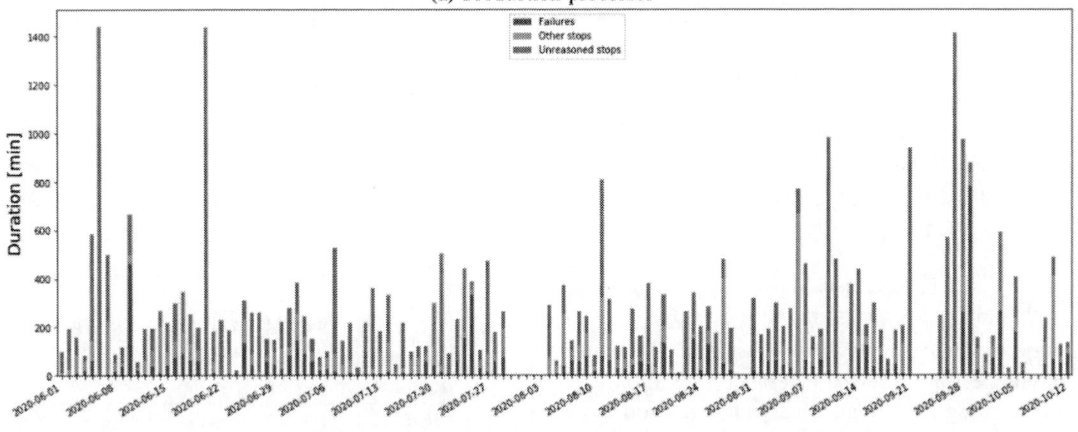

(b) Unplanned stops

Fig. 2: Duration of production processes (a) and unplanned stops (b) aggregated by day.

the duration (Duration, in seconds). It is important to notice that stop timestamps have minute resolution (seconds = 00), which leads to small inaccuracies when analyzing sequences of stop events during the processing of fabrics, and to the presence of records with identical StartTime and in many cases also EndTime timestamps. The indexes OrderID and StopID were added to uniquely identify each record in the tables. BatchNumber in the production table might not be unique due to one of two reasons: reprocess of bleaching when obtained whiteness degree is not acceptable (Repairment process), and reuse of BatchNumber once the processing of a fabric through all required machines in the plant is complete. The StopReason is introduced by the operators through the PLC screen of the machine, by choosing the proper option from the full list which is shown when the machine stops. The following is the list of the 17 stop reasons present in the dataset, classified as Planned and Unplanned:

- Planned stops (4): Planned maintenance, Cleaning, No production, Holiday.
- Unplanned stops (13): Unreasoned stops, Recipe change, Fabric rupture, Waiting for batch frame trolley, Fabric wrapped around a cylinder, Refreshing Stitching, Fabric construction changing, Color OK, Water changing, Mechanical Failure, Electronic failure, Electrical failure, Power failure.

The two tables integrate a total of 2050 hours of production and 1235 hours of stop events. Bleaching and Bleaching + Emulsion processes comprise the 81% of all production orders. Bleaching + Emulsion is the bleaching process executed for a specific type of fabric. More than half of the stop time corresponds to the Planned stops, mainly to the No production reason. Near 55% of the orders processed in the reported period presented unplanned stops, with a total stop duration of almost 300 hours. The large number of registered stops is due to the presence of numerous sequences of microstops of few seconds duration, usually labelled as Unreasoned stops, that should be conveniently considered as unique longer chains of these events. The duration of near 48.5% of stops does not exceed 60 seconds, whereas 81.5% last less than 5 minutes. Total stop time due particularly to the four failure types rises to 107 hours, 72 of which correspond to the mentioned critical condition. The Unreasoned stops are largely the most frequent in the dataset, reaching 67% of all stop events and 30% of the full stop time. Figure 2 shows the duration of production processes (a) and unplanned stops (b) aggregated by date. The eight stop reasons other than Unreasoned stops and Failures are combined and shown in the picture as Other stops.

IV. EVENT-BASED MODELLING APPROACH

The approach proposed in this paper aims to transform the above mentioned production and stop data in a series of timestamped events, using a format that enables to exploit the application of the pipelines typically implemented in log-based predictive maintenance modelling. These pipelines include feature engineering steps in which the learning instances are generated by processing and aggregating data within a features window preceding each prediction instant, i.e., the instance point, subdivided into a number of time windows. Features are extracted from this time frame by applying strategies like rolling windows with different aggregation functions and temporal coverage, identification and counting of patterns, among others. A label window used to generate the instance labels is also created from each of those instants. One instance is formulated for each instance point, which is moved ahead in time along with the features and label windows by a predefined time step, in order to generate the full set of training and testing instances.

The three big steps implemented in this approach and described in the next subsections are the following:

- Data preprocessing: Events formulation and alignment
- Feature engineering: Instance and label generation
- Machine learning modelling: Binary classification model training and testing

A. Data Preprocessing

The production and stop records present in the data sources have start and end timestamps, and in order to transform these records in a streaming of events, what we have done is to consider both start and end of the records as two separate events: Start Production/Stop and End Production/Stop. This sequence of events, correctly arranged by order of occurrence, is in fact the proper input data format needed for the future training and scoring of the model in production using streaming data in real-time. The collected data show that more than 70% of the registered stops occur during production processes, i.e., while the machine is in operation. This means that a failure starting after the StartTime and finishing before the EndTime of a production record splits this process into two pieces, one previous and the other subsequent to the failure. In terms of the events formulation depicted above, a situation like this one gives place to six different events, namely Start Production, Stop Production, Start Failure, End Failure, Re-start Production and End Production. Depending on the number of stops registered during the process, production records could be splitted in more than just two parts. Figure 3 shows an example of the events generated from the occurrence of two stops/failures during two production processes.

With the aim of applying this principle to the whole available dataset, we had to perform several steps of data

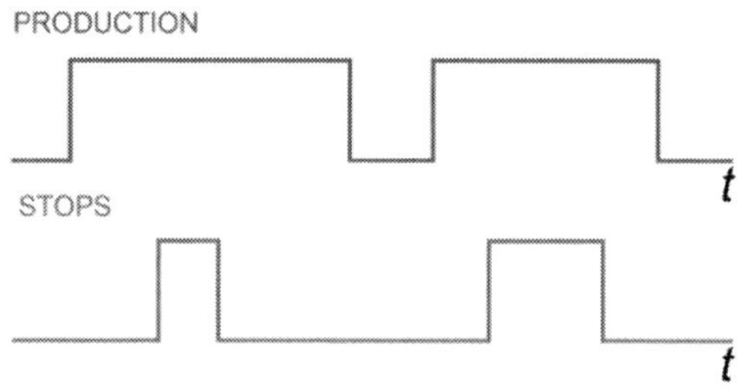

(a) Production and stops records

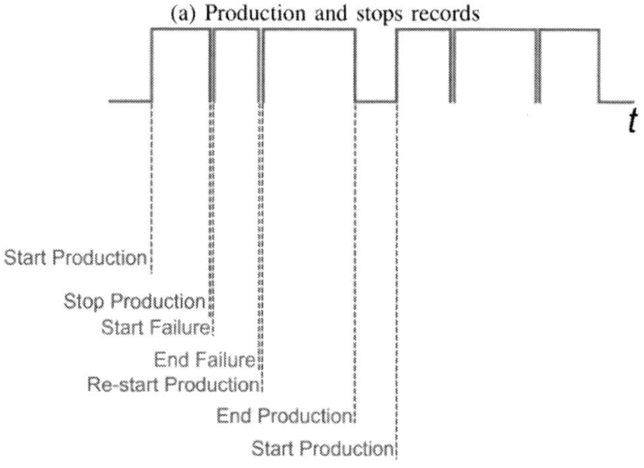

(b) Data alignment and events creation

Timestamp	Event
16/06/2020 08:12	Start Production
16/06/2020 09:14	Stop Production
16/06/2020 09:15	Start Failure
16/06/2020 10:01	End Failure
16/06/2020 10:02	Re-start Production
16/06/2020 12:23	End Production
16/06/2020 12:28	Start Production
16/06/2020 13:56	Stop Production
16/06/2020 13:57	Start Failure
16/06/2020 16:22	End Failure
16/06/2020 16:23	Re-start Production
16/06/2020 18:41	End Production

(c) Sequence of events

Fig. 3: Example of events generation after alignment of records and splitting of production processes.

preprocessing before, to obtain a clean and consistent stream of events. In addition, we categorized the stops as those occurring during or outside the production processes. The preprocessing steps involved were:

- Chaining of stops: Trains of consecutive short stops of the same type (StopReason) were permanently joined into single and longer stop chains of identical type, and duration given by the sum of the duration of all stop components.
- Chaining of chains of stops: Consecutive and very close

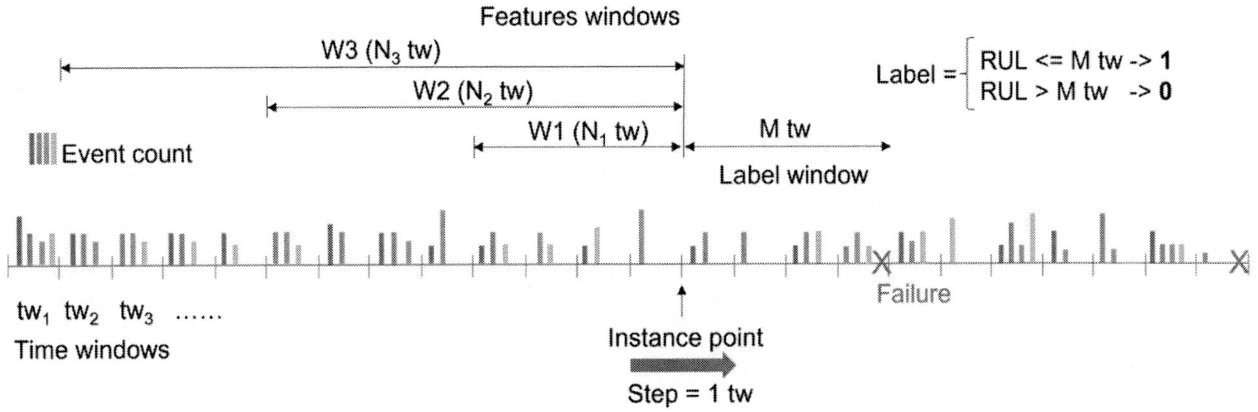

Fig. 4: Scheme applied to the generation of the training instances.

chains of stops of identical or different type were temporarily joined in order to avoid the generation of very short pieces of production records when splitting for events formulation.

- Categorization of stops: Every stop or stop chain occurring exclusively during a production process, i.e., for which StartTime (stop) > StartTime (production) and EndTime (stop) < EndTime (production) was denominated Stop Type I (inner stops). All remaining stops were categorized as Stop Type II (outer stops).
- Adjustment of stops EndTime: Given the minute resolution of the stop timestamps, there are many records with equal StartTime and also with identical StartTime and EndTime (around 2k), and in all cases the time gap between timestamps does not reflect the real duration of the stops. To solve this, we assumed the registered StartTime of all stops records as correct and adjusted the EndTime as StartTime + Duration. Despite this leads to slight inaccuracies regarding the exact time of occurrence of stop events, it contributes to generate a more consistent dataset.
- Partial overlapping between production and stop records: StartTime and/or EndTime timestamps of production records were slightly shifted in the cases of the frequently observed short overlapping with previous or subsequent stop records (Type II). The choice of shifting the production records was supported by the fact that registration of the start and end times of these processes is carried out manually by the operators, which means that timestamps are prone to involuntary errors and less reliable, contrarily to the stop records stored automatically by the PLC.

After all these operations, we finally proceeded with the generation of the events. The algorithm roughly consists of the following steps:

- Integrate Production and Stop data
- Detect Type I stops, split Production records and label events
- Label remaining events
- Unchain the temporary stop chains
- Separate instances in start and end events and relabel accordingly

B. *Feature engineering*

The decomposition and sorting of all production and stops processes following the actions explained above give place to a chronological sequence of discrete events. This dataset is substantially a time series of all events occurring in the bleaching machine, including the target failure event that we plan to predict by training a machine learning model. The dataset contains clean and ordered data, but it is not suitable yet for training a binary classification model for failure prediction. The next step in the pipeline is the generation of the training instances, each one containing a set of features and a label, through adequate feature engineering techniques. Figure 4 shows the scheme used for instances generation, in line with those presented in [16]–[18]. The instances are formulated at specific points in time, separated by fixed time intervals determined by the size of the time windows in which the features window and the label window are subdivided. The point in time associated to an instance is referred to as an instance point, and the features window is a time interval set before it, that finishes at the instance point and has an extension of N time windows. All the events occurring within the features window of an instance point are involved into the determination of the values of the features associated to that instance. In this work we applied the counting of the events to calculate the feature values, but other aggregation functions, statistics and strategies can be used to enrich the feature spectrum. The concept of the feature window implemented in this way is clearly the same of the rolling window commonly applied in time series analytics. All the unique events generated in the Data preprocessing step are converted in features of the learning dataset when following this method. As showed in the figure, multiple features windows can be used for each instance point, with different sizes in terms of time windows, which in turn multiplies the number of features

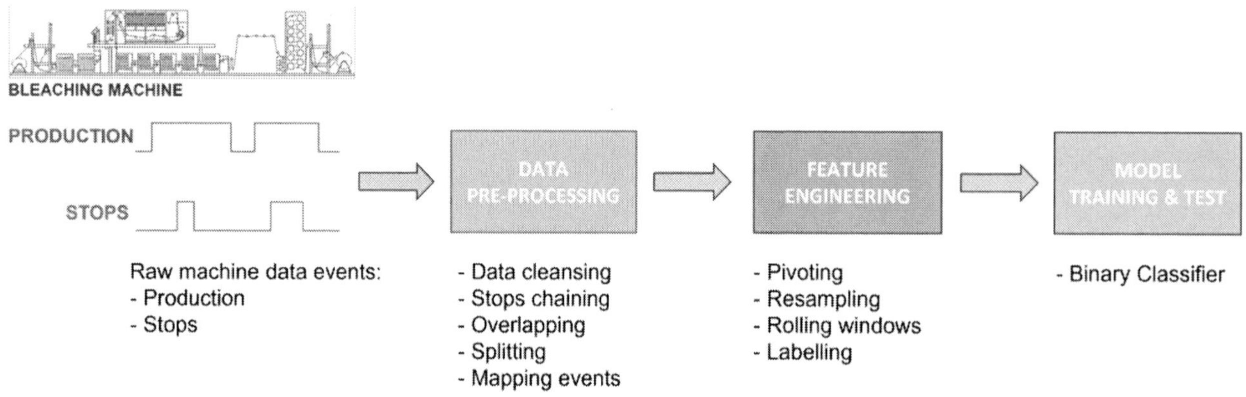

Fig. 5: Steps implemented in the present event-based approach for predictive maintenance.

created. The label window is set from the instance point and has a length of M time windows. The presence of at least one event of the targeted failure inside the label window of an instance point dictates the assignment of a positive label to that instance (class 1), otherwise of a negative one (class 0). It is worth mentioning that within the features window, the target failure events are treated identically to the rest of the stops. Once the features and label are generated and an instance is created, the instance point and the windows are moved ahead by a step of one time window in order to generate the next learning instance. By iterating through this process, we construct the entire dataset for the subsequent training of the failure prediction model.

C. Machine Learning modelling

The tool selected to conduct the modelling experiments is LightGBM [25], a gradient boosting decision tree framework that supports different algorithms, i.e., regression, classification and ranking. We applied this framework for binary classification, in order to predict the RUL of the machine under study considering the two classes (0 and 1) introduced in the previous subsection. A prediction of 1 raised by the model indicates the prediction of occurrence of the targeted failure event in the next period of time given by the duration of the label window, starting from the current instance point. LightGBM is a state-of-the-art framework and has demonstrated to be faster and more robust with respect to other tree-based algorithms, enabling explainability and distributed computation.

V. Results

All the steps outlined in Section IV are graphically summarized in Figure 5. We applied this approach to the production and stops data of the bleaching machine, described in Section III B. Having 4 production processes and 17 stop reasons, and considering that up to four events can be generated from every production and stop record (Start, Stop, Re-start, End for production and Start Type I, End Type I, Start Type II, End Type II for stops), we managed to formulate a total of 80 events from the integrated dataset. The size of the events table is independent of the number of the different events created, and it is around 16k records. On the other hand, each event represents one feature within each features window used to construct the training dataset. Anticipating a time window size of 1 hour and the setting of 3 features windows to proceed with the feature extraction process, a training dataset of around 3k instances with 240 features would be obtained. To prevent dimensionality issues, we decided to reduce the number of possible distinct events so as to get a larger ratio between the training dataset size and the number of dimensions. To do this we mapped the processes and stops into 9 groups, as shown in Table I, and joined the Type I and Type II stop categories, to finally reach a total of 20 features. Despite knowing their importance in log-based approaches, a thorough implementation of feature selection techniques was not in the scope of this first version of the work.

The parameters of the feature extraction scheme selected to conduct the experiments are the following:

- Time windows size = 1 hour
- Number of features windows = 3
- Sizes of features windows (N) = 12, 24, 36 time windows
- Size of label window (M) = 12 time windows

The size of the time windows is the parameter that defines the quantity of instances composing the ultimate dataset that is used to train and test the model. A size of 1 hour is reasonable given the typical duration of the production processes and the frequency of occurrence of the unplanned stops and failures. Considering the parameters detailed above, the final dataset consists of 3161 records, 60 features and the label. The event selected as the target failure to construct the label is the Start Mechanical Failure, whose relevance was highlighted in Section III A. The resulting ratio between classes is approximately 1:5, being the minority class the positive one, i.e., the class indicating the occurrence of at least one Start Mechanical Failure event in the next 12 hours from an instance point. Although a slight imbalance between classes is observed, it is not large enough as to consider the problem a severely imbalanced classification.

The LightGBM binary classifier was trained and evaluated

TABLE I: Mapping of production and stop records into groups.

Process or stop reason	*Group*
Bleaching, Bleaching+Emulsion, Repairment, Washing	Production
Planned maintenance, Cleaning, No production, Holiday	Planned
Electrical failure, Power failure	Electrical/Power Failure
Fabric construction changing, Water changing, Recipe change, Color OK	Change
Fabric wrapped around a cylinder, Fabric rupture, Refreshing Stitching	Fabric issue
Unreasoned stops	Unreasoned stops
Waiting for batch frame trolley	Waiting for batch frame trolley
Mechanical Failure	Mechanical Failure
Electronic failure	Electronic failure

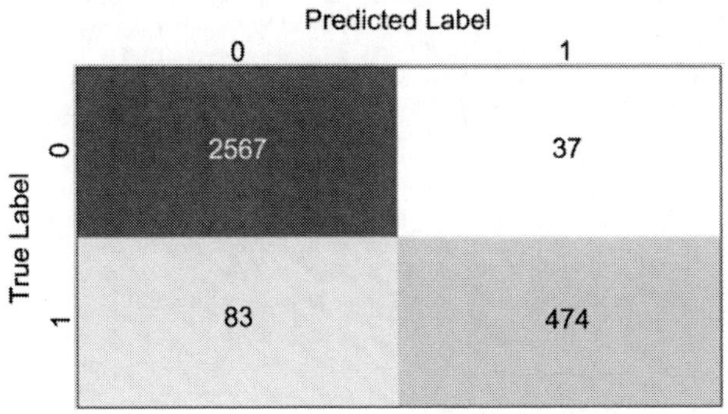

Fig. 6: Confusion matrix.

by applying cross-validation with 5 folds. Hyperparameter tuning was conducted using a grid search to find the model with better performance. Due to the observed class imbalance, the macro average of Area Under Receiver Operating Characteristic Curve (AUC), Precision and Recall metrics were calculated in order to weight equally both the minority and majority classes. The following are the obtained values:

- Accuracy = 0.962
- AUC(macro) = 0.987
- Precision(macro) = 0.948
- Recall(macro) = 0.918

As can be corroborated the metrics are very encouraging. When considering only the minority class, the Recall metric falls to 0.85. This is due to the non-negligible number of false negatives predicted by the model, as can be noticed from the confusion matrix shown in Figure 6. There are 474 and 83 positive samples predicted correctly and wrongly, respectively. There is room to improve even more the classification quality, for example, by deepening the search of the optimal hyper-parameters of the model and conducting experiments with different classificators.

VI. Conclusion and Future Work

Knowing the principles of the log-based approaches for predictive maintenance, we decided to transform the available production and stops data from a textile machine in a large sequence of events having a similar format to the events typically extracted from log files, then apply the proper preprocessing, feature engineering and labelling steps, and finally train a supervised machine learning classificator to predict the time to mechanical failure of the equipment.

The preliminary results evidence the potentiality of the proposed method for the predictive maintenance of industrial machines, and its extreme utility in scenarios in which the lack of collections of sensor measurements and log files prevents the application of more traditional data-driven schemes. Despite the approach has been proven to be effective in a particular use case, we consider that the application can be extended to a wide variety of manufacturing sectors in which the predictive maintenance of the equipment is known to deliver a high business impact.

The work also shows the high extra value that the production and failure data of a machine might provide to a manufacturer. These data are commonly available in industrial plants at all scales, and the study contributes to highlight the reasons because data are considered so valuable assets in the era of Industry 4.0.

It is worth mentioning that the unavailability of detailed and quality maintenance data regarding repairing, reconditioning or replacement of specific mechanical components of the bleaching machine, addressed the study to the RUL prediction of the roller bearings as a whole subsystem. Based on their experience, the domain experts and senior operators can exploit these predictions to elucidate what are the most probable roller bearings to fail when an alert is raised by the model.

The future work will be focused not only on the improvement of the prediction performance of the model by hyperparameters tuning and feature selection, but also on the exploration of the incidence of different combinations of parameters in the feature extraction method, namely the size of the time windows, the number and size of the features windows and the size of the label window. In addition, efforts will be addressed to investigate other aggregations and featuring strategies to apply to the events enclosed into the features windows.

Acknowledgement

This work was developed in the framework of the project "RECLAIM- RE-manufaCturing and Refurbishment LArge Industrial equipMent" and received funding from the European Union's Horizon 2020 research and innovation programme under grant agreement No 869884. The authors would like to acknowledge the valuable collaboration of Zorluteks, for providing data and domain expert support.

REFERENCES

[1] C. Ji, Q. Shao, J. Sun, S. Liu, L. Pan, L. Wu, and C. Yang, "Device data ingestion for industrial big data platforms with a case study," *Sensors*, vol. 16, no. 3, 2016.

[2] G. Peralta, M. Iglesias-Urkia, M. Barcelo, R. Gomez, A. Moran, and J. Bilbao, "Fog computing based efficient iot scheme for the industry 4.0," in *2017 IEEE International Workshop of Electronics, Control, Measurement, Signals and their Application to Mechatronics (ECMSM)*, 2017, pp. 1–6.

[3] J. Lee, F. Wu, W. Zhao, M. Ghaffari, L. Liao, and D. Siegel, "Prognostics and health management design for rotary machinery systems—reviews, methodology and applications," *Mechanical Systems and Signal Processing*, vol. 42, pp. 314–334, 01 2014.

[4] A. Mathur, K. F. Cavanaugh, K. R. Pattipati, P. K. Willett, and T. R. Galie, "Reasoning and modeling systems in diagnosis and prognosis," in *Component and Systems Diagnostics, Prognosis, and Health Management*, P. K. Willett and T. Kirubarajan, Eds., vol. 4389, International Society for Optics and Photonics. SPIE, 2001, pp. 194 – 203.

[5] L. Barajas and N. Srinivasa, "Real-time diagnostics, prognostics and health management for large-scale manufacturing maintenance systems," *Proceedings of the ASME International Manufacturing Science and Engineering Conference, MSEC2008*, vol. 2, 01 2008.

[6] J. Sikorska, M. Hodkiewicz, and L. Ma, "Prognostic modelling options for remaining useful life estimation by industry," *Mechanical Systems and Signal Processing*, vol. 25, no. 5, pp. 1803–1836, 2011.

[7] M. Ben-Daya, S. Duffuaa, A. Raouf, J. Knezevic, and D. Ait-Kadi, *Handbook of Maintenance Management and Engineering*, 01 2009.

[8] R. L. de Moura, L. B. Werner, and A. Gonzalez, "Management and ownership: A data strategy in the industry 4.0 context," in *Proceedings of the 3rd International Conference on Big Data and Internet of Things*, ser. BDIOT 2019. New York, NY, USA: Association for Computing Machinery, 2019, p. 23–28.

[9] Y. Peng, M. Dong, and M. Zuo, "Current status of machine prognostics in condition-based maintenance: a review," *Int J Adv Manuf Technol*, vol. 50, p. 297–313, 2010.

[10] Z. Gao, C. Cecati, and S. X. Ding, "A survey of fault diagnosis and fault-tolerant techniques—part i: Fault diagnosis with model-based and signal-based approaches," *IEEE Transactions on Industrial Electronics*, vol. 62, no. 6, pp. 3757–3767, 2015.

[11] Y. Yuan, X. Tang, W. Zhou, W. Pan, X. Li, H.-T. Zhang, H. Ding, and J. Goncalves, "Data driven discovery of cyber physical systems," *Nature Communications*, vol. 10, 10 2019.

[12] Y. Yuan, H.-T. Zhang, Y. Wu, T. Zhu, and H. Ding, "Bayesian learning-based model-predictive vibration control for thin-walled workpiece machining processes," *IEEE/ASME Transactions on Mechatronics*, vol. 22, no. 1, pp. 509–520, 2017.

[13] H. M. Hashemian, "State-of-the-art predictive maintenance techniques," *IEEE Transactions on Instrumentation and Measurement*, vol. 60, no. 1, pp. 226–236, 2011.

[14] W. Zhang, D. Yang, and H. Wang, "Data-driven methods for predictive maintenance of industrial equipment: A survey," *IEEE Systems Journal*, vol. 13, no. 3, pp. 2213–2227, 2019.

[15] M. Canizo, E. Onieva, A. Conde, S. Charramendieta, and S. Trujillo, "Real-time predictive maintenance for wind turbines using big data frameworks," in *2017 IEEE International Conference on Prognostics and Health Management (ICPHM)*, 2017, pp. 70–77.

[16] C. Gutschi, N. Furian, J. Suschnigg, D. Neubacher, and S. Voessner, "Log-based predictive maintenance in discrete parts manufacturing," *Procedia CIRP*, vol. 79, pp. 528–533, 2019, 12th CIRP Conference on Intelligent Computation in Manufacturing Engineering, 18-20 July 2018, Gulf of Naples, Italy.

[17] J. Wang, C. Li, S. Han, S. Sarkar, and X. Zhou, "Predictive maintenance based on event-log analysis: A case study," *IBM Journal of Research and Development*, vol. 61, no. 1, pp. 11:121–11:132, 2017.

[18] M. Calabrese, M. Cimmino, F. Fiume, M. Manfrin, L. Romeo, S. Ceccacci, M. Paolanti, G. Toscano, G. Ciandrini, A. Carrotta, M. Mengoni, E. Frontoni, and D. Kapetis, "Sophia: An event-based iot and machine learning architecture for predictive maintenance in industry 4.0," *Information*, vol. 11, no. 4, 2020.

[19] R. Sipos, D. Fradkin, F. Moerchen, and Z. Wang, "Log-based predictive maintenance," in *Proceedings of the 20th ACM SIGKDD International Conference on Knowledge Discovery and Data Mining*, ser. KDD '14. New York, NY, USA: Association for Computing Machinery, 2014, p. 1867–1876.

[20] S. Xiang, D. Huang, and X. Li, "A generalized predictive framework for data driven prognostics and diagnostics using machine logs," in *TENCON 2018 - 2018 IEEE Region 10 Conference*, 2018, pp. 0695–0700.

[21] O. Maron and T. Lozano-Pérez, "A framework for multiple-instance learning," in *Advances in Neural Information Processing Systems*, M. Jordan, M. Kearns, and S. Solla, Eds., vol. 10. MIT Press, 1998.

[22] Y. Lei, N. Li, L. Guo, N. Li, T. Yan, and J. Lin, "Machinery health prognostics: A systematic review from data acquisition to rul prediction," *Mechanical Systems and Signal Processing*, vol. 104, pp. 799–834, 2018.

[23] S. Khan and T. Yairi, "A review on the application of deep learning in system health management," *Mechanical Systems and Signal Processing*, vol. 107, pp. 241–265, 2018.

[24] T. Xia, Y. Dong, L. Xiao, S. Du, E. Pan, and L. Xi, "Recent advances in prognostics and health management for advanced manufacturing paradigms," *Reliability Engineering & System Safety*, vol. 178, pp. 255–268, 2018.

[25] G. Ke, Q. Meng, T. Finley, T. Wang, W. Chen, W. Ma, Q. Ye, and T.-Y. Liu, "Lightgbm: A highly efficient gradient boosting decision tree," in *Advances in Neural Information Processing Systems*, I. Guyon, U. V. Luxburg, S. Bengio, H. Wallach, R. Fergus, S. Vishwanathan, and R. Garnett, Eds., vol. 30. Curran Associates, Inc., 2017.

Analyzing the United State's Nationwide Opioid Crisis and Socio-economic Factors using K-Means Clustering

Ryan McGinnis
Thomas Jefferson College of Biomedical Sciences
Thomas Jefferson University
Philadelphia, PA, USA
Email: ryan.mcginnis@students.jefferson.edu

Les Sztandera
Kanbar College of Design, Engineering, and Commerce
Thomas Jefferson University
Philadelphia, PA, USA
Email: les.sztandera@jefferson.edu

Abstract— **In this paper, we lay out the severity of the opioid crisis by focusing on the current literature of socio-economic addiction factors. We also discuss how opioids have become so prominent in the US. The analysis was done by taking data from one major city per state, totaling 50 cities, and putting them through a K means clustering analysis. Our findings revealed that commute times and average annual income had proportional increase and decrease to their cities opioid death rates. This builds to the current literature of the different quality of life factors that contribute to one's likelihood to develop an addiction.**

Keywords – opioid; k-means; clustering; socio-economic; factors; statistical analysis.

I. Introduction

Over the past several decades, the number of deaths due to opioid use has been rising at an alarming rate. It has reached a critical level where deaths related to opioid use surpass the number deaths due to motor vehicle accidents, gun violence and HIV [3]. This means that opioids can be considered the third leading killer in the United States, beaten only by heart disease and cancer. The opioid epidemic has grown from multiple issues. There are several different reasons someone would use opioids. Opioids are used either by prescription for pain management, or as a result of addiction.

Opioids have become a widely used pain management medication for patients with acute or chronic pain. Opiates are prescribed to those who may be recovering from an injury or surgery and will use opioid to better manage their pain. They are also prescribed for those with chronic pain and patients that need pain management medication for long durations of their lives. It is not uncommon for some of these patients to take the wrong dosage of medication, or forget they already took their medication, and accidentally overdose [2] [4]. In addition to this, they are highly addictive medication and considered a controlled substance by the Food and Drug Adminstration (FDA). It is very common for patients who are prescribed opioids for pain management to become dependent on them [7]. As a result, patients will recover from their injuries addicted to opioids.

Outside of prescription medication, there are many forms of opioid abuse from illicit drugs. Prescription opioids, heron, fentanyl, and other synthetic opioids are often illegally sold on the streets to those suffering from addiction. Opioid addiction being a large contributor to the opioid death tool, it is much more dangerous using the street version of these drugs because they are often diluted with fillers or other drugs. Part of this is because of how accessible opioids and their synthetic counterparts have become. There has been network analysis done to track the distribution of opioids coming from South American countries into the United States [5]. It is no question that the East Coast has been hit the hardest in opioid epidemic simply because that is where the supply is being distributed.

The opioid epidemic also stays out of the public's eye because of how it is factored by the Center for Disease Control (CDC). The CDC considers any opioid related death an "accidental poisoning" and, therefore, falls in with many other categories of death that are considered accidents. This category of accidental deaths is the third leading killer in the United States. Breaking down the different accidents in this category, opioid related deaths would have the highest death toll. Because of this, opioid deaths have surpassed motor vehicle accidents, gun violence, and HIV [3]. However, all opioid accidents are avoidable, and addiction can be treated. With better management for pain treatment, opioid prescription frequency, and how we manage addiction in our cities, it is possible to minimize the opioid death toll.

There are many retrospective studies that have been done that analyze and discuss what demographic factors influence addiction. One study looked at 5,483 overdose patients and laid out all demographic factors for analysis [9]. The most significant finding was that more than half of the patients had an opioid prescription within 90 days of their death. This tells us that opioid prescription history is a massive contributor to one's likelihood to overdose. Having the initial exposure to opioids opens the gate to addiction that the patient otherwise would never have if they were prescribed a different medication. In addition to opioid prescription history, the results showed that the majority of the patients were white/non-Hispanic. Although it is difficult to confirm, many papers analyze ethnic backgrounds of their patients for trends. The challenge that this brings is the diversity of factors that could be influencing the data, outside of the scope of the experiment. For example, ethnic ratios are not likely to be proportionate in each city/state/country where the study is done and this will influence the discussion around the results. It is best to take ethnic background data on the opioid epidemic lightly until there is a larger collection of studies analyzing the data with different factors. Some interesting factors that were studied in the paper reference were education background and marital status. The highest overdose rates came from those with only a high school diploma. The rate of overdoses declined with each higher level of education, bachelor's degree, master's etc. Marital status opioid rates were relatively the same across married, divorced, or single, however there was a steep drop off in the widowed category. Those who were widowed were far less likely to overdose on opioids. Factors like these raise questions as to what exactly can lead one to an opioid dependency, and thus are important to analyze with as many studies as we can.

In "Analyzing the relationships between city opioid deaths and socioeconomic factors" [6], we looked at one major city from each state's opioid death toll, average commute time, budget for roads, and budget for arts and culture in 2018 for a total of 50 cities their respective variables. We also collected data from 2017 however not the full 50 cities due to the fact that budgets and their timelines are allocated differently for each city. The reason we collected these variables was so that we could analyze what different socio-economic factors were related to the opioid death toll, speculate as to how they factored into addiction, and reference other studies that were done to support our findings. The data was analyzed via ANOVA tests and Logistical Regression Tests. Logistical Regression was chosen for this experiment because it showed the trendline for the data. Our findings revealed that commute time yielded significant results in nearly all of the tests it was included in. This was complimented by budget for roads yielding significant results in some of the tests, while budget for arts and culture showed occasional significant results but with no pattern. This shows that commute times had a strong relationship with one's likelihood to overdose on opioids. Since the city's commute times are most likely determined by their respective budget for roads, it makes sense that that variable also share some significant results with commute time. We concluded that commute time and its opioid addiction relationship is connected by a quality-of-life factor.

The significance of these papers that analyze external factors form opioid deaths is that they are a novel approach to uncovering what drives addiction. There is already a massive quantity of papers that look at addiction related deaths retrospectively and compare what each patient had in common [8]. They often look at factors like ethnicity, financial status, education, or career, but they leave out all of the external factors. External factors may prove to be critical in identifying one's likelihood of addiction. External factors are what people are exposed to on a regular basis that can influence addiction, regardless of their demographic factors. By analyzing as many different factors as we can, we can create a foundation of external factors that are known to influence addiction. This will take many more studies of replication and novel approaches to build this foundation, but it will play a critical role in prediction and prevention in the world of addiction medicine.

In this paper, we aim to look at how external factors in one's surroundings may be a contributing factor to their likelihood of using opioids [1]. We will look at average commute times, budgets for roads, and budgets for arts and culture within each city and compare them their opioid death count of 2018. The significance of this, is that it gives cities predictor and preventative models to both prepare and avoid increasing opioid deaths. With K means cluster analysis we can group cities into different categories base on their average commute times and how they allocate their budget.

We will also compare the results with Cluster Mapping data from Harvard Business School and US Economic Development Administration, 2018 [8]. This allows us to look at the country by metropolitan county and see if there are any patterns that are comparable with our results. In Figure 1, we can see the average annual wage, clustered into their respective metropolitan regions. The different annual wage averages can give us some insight as to whether or not it has any effect on one's likelihood of opioid abuse. Looking to see if there are any financial thresholds where cities above or below any certain amount of funding could show some consistency with our clustering data. By comparing these patterns without clustering data, we could reason that financial status does play a role in a city's opioid crisis. If wealthier cities reflect to have higher opioid death rates, this can be used as predictor model.

II. Materials and Methods

For this experiment, we looked at each state in the US and took one major city from them. For each of those cities, we took the following data from 2018: total opioid death toll, average commute time, budget for roads, and budget for arts and culture. We used IBM Statistical Package for the Social Sciences (SPSS) statistical software version 25 to analyze the data.

The first thing we did was standardize all the variables so that they could be compared to each other. This was done by converting them all to their Z scores. In SPSS, a descriptive test was run with all of the variables, and metrics set to their default settings.

With the Z scores collected, the K means cluster analysis was ready to be run. The Z scores were added to the variable list with their labels classed by cities. The maximum number of iterations was set to 99. This is because with

TABLE 1. EACH CITY WITH THEIR RESPECTIVE CLUSTER LABEL FROM THE K-MEANS CLUSTER ANALYSIS.

City	Cluster
Philadelphia	1
Chicago	1
Phoenix	1
Baltimore	1
New York City	2
Detroit	3
Portland	3
Houston	3
Los Angeles	4
Boston	4
Providence	4
Newark	4
Charlotte	4
Indianapolis	4
Las Vegas	4
Atlanta	4
Seattle	4
Orlando	5
Charleston	5
Manchester	5
Louisville	5
Columbus	5
Albuquerque	5
Salt Lake City	5
Nashville	5
Portland	5
Wilmington	5
Hartford	5
Burlington	5
Milwaukee	5
St Louis	5
Columbia	5
Richmond	5
Anchorage	5
Oklahoma City	5
Denver	5
New Orleans	5
Birmingham	5
Cheyenne	5
Minneapolis	5
Des Moines	5
Little Rock	5
Jackson	5
Boise	5
Wichita	5
Fargo	5
Sioux Falls	5
Billings	5
Honolulu	5
Omaha	5

enough iterations that clusters will develop a pattern and average out. The cluster membership was set to save so in retrospect we could analyze which city fits in which cluster. The number of clusters was set to 5. The reason 5 clusters were chosen was because during the initial testing, too few didn't offer enough variation across clusters. Anymore than 5 clusters and we saw that groups started to replicate with no significant difference. 5 clusters gave us a good variation of the different groups that could emerge from the different ways commute time and budget allocation factors into opioid deaths. The ANOVA table was also saved to analyze variance and significance scores of the variables. All other metrics were set to their default settings.

III. Results

In Table 1, we can see how the software categorized the different clusters. The software plotted all of the data points of the variables and grouped them into 1 of 5 clusters based on these generated values. With each iteration, there comes 5 new locations for where the clusters are centered. Each iteration offers a different way to group these cities into clusters. The more iterations that are done helped the software find an average cluster for each city until the city's cluster assignments become redundant. Once the software finds the average cluster that all the cities are assigned, the iterations end, and results are shown. From here we can analyze where each city falls in relation to the clusters.

In Table 1, we can see each city and in which cluster they were categorized. It is worth noting that the opioid crisis is so severe in New York City, that it is the only one in Cluster 2.

IV. Discussion

There are a few key takeaways that this data reveals to us. Initially, it is clear that cities with higher populations tend to lean towards clusters 1, 3 or 4, while smaller cities tend to fall into cluster 5. A simple predictor of the opioid death toll can be population. The more people, the more likely there will be a higher opioid death toll.

In Figure 2, the commute time always sits next to the opioid death toll. This can infer that in many circumstances, the opioid death toll of a city could be predicted by looking at the average commute time for that city. Knowing this, cities can use this as a predictor model for gauging and preparing opioid casualties in their respective cities. The measures that could be taken can be to increase the amount of naloxone supply that emergency responders carry or increasing patrols in high-risk opioid overdose areas. Knowing that commute times are not something that can create addiction, we must ask ourselves how this factor is consistent with opioid deaths across cities. Like many other contributors of addiction, it is a reflection of the quality of life. For the portion that initially seek opioids in their illegal

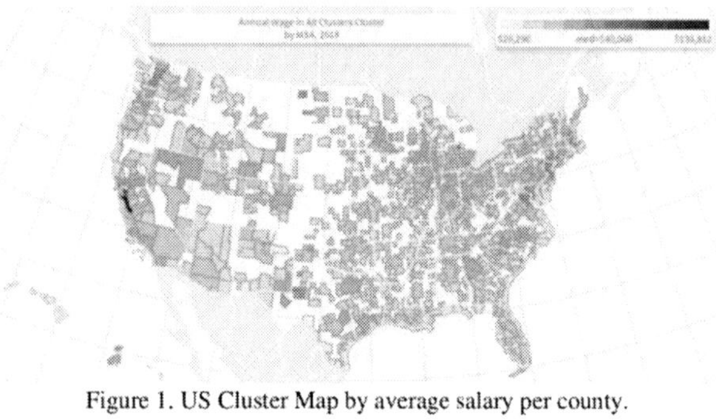

Figure 1. US Cluster Map by average salary per county.

forms or those that have addiction issues prior to their opioid prescription, quality of life is something that has major effects on one's likelihood of developing addiction.

Alternatively, we can see that the city's budget for arts and culture do not show any consistent patterns together. In all clusters, we can see that opioid deaths and budget for arts and culture are inconsistent with each other. As opioid deaths rise and fall, budget for arts does not rise or fall or vice versa with it. This means that budget for arts and culture acted as our control group. By showing us that some groups have no relationship, we can focus on the groups that show relationships like opioid deaths and commute times. Looking at Figure 1, we can see the annual wage averages by metropolitan area of 2018. By comparing the cluster groups to their city's annual wage, we can see that almost all of the high annual wage cities have a proportional relationship with high opioid death tolls. New York City, being in cluster 2 has one of the highest annual wages of $73,000. Close to New York there is Philadelphia in cluster 1 with an annual wage of $59,000 and Baltimore in cluster 1 with an annual wage of $57,000. The surrounding metropolitan areas have a lower annual wage and by more than $10,000 and lower opioid death counts. However, if we look at Los Angeles in cluster 4, it has an annual wage of $60,000. The opioid crisis, being as complex as it is, leads us to believe that this cannot be predicted by commute time, roads, or wage alone, but by a combination of actors. Knowing that the opioid crisis is worse on the East coast, we can see that reflected here by how death rates are higher in wealthier cities along the East Coast with harsher commute times, but not along the West coast.

Illicit opioids and their synthetic counterparts are some of the most lethal illegal drugs in the US right now. With massive amounts of opioids being brought into the US internationally and devastating the east coast, it has become a two pronged attacked on those susceptible to addiction. Not only do those who work their tolerance up eventually become addicted to opioids, but it is very common who have finished their prescription with a dependence on the drug, continue to seek, use and thus turning to the more accessible and cheaper illegal sources. For these illegal opioids, it is not simply a matter of population density, otherwise we would see different results in our study. For example, Los Angeles being in cluster 4 but having one of the highest populations in the country. Illegal opioids are much more widely distributed along the East Coast. Synthetic opioids can be cheap or diluted to be sold at a margin of their price, however purchasing prescription opioids on the street are far more expensive. Knowing this, we must also consider the economic state that some of these critically hit areas are in.

Looking at Figure 2, we can see that the majority of our critically impacted cities, being in clusters 1 or 2, are all metropolitan areas that average over $55,000 annual wage. Knowing this, it stands to reason that these areas have the financial means to afford these opioids either via prescription or illegally. Looking at other cities on the chart, it is interesting to see how as soon the average wage falls roughly below the $55,000 annually, these cities end up in clusters 3, 4, and 5. This tells us that economic status can play a significant role in one's likelihood of addiction to opioids. This is most likely due to the fact that opioids are one of the most expensive drugs to abuse both legally and illegally. Naturally those that cannot afford prescription opioids, or their illegal street counterparts, will not have the same level of exposure as those that can. Those that can afford opioids both in their prescription form or their illegal street form have a much higher risk of becoming addicted. If one is in a pain management situation and can afford an opioid prescription, they are at a much higher risk than it may seem. If they can afford the opioid prescription, they have the risk of developing a dependency. Not only are they at the initial risk from their prescription but following their prescription their odds of developing an addiction only increase if they live in one of these wealthier cities, on the East coast, and make an average income greater than $55,000.

Knowing that those making above $55,000 annually may be a factor contributing to addiction, we can compare that to the findings of the study discussed earlier in this paper. There is a steady decline in overdose likelihood with degree of higher education. Typically, higher salaries are earned by those with a strong educational background. Naturally there are exceptions, but there must be some middle ground of those with only a high school diploma, although still in a high-income job. It is possible that the patients that made up the high school diploma category are from an older generation when going to college was not a standard. This generation would fit the age group where it is very common to take the wrong dose of opioid medication and passing away in their sleep. This means they would also fit the category of having an opioid prescription within 90 days of their death. Evidently, knowing what factors contribute to addiction helps us build the circumstances as to one's likelihood of overdosing.

V. Conclusion

When considering strategies to minimize the death toll of opioids, one must first consider the complexity what

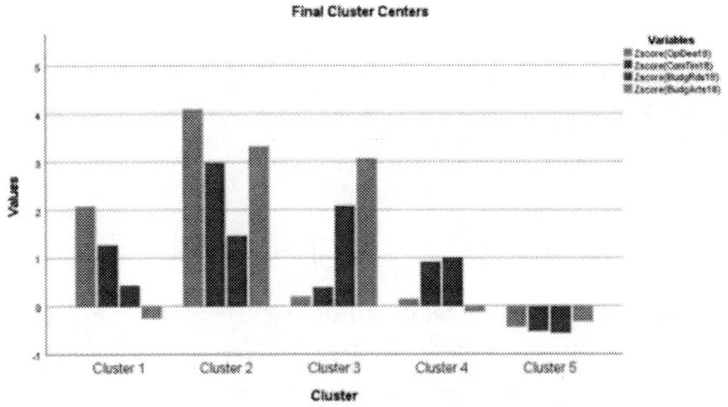

Figure 2. Results from k-means cluster analysis.

influences it. We know that they are a pillar of pain management in modern day society, highly addictive, and have little to no substitutes for chronic pain. They are so addictive that prescribed patients are likely to develop some level of dependence of these drugs, either causing addiction to the prescription opioids themselves or starting a lifestyle of addiction to similar drugs. In addition to having a prescription to an opioid, there are demographic factors that contribute to one's likelihood of addiction. This gives insight as to who is likely to become dependent on their opioid prescriptions and developing addiction, however using this information to prescribe opioids and their strength is at the discretion of the provider and is not uniform. Because of all this, it is to be expected that opioid deaths are to be higher in more densely populated areas. The more people, the more doctors, the more circumstances there will be to prescribe opioids. However, this is not the only pathway that opioids contribute to their death toll.

Opioids have proven to become one of the most dangerous drugs in our society. Being one of the only medications on the market suitable for pain management and its high likelihood of developing a dependency, it creates a high volume of addiction in our society. In addition, opioids are being illegally distributed across our country granting even easier access to them. Legally or illegally, opioids are one of the strongest and easiest drugs to get a hold of in this country. With opioid deaths only continuing to rise, the best thing we can do is uncover what are the factors that drive this epidemic. From this paper, we discovered that a city's commute plays a major role in their opioid death toll. As commute times increased or decreased, the death followed. We also found that annual income is also a factor. Having the financial means to afford these drugs, either legally or illegally, only builds to the accessibility of these drugs. The opioid epidemic is driven by many compounding factors. Knowing that commute times and annual income rates are some of these factors can give cities more insight to prepare and manage their populations.

Further studies can be done that analyze other quality of life factors to see if any of them have a proportionate role in opioid death rates. The model of the study could also be changed. Instead of looking at cities, additional studies could analyze the data by zip code or county. One of the difficulties that this study faced is that, although we analyzed city's budget for roads and arts and culture, there was no way knowing exactly where these funds were allocated to. In 2018, it is possible that a large portion of the budget went to one project as opposed to spread evenly across the city. Because of this, it would be interesting to look at these cities on a smaller scale. If the data is available, analyze where the budgets were allocated (filling potholes, new bridges, multi neighborhood) and compare to how the opioid death toll was affected. One could also use the Harvard Business School Clustering Map, to analyze other factors that may be proportional to a location's opioid death rate. There is more work to be done in order to have a better understanding as to all the different factors that influence addiction and opioid death rates.

REFERENCES

[1] A. Alalawi and L. Sztandera, "Leveraging Statistical Methods and AI Tools for Analysis of Demographic Factors of Opioid Overdose Deaths." International Journal on Advances in Life Sciences: 12(1&2): 24 – 33.

[2] J. Baird et al., "A retrospective review of unintentional opioid overdose risk and mitigating factors among acutely injured trauma patients." Drug Alcohol Depend. 2017; 178: 130 - 135. DOI: 10.1016/j.drugalcdep.2017.04.030.

[3] D. Ciccarone, "Fentanyl in the US heroin supply: A rapidly changing risk environment." The International Journal on Drug Policy. 2017 Aug; 46:107-111. DOI: 10.1016/j.drugpo.2017.06.010.

[4] P. Dilokthornsakul et al., "Risk factors of prescription opioid overdose among Colorado Medicaid beneficiaries." J Pain. 2016; 17 (4): 436 - 443. DOI: 10.1016/j.jpain.2015.12.006.

[5] L. Giommoni, A. Aziani and G. Berlusconi, "How do illicit drugs move across countries? A network analysis of the heroin supply to Europe." J Drug Issues 2017; 47 (2): 217 - 240. DOI:10.1177/0022042616682426.

[6] R. McGinnis, L. Sztandera, R. Vadigepalli, and J. Ruane, "Analyzing the relationships between city opioid deaths and socioeconomic factors" J Opioid Mgmt. 2021; 17(5): 363-382. unpublished.

[7] S. Nechuta, B. Tyndall, S. Mukhopadhyay and M. Mcpheeters, "Sociodemographic factors, prescription history and opioid overdose deaths: A statewide analysis using linked PDMP and mortality data." Drug Alcohol Depend. 2018; 190: 62 - 71. DOI: 10.1016/j.drugalcdep.2018.05.004.

[8] US Cluster Mapping. Harvard Business School. Retrieved June 12, 2021 from https://clustermapping.us/region

[9] B. Zedler et al., "Risk factors for serious prescription opioid-related toxicity or overdose among veterans' health administration patients." Pain Med. 2014; 15 (11): 1911 - 1929. DOI:10.1111/pme.12480.

Data Merging Technique in Cataract Patients in Telangana for Enhancing Public Awareness of Visual Impairment

Amna Alalawi
Strategic Leadership Program
Thomas Jefferson University
Philadelphia, PA, USA
Email: alalawiaj@gmail.com

Les Sztandera
Kanbar College of Design, Engineering, and Commerce
Thomas Jefferson University
Philadelphia, PA, USA
Email: les.sztandera@jefferson.edu

Abstract—**Data merging is a creative technique used in big data analysis and is considered a model in strategic leadership thinking, one which is used in integrating and applying strategy to resolve complex problems. In addition, data merging can draw a blueprint for effective decisions, especially when harnessing data in healthcare to clarify ambiguity on complex issues. The objective of this study was to examine the data merging technique using the Electronic Medical Record (EMR) in LV Prasad Eye Institute (LVPEI) in India, for the aim of contributing to the management of patient care, and ultimately spreading public awareness of cataracts. Our findings revealed that there is a high presence of cataract in the state of Telangana, mostly in rural areas and throughout the different weather seasons in India. Men tend to be the most affected, while home makers make the most visits to the hospital, in addition to employees, students, and laborers. While cataract is most dominant in the older age population, diseases such as astigmatism and conjunctivitis are more present in the younger age population. The study appeared useful for taking preventive measures in the future to manage the treatment of patients who present themselves with eye disorders in Telangana.**

Keywords -data merging; visual impairment; data analysis; public awareness.

I. INTRODUCTION

India is home to over 8.3 million people with Vision Impairment (VI), the highest in the world [1]. Even though, in 1976, India became the first country in the world to start a national program for control of blindness with the goal to reduce blindness prevalence to 0.3 percent by 2020, the prevalence of blindness still stands at 1.99 percent, according to the National Blindness and Visual Impairment Survey, released in October 2019 [2] by the Union Ministry of Health and Family. The prevalence of blindness and visual impairment is one of the highest in Telangana, a state in Southern India, as inferred from survey [2]. The significant reasons indicated in the survey were due to cataract and refractive error [3].

All surveys in the country have shown that cataract, which is a clouding of the lens – turning the lens from clear to yellow, brown, or even milky white, is the most common cause of blindness and all prevention of blindness programs have been "cataract-oriented." However, it has recently been recognized that the visual outcome of the cataract surgeries as well as the training of ophthalmologists has been less than ideal.

This study uses Artificial Intelligence (AI) and machine learning techniques to explore a dataset containing information on 873,448 patients who visited LV Prasad Eye Institute (LVPEI), a multi-tier ophthalmology hospital network, based in Hyderabad. LVPEI operates out of 106 locations, 86 of them being primary eye care centers located in remote rural villages [10]. For the past 24 years, it has served over 14 million people, over 50 percent of them entirely free of cost, irrespective of the complexity of care needed. To date, LVPEI has trained over 13,000 eye care professionals; its faculty has been awarded 22 PhDs with over 1,000 research paper publications, its sight enhancement and visual rehabilitation services served over 100,000 people, and its eye bank services have harvested about 34,000 donor corneas, and it has transplanted more than 17,000 of them to needy patients [10].

The data used in this study was extracted from EyeSmart, the hospital's EMR and health management system, and then merged with climatic factors to test the correlation between climatic variables and ocular diseases presented by the patients [1]. Studying risk factors, primarily associated with climate and the environment can lead to a better understanding of the causes, diagnosis, and treatment of several eye diseases [4].

The goal of an EMR in general is to enable electronic documentation of patients for faster retrieval and research purposes, as well as to transform the entire network into a paperless eco-friendly environment. LVPEI states that Eye Smart is an effective EMR that is enabled for viewing on various digital platforms, such as iPads, iPhones and other tablets. It has also evolved into an effective educational tool for students and fellows who train at the institute. The standard procedures, classifications, evidence-based medicine protocols integrated into the system help to deliver more effective care, and to also aid in teaching.

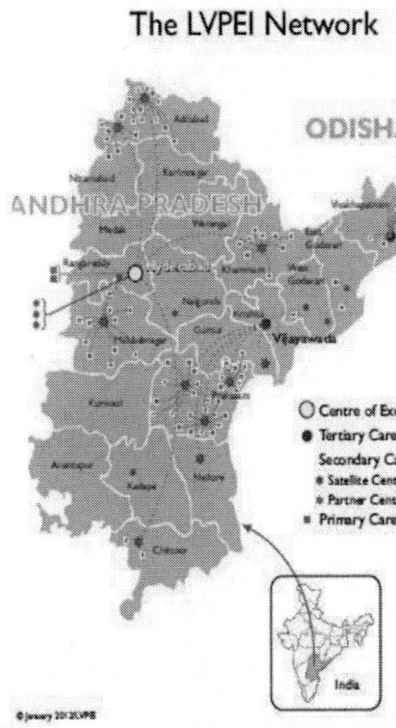

Figure 1. LVPEI Area Map

Figure 1 shows the different centers of LVPEI in the state of Telangana and the total area that it covers in offering eye care to all patients. The map is important to view as the different districts of where patients come from have been examined alongside cataract development.

In Section II of the paper, we explain the data merging technique that was used to merge weather variables with datasets from Eye Smart, to enhance the findings that relate to the development of cataracts in patients, and to potentially offer preventative measures of the development of the disease. The aim is to use knowledge management to gain insight into socio-demographic and environmental factors to shed light on the causes, diagnosis, and treatment of cataracts to enhance ophthalmology practice. In this case, the knowledge management technique consists of applying computational intelligence software to patient data and environmental factors such as race, culture, and climate.

The need for an interconnected health network has reached its peak. Using electronic health records dramatically increases the quality of care for patients and the efficiency of the health care systems. Looking at electronic health systems independently can show limited information about patients. The methodology, which was based on a design thinking approach, offers ways in which EMRs can be studied collectively and holistically to bridge the gap that currently exists between knowledge and practice, and to enhance and improve public awareness of visual impairment.

The rest of the paper is organized into discussing methodology of the research in Section 2, analysis and findings of the data trends in relation to the development of cataracts in Sections 3 and 4, and conclusion including recommendations for preventative measures in Section 5.

II. METHODOLOGY

To gain insight into the climatic and socio-demographic factors that correlate to the risk of ocular diseases in the State of Telangana, we used multiple approaches utilizing AI and statistical software and programming languages, including Microsoft Power BI and Python to explore the dataset, which contained information on 873,448 patients complaining of eye disorder symptoms across multiple categories of ocular diseases. Publicly available climatic variables were obtained and aligned to the dataset through a process called column mutation, and then examined by Microsoft Power BI, which heavily relies on visual illustrations and statistical storytelling to present findings and new insights. It should be noted that Microsoft Power BI is considered an assortment of software or apps which all together works in amalgamation to transform the unrelated sources of data into a visually pattern oriented, continuous and dynamic insights.

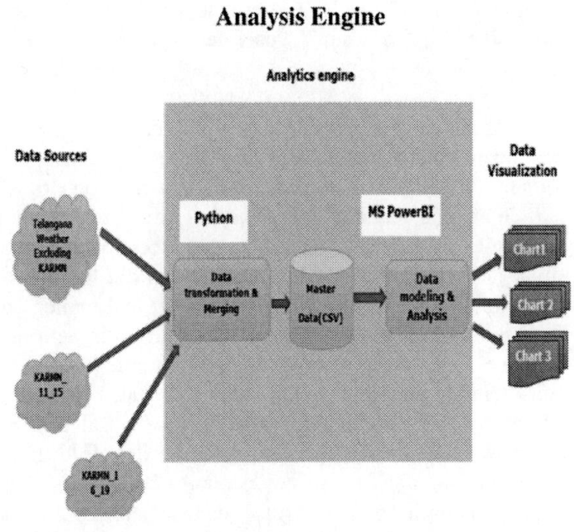

Figure 2. Data Analytics Engine

The purpose of Figure 2 is to explain the process of the data analytics engine that was applied in the research, and that achieved enhanced visibility of patterns and findings. The environment for any data analytics application creation should provide for the following: storing data, processing data, and data analysis alongside visualization. To this end, the process contributed to knowledge expansion of the causes that develop cataract in patients and showed the relationships between all the co-factors studied. Researchers and practitioners in the big analytics sector can use this diagram to understand how data merging can be processed and can lead to potential strategies for greater impact of result findings. The main advantage to data merging is that, in addition to storing big data, it provides a process through which large pools of data can lead to intelligent insight and perform informed decisions based on variables that are merged alongside each other. The outcome led to decisions that can drive recommendations, growth, planning and prevention, which can be defined as the "wisdom" that is created.

Trends in the IT industry have been transformational in the way data is collected and analyzed through AI techniques. There was an era when people were moving from manual computation to automated, computerized applications, then moved into an era of enterprise level applications, which ultimately gave birth to architectural models such as Software as a Service (SaaS) and Platform as a Service (PaaS). Now, we are in the big data era, which can be processed and analyzed in cost-effective ways [5], such as through Microsoft Power BI. The world is moving towards open source to get the benefits of reduced license fees, data storage, and computation costs. It has really made it lucrative and affordable for all sectors and segments to harness the power of data. This is making Big Data synonymous with low cost, scalable, highly available, and reliable solutions that can churn huge amounts of data at incredible speed and generate intelligent insights.

III. Analysis

The scheme of Cynefin Framework acts as a guidance to healthcare practitioners and researchers because of its foundation in the management of information [6]. This particular tool was developed with an aim to offer support and right direction in the process of decision making for situations where the existing intricacy within the outcomes affect the nature of knowledge, forecast, and choice [6]. It has varied domains which necessitate different actions, for instance, the straightforward and complex context is considered equivalent to an "ordered state" of universe which can be interpreted based on the causal and effect association of the facts or findings, and therefore the right orientation or pattern can be decoded [7]. However, in the case of "complicated or chaotic" data, where researchers or healthcare practitioners are unable to formulate a definitive cause and effect association, there is no such immediate conceivable relationship, thus, the Cynefin Framework guides professionals to choose the right orientation based on the "emerging patterns" [7]. This means that the chaotic or unordered state of the world requires pattern dependent management for proper orientation and right decision making [7].

This framework proved very useful in this study as it served as a guide to simplify the complex data in a format that could be studied and explored for suggesting reasons that are associated with the development of cataracts, with the hope of taking preventative measures in the future in patient treatment.

Cynefin Framework

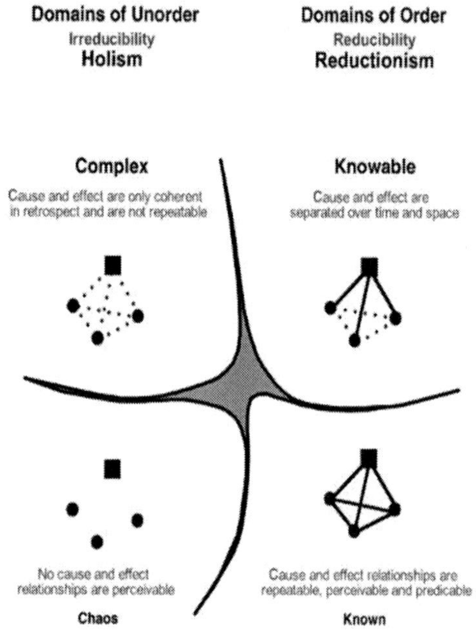

Figure 3. Cause Effect Association Interpretation Using Cynefin Framework

Figure 3 refers to the cause and effect association between the parameters decoded with the aid of the Cynefin Framework [8]. In the figure, the square block indicates the "causal agent", and the dots indicate the "effect agent" [8]. The proper lines refer to the direct association in between the two agents whereas the dotted lines refer to the weak or probable association in between the two agents. When the relation or the conduct of the components of the complex adaptable systems cannot be perceived in direct terms, it is said to be emergent and active in nature. Moreover, these factors again show alterations with time and pressure of the surrounding environment due to which it develops into a new form [8].

The master dataset or the big data, which was explored and analyzed, covered clinical visits between the year 2011-2019, and included demographic information of the patient, including age, gender, profession, data of visit, district of resident, and symptoms and diagnosis of the patient in relation to eye disease. To look further into this issue, we merged climate variables to the dataset to explore the relationship with eye disorders. The AI approach can be of varied types, namely conventional symbolic AI, Computational intelligence, and statistical tools, or the combination of all of the above. Here, in the present assignment, the Computational intelligence approach has been adopted for the analytical purpose [9].

The climate variables we examined were average temperature, minimum temperature, maximum temperature, humidity, rainfall, and solar radiation. This data was retrieved from the Telangana State Development Planning Society in the state of Telangana. The findings that relate to temperature and its effect on cataract in older age was consistent in high and low temperatures.

We followed the model of the Cynefin Framework as a blueprint for analysis to take complicated data into a simplistic form for exploration. By transforming the data into information, we gained certain knowledge about the topic which then was transformed into wisdom that helped us in not only conducting the investigation effectively, but also to gain effective understanding about the research topic. The readers can also rely on this wisdom to gain conceptual clarity and understanding of the subject matter.

IV. Summary of Findings

This section highlights key findings of the study, as well as trends in relation to the subject matter as per the demographic and climatic variables tested, which as discussed in the previous section were were average temperature, minimum temperature, maximum temperature, humidity, rainfall, and solar radiation. This data was retrieved from the Telangana State Development Planning Society in the state of Telangana, and then merged with the EMR of patient records using data merging as the main technique for analysis.

The analysis shows that astigmatism (irregularity in the shape of the cornea) and conjunctivitis (inflammation or infection of the conjunctiva) are the most prevalent eye diseases among the youth population (ages 21-40) in Telangana. For older adults, (ages 41-70), the analysis shows that cataract and pseudophakos are the most prevalent eye diseases. Paloncha, Kothagudam, Kothagudam Bazar, Bhadrachalam, Mauguru, Madhapur, Kondapur, Adilabad, Yellandu, Kondapur and Tekulapalli are the top ten locations with the highest number of hospital visits, with Paloncha being identified as a high-risk location because of the presence of the state-run thermal power plant. In addition, the analysis shows a consistent pattern for high prevalence of cataract within the minimum ranges of temperature (20°C - ~30°C). The analysis also shows that cataract is the most prevalent eye disease in the rainfall season.

Influence Diagram - Taking Knowledge to Wisdom

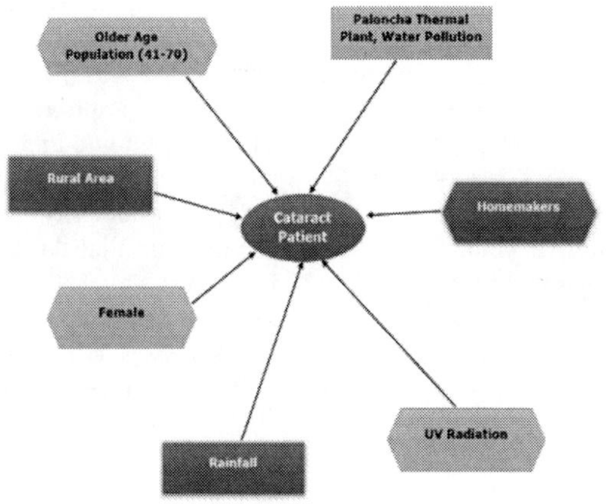

Figure 4. Influence Diagram of Cataract Patients and Co-Factors Affecting Cataract

Figure 4 depicts the summary of findings in a form of an influence diagram. Influence diagrams are closely related to decision trees and often used in conjunction with them. An influence diagram displays a summary of the information contained in a decision tree. It involves four variable types for notation: a decision (a rectangle), chance (an oval), objective (a hexagon), and function (a rounded rectangle). Looking at the data analysis holistically through Figure 4 creates the ease to depict the main causes of the development of cataracts.

V. Conclusion

As concluded from the research, the healthcare EMR system is large and complex, one that does not naturally lend itself to easy analysis, design or even understanding. In the case of studying the patients' data in Eye Smart, and summarizing the co-factors that play a role in the development of cataracts in Telangana, an influence diagram was created to show the different co-factors that lead to cataract according to the findings generated. This was further analyzed with a systems thinking approach, a method that allows consideration of the whole rather than individual elements of representation of the related co-factors.

The mission of data merging is to try to improve societal outcomes by developing, integrating, and using appropriate analytical tools in these new approaches, to offer healthcare practitioners the opportunity to design better patient-care policies and well-targeted regulations to lower the burdens of the economic and social problems associated with diseases, such as cataracts. An important starting point is to understand how data analysis and its results can be incorporated into the actual decision-making process. decision-making process.

Visual impairment imposes substantial costs on society, particularly to individuals with visual impairment and their families. Eliminating or reducing disabilities from visual impairment through public awareness of preventive care, early diagnosis, more intensive disease treatment, and new medical technologies could significantly improve the quality of life for people with visual impairment and their families, while also potentially reducing national health care expenditure and increasing productivity in the underdeveloped world. We recommend that the authorities spend more time and funds on creating awareness to educate individuals and families about the visual impairment crisis in Telangana. Creation of awareness is one of the most comprehensive approaches to sensitize communities concerning the consequences of eye disorders, but also one of the avenues to equip individuals with knowledge, skills and correct attitudes towards a healthier lifestyle.

Besides creation of awareness, this study also recommends ophthalmologists' understanding of all factors that influence a disease other than medical history, and to look at each patient uniquely in terms of social income, cultural upbringing and offer a more individualistic approach in educating a patient from the criticality of self-care, to help patients deviate away from high risk situations that can cause eye disorders, and to find ways from an earlier age for more effective preventative results that can reduce the number of individuals with vision impairment.

REFERENCES

[1] S. Marmamula, R. Khanna, and G. Rao, "Unilateral visual impairment in rural south India–Andhra Pradesh Eye Disease Study (APEDS)", *International Journal of Ophthalmology*, *9* no.5, pp.763, 2016.

[2] G. Rao, N. Khanna, and A. Payal, "The global burden of cataract," *Current Opinion in Ophthalmology*, *22* no. 1, pp. 4-9, 2011.

[3] A. Das, P. Kammari, and S. Ranganath Vadapalli, "Big data and the eyeSmart electronic medical record system-An 8-year experience from a three-tier eye care network in India," *Indian Journal of Ophthalmology*, *68* no. 3, pp. 427, 2020.

[4] A. Clark, J. Ng, N. Morlet, and J. Semmens, "Big data and ophthalmic research," *Survey of Ophthalmology*, *61* no.4, pp. 443-465, 2016.

[5] S. Gupta, Real-Time Big Data Analytics. Packt Publishing Ltd. 2016.

[6] D.J Snowden and M.E Boone, A leader's framework for decision making. *Harvard Business Review*, 85(11), p.68. 2007.

[7] G. Kempermann, Cynefin as reference framework to facilitate insight and decision-making in complex contexts of biomedical research. *Frontiers in Neuroscience*, 11, p.634. 2017.

[8] J.P. Sturmberg and C.M. Martin, Complexity and health–yesterday's traditions, tomorrow's future. *J Eval Clin Pract*, 15(3), pp.543-548. 2009.

[9] R. Ackoff,. "From Data to Wisdom." *Journal of Applied Systems Analysis,* 16.1 pp. 3-9. 1989.

[10] A Das, P Kammari, R Vadapalli, and S. Basu. Big Data and the Eyesmart electronic medical record system. *Indian Journal of Ophthalmology*. pp. 427-432. 2020.

How Do Socioeconomic Factors Correlate to COVID-19 Cases and Deaths?

Anthony Rene Guzman, Jin Soung Yoo
Department of Computer Science
Purdue University Fort Wayne
Fort Wayne, IN, United States of America
Email: guzmar01@pfw.edu, yooj@pfw.edu

Abstract—**The COVID-19 pandemic has spread around the world and had significantly affected every aspect of our day-to-day lives. Non-clinical socioeconomic factors may be important explanatory variables of COVID-19 cases and deaths. This work explores the correlations between various socioeconomic factors and the number of cases and deaths resulting from COVID-19. The study was conducted with county-level data from the U.S. Census Bureau and John Hopkins University, and examined the impact of ten different socioeconomic factors regarding population size, poverty, median household income, employment and education levels on COVID-19 prevalence across all counties in the United States. Correlation coefficients were computed between each of the socioeconomic factors and the total number of cumulative COVID-19 cases and deaths using various correlation analysis methods such as the Pearson, Kendall, and Spearman formulas. The results of the analyses echo the findings of similar research regarding COVID-19 and are visualized and discussed.**

Keywords- COVID-19; socioeconomic factors; correlation analysis.

I. INTRODUCTION

Coronavirus disease-19 (COVID-19) is a novel coronavirus that was first identified in Wuhan, China, in early December of 2019 [1]. Since its discovery, COVID-19 has affected world economies and lives across the globe. Due to the unknown and rapidly developing nature of the pandemic, governments, scientists and researchers have been working nonstop to develop a vaccine and understand more about this novel virus.

So far, old age and pre-existence of chronic conditions have been linked to more severe COVID-19 symptoms [2]. Other potential factors such as race/ethnicity and socioeconomic factors may also play an important role in the COVID-19 pandemic. The socioeconomic gradient in health is ubiquitous and has been described across pathologies, in life expectancy and mortality [3]. Low income might affect living conditions in many ways, such as residence in more deprived neighborhoods and housing conditions. A lower education level can be indirectly associated with several factors that may increase the risk of developing severe forms of COVID-19. However, the influence of socioeconomic factors on COVID-19 transmission, severity and outcomes is not yet known and is subject to scrutiny and investigation.

This study aims to identify any correlation between various socioeconomic factors and the number of cases and deaths resulting from COVID-19 across all counties in the United States. For this research, many socioeconomic data sets were considered and included various topics such as poverty, race, income, method of transportation, and more. The data for some factors, such as method of transportation to work and field of occupation, were not available on a granular level and were excluded from the analyses. Out of these many factors, ten were chosen to be considered for the correlation analysis. These socioeconomic factors were selected to correlate with COVID-19 cases and deaths due to their high data availability and novelty, Federal Information Processing Standards (FIPS) code-level data granularity, and prevalence in existing pandemic research. These factors are (1) total population size, (2) median household income, (3) population and percentage of population in poverty, (4) total employed population size, (5) total unemployed population size, (6) unemployment rate, (7) population and percentage of population without a high school diploma, (8) population and percentage of population with only a high school diploma, (9) population and percentage of population with some college education or an associate's degree, (10) population and percentage of population with a bachelor's degree or higher. This work explores each socioeconomic factor separately and analyzes the relationship with COVID-19 cases and deaths. The ten socioeconomic factors were grouped together based on the socioeconomic topic they fall under, which resulted in four groups: *population size*, *income and poverty*, *employment*, and *education*. Socioeconomic status might be one determinant that can tell us which regions are more vulnerable and high risk to the coronavirus disease. If we can find correlations between socioeconomic factors and COVID-19 outcomes, the findings will be useful in determining what regions may benefit most from a strategic allocation of health care resources.

This research used official county-level data sets gathered from the U.S. Census Bureau, U.S. Department of Agriculture (USDA) [4], and John Hopkins University [5]. The COVID-19 data sets provided by John Hopkins University contain time-series data for cumulative COVID-19 related cases and deaths, separated by county. Socioeconomic data sets provided by the U.S. Census Bureau and processed by the USDA contain data regarding education, population, poverty, and unemployment for each county of the United States in 2019.

The biggest challenge encountered when conducting this research was determining the best way to quantify the relationship between socioeconomic factors and COVID-19 cases and deaths. There are many different data mining tasks that could lead to interesting results, such as rule-based classification, time-series analysis, or clustering [6]. Another challenge of this research was determining how to correlate socioeconomic factors with COVID-19 cases and deaths. Quantitative values for socioeconomic factors are gathered infrequently and represent a value for a certain point in time (e.g., percentage of population in poverty in 2019). COVID-19 cases and deaths, on the other hand, take the form of a time-series with high variations in case and death frequency. These variations can be attributed to the time of the year, trends in social distancing, and changes in government ordinances. The last difficulty was that data on individual-level socioeconomic position are not being collected. The World Health Organization standard COVID-19 case report form only asks for each patient's age, sex/gender, place where the case was diagnosed, and usual place of residence. This impedes the sophisticated analysis of impact of socioeconomic factors.

This study uses Pearson, Kendall, and Spearman correlation coefficients in order to determine the relationships between socioeconomic factors and COVID-19 cases and deaths. By analyzing each socioeconomic factor separately, we investigated which factors most strongly correlate to COVID-19 cases and deaths. This research differentiates itself by using various correlation methods and is novel in the sense that the data being analyzed is more accurate due to its granularity. Similar research in this field has been done by using state-level data, but the data in this research is at the county level. Our analysis results offer some interesting findings. Visualization is also used to determine which geographical regions of the country are most vulnerable in the event of a pathogenic outbreak.

The following section describes the related literature. Section 3 describes the data and data preprocessing methods used. Section 4 describes correlation analysis and the methods used in detail. Section 5 describes the results of the research. Section 6 discusses the findings, and Section 7 concludes this paper.

II. Literature Review

Recently, there has been an abundance of research with respect to COVID-19 and data analysis. Applications for COVID-19 include COVID-19 detection and diagnosis, tracking and identification of the outbreak, infodemiology, biomedicine, and pharmacotherapy [7]. This section describes some related work in the field of statistically driven COVID-19 analysis.

Kurian et al. [8] evaluated the correlation between COVID-19 cases and Google Trends data on a state-by-state basis using the Pearson correlation method. Their findings suggest that certain keywords searched online were linked to high COVID-19 activity in the time leading up to spikes in cases, such as *face mask*, *Lysol*, and *COVID stimulus check*.

Shi et al. [9], using data on occupational position from 484 COVID-19 patients in Zhejiang Province of China, reported that severe cases were more likely to be agricultural workers and less likely to be self-employed than mild cases. Oh et al. [10] analyzed various socioeconomic factors of the South Korean population using a multivariable logistic regression model to determine if a lower socioeconomic standing increases the risk of contracting COVID-19.

Huang et al. [11] used k-means clustering ($k = 3$) to show how socioeconomically disadvantaged groups were disproportionately affected by stay-at-home orders. The results of their research showed that those who were more likely to stay at home were typically white, wealthy, well educated, and resided in regions with low unemployment and high median household income. Research conducted by Hawkins et al. [12] echoed these findings, where regions with low socioeconomic status are shown to have higher rates of COVID-19 cases and deaths.

Burton et al. [13] found that African Americans have been disproportionately affected by COVID-19. African American patients in the study were also found to be associated with older age, reside in a low-income area, and have a higher obesity rate. In turn, these socioeconomic factors contributed to their risk of contracting COVID-19. Gangemi et al. [14] also analyzed different socioeconomic factors to determine if significant correlations could be identified. They discovered that Gross Domestic Product (GDP) per capita and number of flights per capita were significantly correlated to the number of COVID-19 cases on a country-level basis.

Hatef et al. [15] developed an Area Deprivation Index (ADI) to measure a ZIP code's composite socioeconomic characteristics, using factors such as population size, age, gender, and race distribution. Populations in ZIP codes with higher ADI scores were found to be more at risk for COVID-19 related cases and deaths than those in ZIP codes with low ADI scores. Roser [16] found that the Human Development Index (HDI), a composite score that measures life expectancy, access to education, and standard of living, is significantly correlated to the number of COVID-19 cases in a country. The Distressed Communities Index (DCI) [17], a comprehensive estimate of a location's socioeconomic status, was used for analyzing COVID-19 case and fatality data in a Mann-Whitney U test.

III. Data and Data Preprocessing

This section describes the data and data preprocessing in detail.

A. Data

Two main data sets were gathered from several sources for use in the correlation analyses. The first main data set contains county-level COVID-19 cases and deaths data and was provided by the COVID-19 Data Repository by the Center for Systems Science and Engineering (CSSE) at John Hopkins University [5]. The COVID-19 Data Repository is a publicly available data source that contains county-level time-series data for cumulative COVID-19 related cases and deaths that is updated daily. The data presents 3,340 counties and county-equivalents. The time series data begins on January 22, 2020 and is updated daily. For this research, we used the data entries up until March 27, 2021. This date was selected to provide the most up-to-date correlation analyses. However, other dates such as thirty or ninety days after an outbreak has been identified may also be useful in determining how cases and deaths will continue to occur.

The second main data was provided by the U.S. Census Bureau and processed by the Economic Research Service of the U.S. Department of Agriculture [4]. There are 3,193 counties represented within this data set. We used the data of 2019. The data set contains county-level data for various socioeconomic factors, including poverty levels, median household income, population size, employment levels, and education levels. For this research, the socioeconomic factors analyzed are:

(1) total population size,
(2) median household income,
(3) population and percentage of population in poverty,
(4) total employed population size,
(5) total unemployed population size,
(6) unemployment rate,
(7) population and percentage of population without a high school diploma,
(8) population and percentage of population with only a high school diploma,
(9) population and percentage of population with some college education or an associate's degree,
(10) population and percentage of population with a bachelor's degree or higher.

B. *Data Preprocessing*

The data sets were first pre-processed for easier formatting. In order to eliminate confusion that may stem from how certain county names could be stored (e.g., "St. Mary's County" versus "Saint Marys County"), the data sources were merged based on FIPS codes [18], such that each FIPS code had a one-to-one relationship with each socioeconomic factor. FIPS codes were developed by the National Institute of Standards and Technology and are used to identify unique geographic regions such as states, counties, and county-equivalents (e.g., parishes, boroughs, and independent cities). Once the data sets were pre-processed and merged based on FIPS, the data sets were formatted and prepared for conducting data analysis.

IV. ANALYSIS METHODS

The primary goal of this study is to determine to what degree relationships exist between various socioeconomic factors and the number of COVID-19 cases and deaths. Correlation coefficients were used in this research to determine the degree to which these relationships exist.

Correlation is a value that describes the degree to which two variables are related [19]. A correlation coefficient falls within the range of -1 and 1. Correlation values closer to 1 describe a positive correlation, which means that as one variable increases, the other variable also increases. Correlation values closer to -1 describe a negative correlation, which means that as one variable increases, the other variable decreases. Correlation values close to 0 have little to no correlation, with a very weak or nonexistent pattern to the two variables [20]. The three correlation analysis methods used in this research were the Pearson, Kendall, and Spearman methods.

The Pearson correlation method is a parametric measure that produces a correlation coefficient r, which measures the direction and degree of relationships between pairs of variables. The Pearson correlation formula is shown below, where r is the correlation coefficient, x_i are the values of the first variable, $\bar{x}$ is the mean of the first variable, y_i are the values of the second variable, and $\bar{y}$ is the mean of the second variable [21]:

$$r = \frac{\sum(x_i - \bar{x})(y_i - \bar{y})}{\sqrt{\sum(x_i - \bar{x})^2 \sum(y_i - \bar{y})^2}}$$

The Kendall rank correlation method is a non-parametric measure that assesses the correspondence between the rankings of pairs of variables. The Kendall correlation formula is shown below, where r is the correlation coefficient, c is the number of concordant pairs, d is the number of discordant pairs, and n is the total number of points. For a pair of points (x_i, y_i) and (x_j, y_j), the pair is said to be concordant if $x_i > x_j$ and $y_i > y_j$, or if $x_i < x_j$ and $y_i < y_j$. If neither condition is true, that pair is said to be discordant [22]:

$$r = \frac{(c - d)}{\binom{n}{2}}$$

The Spearman rank correlation formula is another non-parametric measure that determines the correlation between the ranks of pairs of variables. The Spearman correlation formula is shown below, where r is the correlation coefficient, d_i is the difference between the two ranks of each point, and n is the number of points [23]:

$$r = \frac{6 \sum d_i^2}{n(n^2 - 1)}$$

Fahrudin et al. [24] suggest that the Kendall and Spearman correlation analysis methods are more appropriate for this type of research because they are non-parametric methods. These types of methods do not make any assumptions about the model of the data and can operate on incomplete data, making them better suited for uncertain and rapidly evolving events like pandemics.

V. RESULTS

Correlation coefficients were computed between each of the socioeconomic factors and the total number of cumulative COVID-19 cases and deaths. Because correlation formulas determine the degree of association between two variables, the coefficients were calculated using one socioeconomic factor at a time. For each analysis, the Pearson, Kendall, and Spearman correlation methods were used. When discussing the results of the correlation analyses, we used the average of three correlation coefficients. Table 1 is used to describe the strength of the correlation coefficients [25]:

TABLE I. CATEGORIZATION OF CORRELATION COEFFICIENTS

Correlation Coefficient (*r*)	Degree of Association
[0.8, 1.0]	Very Strong (+)
[0.6, 0.8)	Strong (+)
[0.4, 0.6)	Medium (+)
(0.4, 0)	Weak (+)
(0, -0.4)	Weak (-)
[-0.4, -0.6)	Medium (-)
[-0.6, -0.8)	Strong (-)
[-0.8, 1.0]	Very Strong (-)

A. *Relationship with Population Size*

First, we examined the correlation with the socioeconomic factor of (1) total population size. Total population size with regards to COVID-19 cases has correlation coefficients of 0.970086 (Pearson), 0.842793 (Kendall), and 0.953558 (Spearman) with an average of 0.922146. With regards to COVID-19 deaths, the correlation coefficients are 0.930995 (Pearson), 0.727279 (Kendall), and 0.888893 (Spearman) with an average of 0.849055. The relationship between population size and COVID-19 cases and deaths has a very strong positive correlation.

B. *Relationship with Income and Poverty*

Second, we examined the correlation with the socioeconomic factor of (2) median household income with COVID-19 cases and deaths. Median household income with regards to COVID-19 cases has correlation coefficients of 0.220982 (Pearson), 0.220541 (Kendall), and 0.324824 (Spearman) with an average of 0.255449. With regards to COVID-19 deaths, the correlation coefficients are 0.188385 (Pearson), 0.144611 (Kendall), and 0.214694 (Spearman) with an average of 0.182564. Both show weak positive correlations. Figure 1 shows the relationship between COVID-19 cases and median house income. The socioeconomic factor is mapped in gray, with higher values being more gray and lower values being less gray. The number of COVID-19 cases by county are mapped in green, with counties having many cases being greener than counties with fewer cases. As shown in Figure 1, median household income is not a great indicator of the probability of contracting COVID-19. There are some regions with higher average household income that are greener, but not by a significant margin.

Third, we examined the correlation with the socioeconomic factor of (3) population and percentage of population in poverty. The population size in poverty with regards to COVID-19 cases has correlation coefficients of 0.956651 (Pearson), 0.776574 (Kendall), and 0.925292 (Spearman), with an average of 0.886172. With regards to COVID-19 deaths, the correlation coefficients are 0.93817 (Pearson), 0.731511 (Kendall), and 0.893441 (Spearman), with an average of 0.854374. Both show very strong positive correlations. In contrast, the percentage of a population in poverty with regards to COVID-19 cases has average correlation coefficients of -0.104471 and -0.044366, respectively, which show weak negative correlations.

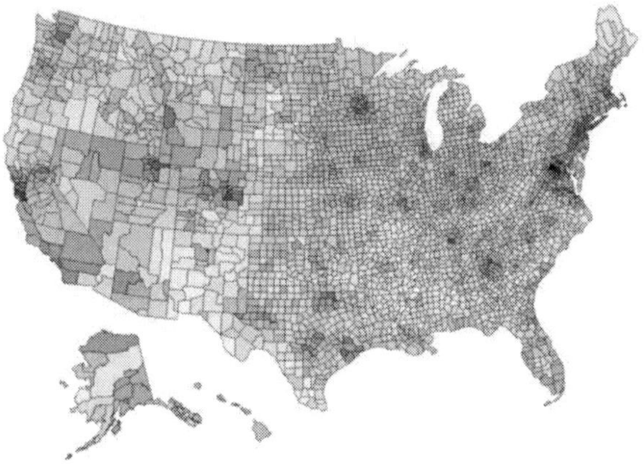

Figure 1. Relationship of Median House Income and COVID-19 Cases

C. *Relationship with Employed and Unemployed*

Fourth, we then examined the correlation with the socioeconomic factor of (4) total employed population size. Employed population size with regards to COVID-19 cases has correlation coefficients of 0.964435 (Pearson), 0.824678 (Kendall), and 0.945477 (Spearman) with an average of 0.911530. With regards to COVID-19 deaths, the correlation coefficients are 0.921836 (Pearson), 0.704132 (Kendall), and 0.872068 (Spearman) with an average of 0.832679. Both show very strong positive correlations.

Fifth, we examined the correlation with the socioeconomic factor of (5) total unemployed population size. Unemployed population size with regards to COVID-19 cases has correlation coefficients of 0.967212 (Pearson), 0.795141 (Kendall), and 0.933167 (Spearman) with an average of 0.898507. With regards to COVID-19 deaths, the correlation coefficients are 0.942800 (Pearson), 0.707763 (Kendall), and 0.875330 (Spearman) with an average of 0.841964. Both also show a very strong positive correlation.

Sixth, we examined the correlation with the socioeconomic factor of (6) unemployment rate. A region's unemployment rate with regards to COVID-19 cases has correlation coefficients of -0.043564 (Pearson), -0.013928 (Kendall), and -0.012187 (Spearman) with an average of -0.023227. With regards to COVID-19 deaths, the correlation coefficients are -0.018840 (Pearson), -0.025321 (Kendall), and 0.042350 (Spearman) with an average of 0.016277. They show a weak negative and weak positive correlation, respectively.

D. *Relationship with Education*

Seventh, we examined the correlation with the socioeconomic factor of (7) population and percentage of population with less than a high school diploma. The population size without a high school diploma with regards to COVID-19 cases has correlation coefficients of 0.965225 (Pearson), 0.764172 (Kendall), and 0.918743 (Spearman), with an average of 0.882713. With regards to COVID-19 deaths, the correlation coefficients are 0.945272 (Pearson), 0.734748 (Kendall), and 0.897835 (Spearman), with an average of 0.859285. Both show a very strong positive correlation. In contrast, the percentage of a population without a high school diploma with regards to COVID-19 cases and deaths has average correlation coefficients of -0.041244 and 0.017281, which show a weak negative and weak positive correlation, respectively.

Eighth, we examined the correlation with the socioeconomic factor of (8) population and percentage of population with only a high school diploma. The population size with only a high school diploma with regards to COVID-19 cases has correlation coefficients of 0.959932 (Pearson), 0.812512 (Kendall), and 0.943194 (Spearman), with an average of 0.905213. With regards to COVID-19 deaths, the correlation coefficients are 0.938317 (Pearson), 0.735719 (Kendall), and 0.89646 (Spearman), with an average of 0.856832. Both show a very strong positive correlation. In contrast, the percentage of a population with only a high school diploma with regards to COVID-19 cases and deaths has average correlation coefficients of -0.262308 and -0.208336, which show a weak negative and weak positive correlation, respectively.

Ninth, we examined the correlation with the socioeconomic factor of (9) population and percentage of population with some college education or an associate's degree. The population size with some college education or an associate's degree with regards to COVID-19 cases has correlation coefficients of 0.961137 (Pearson), 0.809469 (Kendall), and 0.938058 (Spearman), with an average of 0.902888. With regards to COVID-19 deaths, the correlation coefficients are 0.909433 (Pearson), 0.704526 (Kendall), and 0.871939 (Spearman), with an average of 0.828633. Both show a very strong positive correlation. In contrast, the percentage of a population with some college education or an associate's degree with regards to COVID-19 cases and deaths has average correlation coefficients of -0.113840 and -0.141439, respectively, which show weak negative correlations.

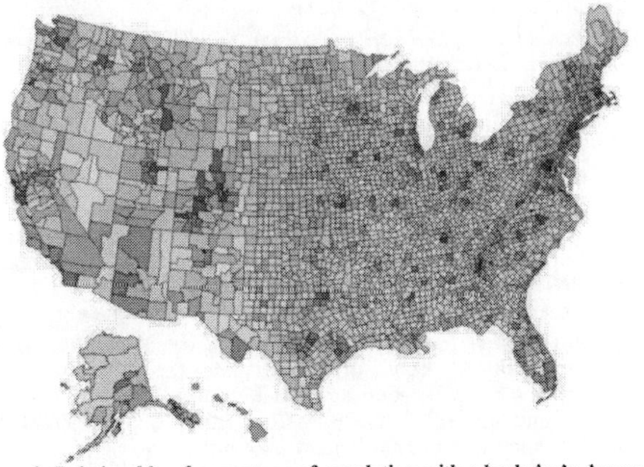

Figure 2. Relationship of percentage of population with a bachelor's degree or higher and COVID-19 Cases

Lastly, we examined the correlation with the socioeconomic factor of (10) population and percentage of population with a bachelor's degree or higher. The population size with a bachelor's degree or higher with regards to COVID-19 cases has correlation coefficients of 0.910476 (Pearson), 0.767488 (Kendall), and 0.912052 (Spearman), with an average of 0.863339. With regards to COVID-19 deaths, the correlation coefficients are 0.882014 (Pearson), 0.658304 (Kendall), and 0.831540 (Spearman), with an average of 0.790619. They show a very strong positive and strong positive correlation, respectively. In contrast, the percentage of a population with a bachelor's degree or higher with regards to COVID-19 cases and deaths has average correlation coefficients of 0.290129 and 0.225420, respectively, which show weak positive correlations. As shown in Figure 2, there is no significant relationship between the percentage of a population with a bachelor's degree or higher and COVID-19 cases and deaths.

VI. Discussion

By analyzing each socioeconomic factor separately, we could determine which factors most strongly correlate to COVID-19 cases and deaths. The strongest correlations among the socioeconomic factors used in the data analysis are *total population size*, *population with only a high school diploma*, and *total employed population size*. The weakest correlations among the socioeconomic factors used in the data analysis are *unemployment rate*, *percentage of population with less than a high school diploma*, and *percentage of population in poverty*. No strong negative correlations were found from the analyses.

While the results of the correlation analyses are mostly expected, they did offer some surprising findings. The correlation coefficients are very similar between total employed population size and total unemployed population size. This could suggest that those that who are employed have roughly the same likelihood of contracting COVID-19 as those who are unemployed. The industry in which those employed work also plays a significant role. For example, someone who uses public transportation and travels to the workplace has a much higher chance of contracting COVID-19 than someone who works from home due to a constant proximity to people outside of their residence. This idea is further supported by the fact that there is no correlation between a region's unemployment rate and the number of COVID-19 cases and deaths.

From the results of the analyses, it is evident that population density is a very strong indicator for the severity of impact caused by COVID-19 in each region. This can be explained by the fact that a region with a higher population density is more prone to airborne transmission of COVID-19. Regions of the country with a higher population density will have more people contributing to economic activity (e.g., people working, shopping, eating out, running chores).

The results of the analyses show that the level of education a person has obtained has little correlation with COVID-19 cases and deaths. This suggests that a person without a high school education has roughly the same likelihood of contracting COVID-19 as someone with a bachelor's degree or higher. Although jobs that require a bachelor's degree or other form of higher education are more likely to offer work-from-home solutions, these solutions have little bearing on the likelihood of contracting COVID-19.

Lastly, the results show that population-based socioeconomic factor values provide much stronger correlation coefficients than percentage of population values. This can be attributed to the fact that cumulative COVID-19 cases and deaths are represented by total counts, while percentages are orders of magnitudes smaller and represent a fraction of the population, rather than the individualistic counts. Further research in this field would benefit most from matching data types. In other words, total COVID-19 cases and deaths should be analyzed with the total number of people with a certain socioeconomic factor. Conversely, socioeconomic factors represented as percentages of a population should be analyzed with percentages of a population affected by COVID-19.

VII. CONCLUSION

The effects of COVID-19 have been far-reaching and ubiquitous; no public health event has taken such a toll on the global community for over a century. This work investigated correlations between various socioeconomic factors and the number of cases and deaths resulting from COVID-19 in the United States. Furthermore, this research showed how statistical computing and visualization can help determine which geographical regions of the country are most vulnerable in the event of a pathogenic outbreak. The information gained from this study will be useful in determining the proper distribution of medical resources when the next pandemic inevitably strikes.

It is imperative that data analysis is further conducted on COVID-19. For future works, this research can be continued by performing rule-based association analysis, which can determine which subsets of variables are most strongly associated with COVID-19 related cases and deaths.

REFERENCES

[1] G. Spiteri et al., "First cases of coronavirus disease 2019 (COVID-19) in the WHO European Region, 24 January to 21 February 2020", *Euro surveillance: bulletin Europeen sur les maladies transmissibles = European communicable disease bulletin* vol. 25,9: 2000178. doi:10.2807/1560-7917.ES.2020.25.9.2000178, pp. 2-7, 2020.

[2] R. H. Shmerling, "COVID-19: If You're Older and Have Chronic Health Problems, Read This." *Harvard Health Publishing*, The President and Fellows of Harvard College. URL : www.health.harvard.edu/blog/covid-19-if-youre-older-and-have-chronic-health-problems-read-this-2020040119396. 2020. [retrieved : September, 2021]

[3] R. G. Wilkinson and K. E. Pickett, "Income inequality and socioeconomic gradients in mortality." *American journal of public health* vol. 98,4, doi:10.2105/AJPH.2007.109637, pp. 699-704, 2008.

[4] J. Pender and E. A. Dobis, Economic Research Service County-level Data Sets. *U.S. Department of Agriculture.* 2021. [retrieved: September, 2021]

[5] E. Dong, H. Du, and L. Gardner, "An interactive web-based dashboard to track COVID-19 in real time". Lancet Inf Dis. 20(5):533-534. doi: 10.1016/S1473-3099(20)30120-1, pp. 544-534, 2020.

[6] J. Han, M. Kamber, and J. Pei, "Data Mining: Concepts and Techniques". Morgan Kaufmann Publishers. 2001.

[7] C. Hertzman, "Putting the concept of biological embedding in historical perspective". Proc Natl Acad Sci U S A. 109 Suppl 2, pp. 17160-17167, 2012.

[8] S. J. Kurian, "Correlations Between COVID-19 Cases and Google Trends Data in the United States: A State-by-State Analysis". *Mayo Clinic Proceedings, 95*(11), pp. 2370-2381, 2020.

[9] Y. Shi et al., "Host susceptibility to severe COVID-19 and establishment of a host risk score: findings of 487 cases outside Wuhan". Critical Care, 24:108. 2020.

[10] T. K. Oh, J. Choi, and I. Song, "Socioeconomic disparity and the risk of contracting COVID-19 in South Korea: an NHIS-COVID-19 database cohort study," *BMC Public Health,* vol. 21, pp. 1-12, 2021.

[11] X. Huang et al., "Time-Series Clustering for Home Dwell Time during COVID-19: What Can We Learn from It?". *ISPRS International Journal of Geo-information, 9*(11), 675, 2020.

[12] R. B. Hawkins, E. J. Charles, and J. H. Mehaffey, "Socio-economic status and COVID-19–related cases and fatalities". *Public Health (London), 189*, pp. 129-134, 2020.

[13] J. Burton, D. Fort, and S. Leonardo, "Hospitalization and Mortality among Black Patients and White Patients with Covid-19," *N. Engl. J. Med.*, vol. 382, (26), pp. 2534-2543, 2020.

[14] S. Gangemi, L. Billeci, and A. Tonacci, "Rich at Risk: Socio-Economic Drivers of COVID-19 Pandemic Spread." *Clinical and Molecular Allergy CMA*, vol. 18, no. 1, 2020, pp. 1–12.

[15] E. Hatef, H. Chang, C. Kitchen, J. P. Weiner, and H. Kharrazi, "Assessing the Impact of Neighborhood Socioeconomic Characteristics on COVID-19 Prevalence Across Seven States in the United States". *Frontiers in Public Health, 8*, 571808, 2020.

[16] M. Roser, "Human Development Index (HDI)." *Our World in Data,* Global Change Data Lab, 25 July 2014, https://ourworldindata.org/human-development-index. [retrieved: September, 2021]

[17] *Economic Innovation Group Distressed Communities Index.* URL: http://eig.org/dci. [retrieved: September, 2021]

[18] J. Holland, "ANSI (FIPS) Codes for Metropolitan and Micropolitan Statistical Areas." *Data.gov Data Catalog*, US Census Bureau, Department of Commerce, 11 Mar. 2021, catalog.data.gov/dataset/ansi-fips-codes-for-metropolitan-and-micropolitan-statistical-areas.

[19] W. M. K. Trochim, "Correlation." *Conjoint.ly*, Analytics Simplified Pty Ltd. URL: conjointly.com/kb/correlation-statistic/. [retrieved: September, 2021]

[20] W. M. LaMorte, "The Correlation Coefficient (r)." *Evaluating Association Between Two Continuous Variables*, Boston University School of Public Health, 21 Apr. 2021, sphweb.bumc.bu.edu/otlt/MPH-Modules/PH717-QuantCore/PH717-Module9-Correlation-Regression/PH717-Module9-Correlation-Regression4.html.

[21] "Pearson's product moment correlation", *Laerd Statistics*, Lund Research Ltd. URL: https://statistics.laerd.com/statistical-guides/pearson-correlation-coefficient-statistical-guide.php. 2020. [retrieved: September, 2021]

[22] "Kendall tau metric". *Encyclopedia of Mathematics*. URL: http://encyclopediaofmath.org/index.php?title=Kendall_tau_metric&oldid=51572. 2021. [retrieved: September, 2021]

[23] S. Glen, "Spearman Rank Correlation (Spearman's Rho): Definition and How to Calculate it", *StatisticsHowTo.com: Elementary Statistics for the rest of us!*. URL: https://www.statisticshowto.com/probability-and-statistics/correlation-coefficient-formula/spearman-rank-correlation-definition-calculate/. 2021. [retrieved: September, 2021]

[24] T. Fahrudin, D. R. Wijaya, and A. A. Agung, "COVID-19 Confirmed Case Correlation Analysis Based on Spearman and Kendall Correlation". *2020 International Conference on Data Science and Its Applications (ICoDSA)*, 1-4, 2020.

[25] Kent State University Libraries. (2021, Mar 22). *SPSS tutorials: Pearson Correlation.* URL: http://libguides.library.kent.edu/SPSS/PearsonCorr [retrieved: September, 2021]

Integrated Architecture of SQL Engine and Data Analytics Tool with Apache Arrow Flight and Its Performance Evaluation

Yuichiro Aoki
Research and Development Group, Center for Technology Innovation - Digital Platform
Hitachi, Ltd.
Tokyo, Japan
email: yuichiro.aoki.jk@hitachi.com

Satoru Watanabe
Research and Development Group, Center for Technology Innovation - Digital Platform
Hitachi, Ltd.
Tokyo, Japan
email: satoru.watanabe.aw@hitachi.com

Abstract—**Data analytics in enterprise systems requires huge amounts of data that are generally stored in databases. Conventionally, Structured Query Language (SQL) engines retrieve the data from the database and data analytics tools, such as Python® scripts, are used to analyze them. In this case, whenever the data moves from the database to the data analytics tools, the data needs to be serialized/deserialized in traditional Open Database Connectivity (ODBC). This is one of the bottlenecks in data analytics performance. In addition, the data needs to be joined for advanced data analytics, and joining the data in the SQL engines takes a lot of time. This is another bottleneck. To remove these bottlenecks, we propose a new architecture integrating the SQL engine and the data analytics tool that reduces the number of data serializations/ deserializations and caches joined results to improve performance of data analytics. Evaluation results show that the data transfer throughput using Apache Arrow/Arrow Flight is 13.1-37.4 times faster than that of a conventional data analytics tool using ODBC. Moreover, this architecture runs 2.4 times faster with the caching mechanism than without it.**

Keywords-relational database; SQL engine; ODBC; Apache Arrow; Apache Arrow Flight; data analytics.

I. INTRODUCTION

Data analytics in enterprise systems requires huge amounts of data that are generally stored in databases. Conventionally, Structured Query Language (SQL) engines, such as Relational DataBases (RDBs), retrieve the data from the database using traditional Open Database Connectivity (ODBC) [6], and data analytics tools like Python® scripts analyze the retrieved data. In such cases, whenever the data moves from the database to the data analytics tool, the data is serialized in the database and deserialized in the data analytics tools. Serialization/deserialization demands many memory copies and takes a lot of time. Thus, serialization/deserialization is a bottleneck in data analytics performance.

In addition, the data needs to be joined for complicated data analytics. Join operations in the SQL engines take a lot of time and are another bottleneck.

In this paper, to address these issues, we propose a new architecture for a data analytics system that integrates the SQL engine and the data analytics tool. It uses Apache Arrow Flight for data transfer between them. Apache Arrow Flight is a brand-new parallel data transfer framework [1]. It uses a column-oriented data format based on Apache Arrow [12]. If the SQL engines, data transfer framework, and the data analytics tools use the same column-oriented data format, the data does not need serialization/deserialization. Thus, the proposed system might be faster than a traditional data analytics system that uses ODBC. In addition, we propose JOIN Result Cache to reduce the number of join operations in the SQL engines. It also improves the performance of the data analytics.

Moreover, we evaluate two types of performance. One is the data transfer performance of the SQL engines using ODBC and Apache Arrow Flight. The other is the performance of JOIN Result Cache.

The rest of the paper is organized as follows. In Section II, we review related work. In Section III, we describe the overview of the proposed architecture of the data analytics system. We show the performance evaluation results in Section IV. In Section V, we make a discussion about the performance, followed by conclusion and future study in Section VI.

II. RELATED WORK

In this section, we review the SQL engines that use Apache Arrow Flight. Dremio [2] is an open-source SQL engine for cloud data lakes. Dremio uses both ODBC and Apache Arrow Flight as a connection with the data analytics tools. Dremio discloses its performance with ODBC and Apache Arrow Flight [3] and Apache Arrow Flight performs 15 times faster than ODBC. In addition, Dremio compares benchmarking results using Transaction Processing Performance Council – Decision Support (TPC-DS) generated data on PrestoDB [4]. On average, Dremio is 3-4 times faster than PrestoDB. However, both results show the overall performance of SQL queries, and the performance of data transfer itself with ODBC and Apache Arrow Flight was not compared.

Li et al. [5] implemented data transfer functionalities using Apache Arrow Flight on the DB-X (currently known as noisepage) database management system [7]. They measured the data transfer throughput using Apache Arrow Flight and Remote Direct Memory Access (RDMA) over

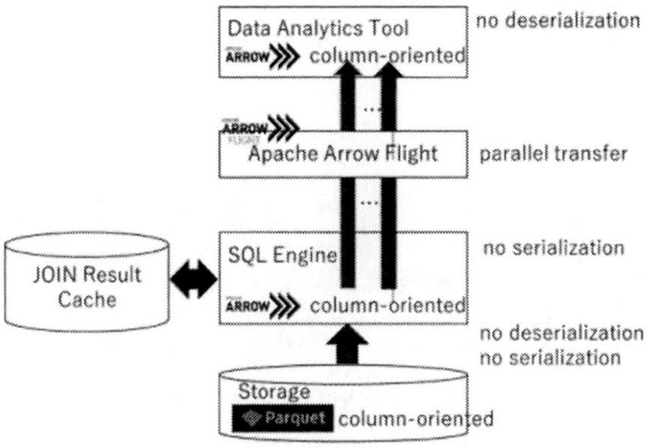

Figure 1. Proposed architecture.

Ethernet. RDMA is slightly faster than Apache Arrow Flight. However, they do not show the overall data analytics system design.

Magpie [8] measured speedups of SQL queries with or without caching data in Apache Arrow Flight. Apache Arrow Flight with caching data runs 2-3 times faster than that without it. However, data transfer time with or without Apache Arrow Flight was not evaluated.

ImmVis [9] is an open-source framework for immersive analytics. It is suggested that data transfer performance may improve if ImmVis uses Apache Arrow Flight. However, the data transfer performance of Apache Arrow Flight was not evaluated.

InfluxData [10] refers to Apache Arrow, Apache Arrow Flight, and Apache Parquet. Data transfer time using Apache Arrow Flight was shown. However, no performance comparison was conducted.

NVIDIA® RAPIDS [11], DataBricks [14], Google BigQuery [16], and Snowflake [17] use Apache Arrow internally. However, they do not use Apache Arrow Flight.

In-database analytics analyzes the data in the RDBs and only the results are transferred to the users [18]. However, in huge results case, the data transfer time is also problematic.

In contrast, we propose a new architecture for a data analytics system that can rapidly transfer the data between the SQL engines and the data analytics tools. In addition, we show the data transfer throughput of both ODBC and Apache Arrow Flight on various SQL engines.

III. Proposed Architecture of Data Analytics System

A. Proposed Architecture

Figure 1 illustrates the proposed architecture. It uses a column-oriented Apache Arrow data format internally. The SQL engine and the data analytics tool are connected via Apache Arrow Flight. Apache Arrow/Arrow Flight decreases the number of serializations/deserializations. In addition, the data is stored in a column-oriented Apache Parquet format in storage [15]. This also decreases the number of serializations/deserializations in collaboration with Apache Arrow in the SQL engine. In this architecture, no serialization and deserialization of the data occurs from bottom to top.

TABLE I. Performance Evaluation Environment

CPU	Intel® Core™ i7-8665U (4 cores / 8threads)	
Memory	32GB	
Storage	1TB SSD	
Host OS	Windows 10 Pro 2004	
Virtual Machine (VM)	Oracle VM VirtualBox 6.1.14	
	VM CPU	4 processors
	VM Memory	16GB
Guest OS	CentOS 7.8	

Moreover, the proposed architecture has JOIN Result Cache next to the SQL engine. JOIN Result Cache reduces the number of join operations.

B. Apache Arrow Flight

Apache Arrow Flight is a brand-new data transfer framework, and 1.0.0 was released in 2020 and 5.0.0 in 2021 [1][13]. Apache Arrow Flight uses Apache Arrow column-oriented in-memory data format [12]. If the SQL engines hold the data in Apache Arrow format in memory, Apache Arrow Flight can use the data for transfer without serialization in the SQL engine. In addition, Apache Arrow Flight transfers the data in parallel using gRPC. The gRPC is an open-source high performance RPC framework using Hyper Text Transfer Protocol/2 (HTTP/2). HTTP/2 enables multiple HTTP requests to be sent on a single Transmission Control Protocol (TCP) connection without waiting for the corresponding responses. Thus, Apache Arrow Flight enables faster data transfer between the data analytics tools and the SQL engines than traditional database connectivity, such as ODBC.

C. JOIN Result Cache

This architecture has JOIN Result Cache beside the SQL engine. Some conventional systems cache the join results without precomputing them. However, this architecture pre-computes them on the basis of join query history before join queries are issued, and caches them. For example, a join query is precomputed if it has the same columns as a previous join query but has different tables. Such cases often appear in daily tabulation of Point-Of-Sales (POS) system. Different daily sales tables have the same column names. The tables are inferred from the history of table usage in previous join queries, because in daily tabulation, tables are often mechanically named in day order, such as sales20210803, sales20210804, etc. Thus, join can be precomputed. The SQL engine uses the results if they are cached. As a result, we could improve the data analytics performance and shorten the Turn-Around Time (TAT) of data analytics.

IV. Performance Evaluation

To prove the effectiveness of the new architecture, we evaluate the data transfer time using ODBC or Apache Arrow Flight. In addition, we make an evaluation of JOIN Result Cache.

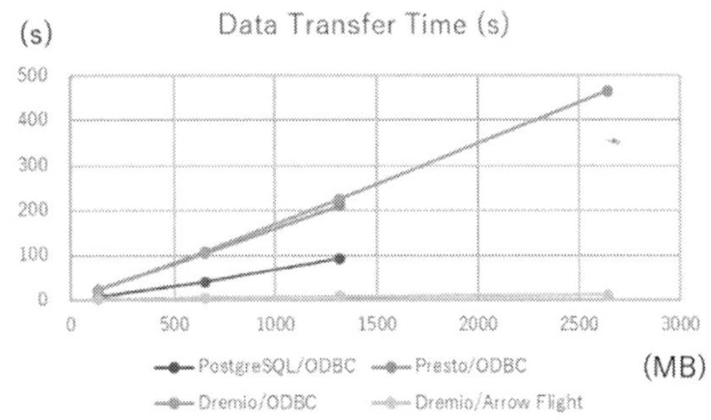

Figure 2. Data transfer time from SQL engine to Python® script.

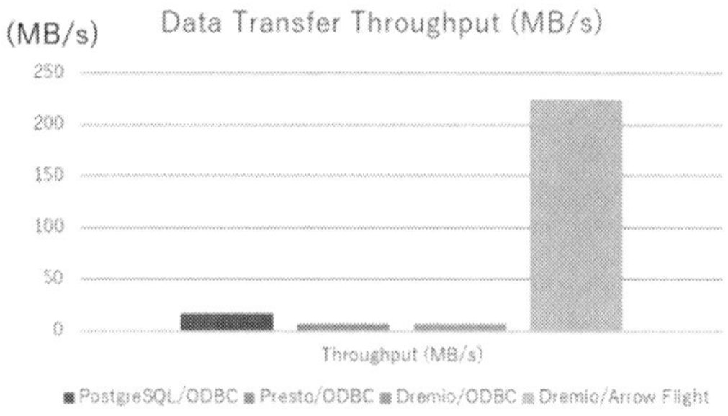

Figure 3. Data transfer throughput from SQL engine to Python® script.

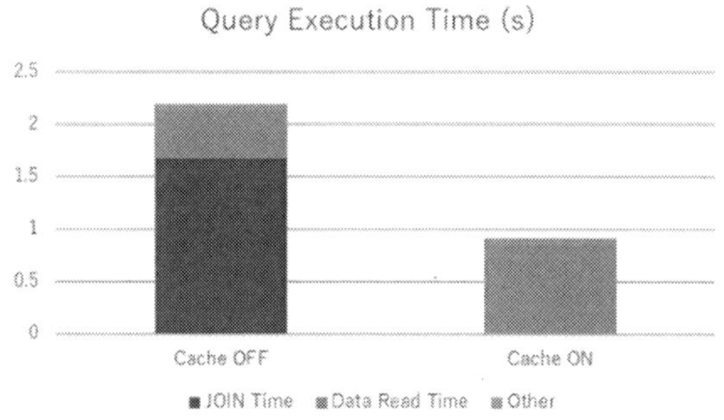

Figure 4. Effect of JOIN Result Cache.

A. *Performance Evaluation Environment*

In this section, we briefly overview the performance evaluation environment. Table I shows details of the environment. We use a virtual machine on Windows 10 for performance evaluation.

B. *Performance Evaluation Targets and Methods*

In this section, we briefly explain performance evaluation targets and methods. We created Python® scripts as an example of the data analytics tool. We imported pyodbc 4.0.30 as connections with the SQL engines in the Python® scripts. It is a Python® wrapper of ODBC. The Python® scripts executed an SQL query in the execute() method and fetched the data from the SQL engines in the fetchall() method. We measured the execution time of this fetchall() method as the data transfer time in ODBC cases.

We also imported pyarrow 2.0.0 as connections with the SQL engines in the Python® scripts. It is a Python® wrapper of Apache Arrow and Apache Arrow Flight. We calculated the data transfer time from the difference between script execution time and SQL engine server's Central Processing Unit (CPU) execution time because Apache Arrow Flight is implemented in C++ libraries of pyarrow and does not use the fetchall() method.

We selected open-source SQL engine Dremio 4.9.1 Community Edition that is enabled to use both Apache Arrow Flight and ODBC [2]. In addition, we also selected PostgreSQL 9.2.24 and Presto 0.250 as ordinary SQL engines that use ODBC.

We generated dummy datasets using Python® Faker package. The datasets have 5 columns (employee ID, first name, last name, age, and education history) and 2.5M, 12.5M, 25M, and 50M rows, respectively. The sizes of the datasets are about 130MB, 650MB, 1315MB, and 2642MB, respectively.

We used SQL queries "SELECT * FROM dataset" for performance measurement. Though they are very simple, we focus on the data transfer time, not the data processing time inside the RDBs, such as GROUP BY operations.

In addition, we measured the effect of the JOIN Result Cache on Dremio. We prepared other thtree datasets with the dataset described above. Two of them are inner-joined and other two are also inner-joined. Lastly, these two inner-joined tables are inner-joined. A Reflection (materialized view in Dremio) of the resulting table was calculated to simulate JOIN Result Cache. The resulting table was queried as "SELECT * FROM table". Its size is about 256 MB.

C. *Performance Evaluation Results*

Figure 2 shows data transfer time from the SQL engine to the Python® script in seconds. Each line means PostgreSQL/ODBC, Presto/ODBC, Dremio/ODBC, and Dremio/Apache Arrow Flight, respectively. We cannot measure the data transfer time of PostgreSQL/ODBC and Presto/ODBC in the 2642MB dataset case because they stopped executing the query with error messages.

In this figure, Presto/ODBC and Dremio/ODBC take almost the same measurement time. PostgreSQL/ODBC runs faster than them. Dremio/Apache Arrow Flight is the fastest in these four measurements.

Figure 3 shows data transfer throughput from the SQL engine to the Python® scripts in MB/s. Each bar means, from left to right, PostgreSQL/ODBC, Presto/ODBC, Dremio/ODBC, and Dremio/Apache Arrow Flight, respectively. The data transfer throughput of Dremio/Apache Arrow Flight is 224MB/s. It is 13.1 times faster than PostgreSQL/ODBC, 36.0 times faster than Presto/ODBC, and 37.4 times faster than Dremio/ODBC.

Figure 4 shows the effect of JOIN Result Cache. In Cache ON case, JOIN time (blue bar) disappeared. As a result, query execution time decreases by 2.4 times.

V. Discussion

ODBC needs data to be serialized and deserialized before and after the data transfer. On the other hand, Apache Arrow Flight uses the Apache Arrow column-oriented in-memory data format that the SQL engine (Dremio) uses internally. Thus, Apache Arrow Flight does not need the data to be serialized before the data transfer. In addition, the Python® script uses the pyarrow module, and the transferred data is retained in Apache Arrow format. Thus, the data do not need to be deserialized. We suppose that this is why Apache Arrow Flight outperforms ODBC.

However, we suppose that, in many cases, the data analytics tools written in Python® use pandas DataFrame, which is not column-oriented. Thus, the data needs to be deserialized when it is analyzed. This could be another overhead of the data transfer. In a simple experiment, for example, the data deserialization of 1315MB Apache Arrow array to pandas DataFrame in Python® takes about 2.6s. This could worsen the data transfer performance by 33.8%. If the time of deserialization linearly depends on the size of the data, 1TB data needs about 40 additional minutes for deserialization. This overhead deteriorates the TAT of data analytics.

After serialization/deserialization disappears, join time is a performance bottleneck. In Figure 4, 76% (blue bar) of the query execution time is join time. The JOIN Result Cache removes join query processing and outperforms Cache OFF case by 2.4 times. The difference between Magpie and the proposed architecture is that the former has cache in Apache Arrow Flight and the latter has cache out of Apache Arrow Flight. It affects the maintenance cost of the system.

The Cache OFF case only reads smaller datasets (296MB) from the storage. However, the Cache ON case reads larger joined table (512MB). That is the cause of the difference in data read time (orange bar) in Figure 4.

In addition, the data analytics system using the proposed architecture can cross the cloud boundaries, because it does not use specific hardware, such as RDMA. This means that data analytics users can distribute the data among usual clouds where the data analytics tools are not installed.

Additionally, if the system resides in one cloud, we can use memory-mapped files in place of file Input/Output (I/O) system calls between storage and the SQL engines. When files are mapped into memory, data in the files is read from and written to the mapped files as if it were in a memory. I/O system calls are usually much slower than memory read/write. Therefore, memory-mapped files can speed up read/write performance of the SQL engines. Thus, in addition to Apache Arrow Flight, memory-mapped files enable us to improve the system performance more and shorten the TAT of data analytics.

VI. Conclusion

We proposed a new architecture for a data analytics system using column-oriented Apache Arrow/Arrow Flight. We compared the data transfer throughput performance between the data analytics tool and the SQL engine using ODBC and Apache Arrow Flight. We found that Apache Arrow Flight transfers the data 13.1-37.4 times faster than ODBC because serialization/deserialization of the data is eliminated. In addition, JOIN Result Cache accelerates the query by 2.4 times using precomputed join results. Thus, our proposed architecture can improve the TAT of the data analytics.

In future work, we will design and implement such a data analytics system using Apache Arrow and Apache Arrow Flight. It may reduce the data analytics time and help data analytics users to gain new insights from the data more rapidly.

References

[1] The Apache Software Foundation, “Arrow Flight RPC” [Online]. Available from: https://arrow.apache.org/docs/format/Flight.html [Retrieved: August, 2021].

[2] Dremio, “Set Your Data Free” [Online]. Available from: https://www.dremio.com [Retrieved: April, 2021].

[3] P. Shrivastava, “Eliminating Data Exports for Data Science with Apache Arrow Flight” [Online]. Available from: https://www.dremio.com/eliminating-data-exports-for-data-science-with-apache-arrow-flight [Retrieved: April, 2021].

[4] S. Leontiev, “Think Presto Is Fast? Dremio is 3,000 Times Faster.” [Online]. Available from: https://www.dremio.com/dremio-vs-presto [Retrieved: April, 2021].

[5] T. Li, M. Butrovich, A. Ngom, W. S. Lim, W. McKinney, and A. Pavlo, “Mainlining Databases: Supporting Fast TransactionalWorkloads on Universal Column-oriented Data File Formats,” arXiv:2004.14471, 2020.

[6] Microsoft®, “What Is ODBC?” [Online]. Available from: https://docs.microsoft.com/en-us/sql/odbc/reference/what-is-odbc?view=sql-server-ver15 [Retrieved: April, 2021].

[7] Database Research Group at Carnegie Mellon University, “noisepage” [Online]. Available from: https://github.com/cmu-db/noisepage [Retrieved: April, 2021].

[8] A. Jindal, et al., "Magpie: Python at Speed and Scale using Cloud Backends," in Proc. CIDR’21, 2021.

[9] F. A. Pedroso and P. D. P. Costa, "ImmVis: Bridging Data Analytics and Immersive Visualisation," Proc. VISIGRAPP 2021, vol.3, pp.181-187, 2021.

[10] P. Dix, “Apache Arrow, Parquet, Flight and Their Ecosystem are a Game Changer for OLAP” [Online]. Available from: https://www.influxdata.com/blog/apache-arrow-parquet-flight-and-their-ecosystem-are-a-game-changer-for-olap/ [Retrieved: June, 2021].

[11] NVIDIA®, “RAPIDS” [Online]. Available from: https://developer.nvidia.com/rapids [Retrieved:]2020.06.04

[12] The Apache Software Foundation, “Apache Arrow” [Online]. Available from: https://arrow.apache.org/ [Retrieved: April, 2021].

[13] Wes McKinney, “Introducing Apache Arrow Flight: A Framework for Fast Data Transport” [Online]. Available from: https://arrow.apache.org/blog/2019/10/13/introducing-arrow-flight/ [Retrieved: April, 2021].

[14] L. Jin, “Introducing Pandas UDF for PySpark” [Online]. Available from: https://databricks.com/blog/2017/10/30/introducing-vectorized-udfs-for-pyspark.html [Retrieved: June, 2021].

[15] The Apache Software Foundation, “Apache Parquet” [Online]. Available from: https://parquet.apache.org/ [Retrieved: May, 2021].

[16] Google, "Download table data in the Arrow data format" [Online]. Available from: https://cloud.google.com/bigquery/docs/samples/bigquerystorage-arrow-quickstart?hl=en [Retrieved: June, 2021].

[17] H. Kapre, "Fetching Query Results From Snowflake Just Got a Lot Faster With Apache Arrow" [Online]. Available from: https://www.snowflake.com/blog/fetching-query-results-from-snowflake-just-got-a-lot-faster-with-apache-arrow/ [Retrieved: June, 2021].

[18] J. Taylor, "In-database analytics," [Online]. Available from: http://www.decisionmanagementsolutions.com/wp-content/uploads/2015/06/In-database-Analytics-Decision-Management-Solutions.pdf [Retrieved: August, 2021].

Analysis of Minimal Clearance and Algorithm Selection Effect on Path Planning for Autonomous Systems

Ronald Ponguillo-Intriago
Dept. of Industrial Systems Engineering and Product Design
Ghent University
Industrial Systems Engineering (ISyE), Flanders Make
Ghent, Belgium
Facultad de Ingenieria en Electricidad y Computacion
Escuela Superior Politecnica del Litoral, ESPOL
Guayaquil, Ecuador
RonaldAlberto.PonguilloIntriago@UGent.be

Payam Khazaelpour
Dept. of Industrial Systems Engineering and Product Design
Ghent University
Industrial Systems Engineering (ISyE), Flanders Make
Ghent, Belgium
Payam.Khazaelpour@UGent.be

Ignacio Querol Puchal
SEAL Aeronautica S.L.
Barcelona, Spain
IgnacioQuerolPuchal@sealaero.com

Silvio Semanjski
SEAL Aeronautica S.L.
Barcelona, Spain
Silvio.Semanjski@sealaero.com

Daniel Ochoa
Facultad de Ingenieria en Electricidad y Computacion
Escuela Superior Politecnica del Litoral, ESPOL
Guayaquil, Ecuador
dochoa@espol.edu.ec

Sidharta Gautama
Dept. of Industrial Systems Engineering and Product Design
Ghent University
Industrial Systems Engineering (ISyE), Flanders Make
Ghent, Belgium
Sidharta.Gautama@ugent.be

Ivana Semanjski
Dept. of Industrial Systems Engineering and Product Design
Ghent University
Industrial Systems Engineering (ISyE), Flanders Make
Ghent, Belgium
Ivana.Semanjski@ugent.be

***Abstract*—There are many path planning algorithms in the literature, with different classifications, domains of use, efficiency to find the shortest path or to make a complete coverage of the area to be studied. In the literature, we can also find evaluations of all these algorithms in terms of their performance in the search for the shortest path, execution time and comparisons between them. In this work, twelve algorithms from the literature were studied to analyze their sensibility to the number of obstacles and the clearance value between them. Data analytics methods were used to make a qualitative study of the sensibility of these algorithms to the constraints studied. For investigation of the problem, two metrics were used, the length of the generated path and the number of iterations used to find the solution. The number of iterations here refers to the number of nodes evaluated by the algorithm when searching for the target node. The results are synthesized in two tables that show the sensibility of the algorithms to the change in the constraints studied and the immunity of others, and the correlation among the algorithms, the constraints and the metrics.**

Keywords*—*robotics path planning, data analytics, clearance analysis, autonomous systems.

I. Introduction

In Robotics Path Planning, there are many algorithms, each one with its particularity to solve a problem under a specific domain and conditions. For example, there are algorithms to discover the shortest path between two points on a map avoiding all obstacles that are on the way. There are also algorithms that do not look for the shortest path between two points, but rather find the route with which they can travel the entire map in the most efficient way, that is, without repeating visited places, or being forced to go back or perhaps generate intersections of traveled segments.

In this work, we analyze algorithms based on the response to different numbers of obstacles and clearance values. We define the clearance value to free space within the robot configuration space, limited in dimensions by the obstacle space. In Figure 1, the idea of clearance is graphically shown.

Twelve algorithms have been chosen from the literature for evaluation. These algorithms are divided into deterministic and probabilistic. The deterministic algorithms considered are A*, bidirectional A*, Breadth First Search (BFS), Bidirectional BFS, Depth First Search (DFS), Dijkstra, Greedy Best First Search, and Visibility Road Map. The probabilistic algorithms analyzed are: Rapidly Exploring Random Tree (RRT), RRT with Path Smoothing, RRT with Sobol Sampler and RRT*.

A common characteristic of all these algorithms is that

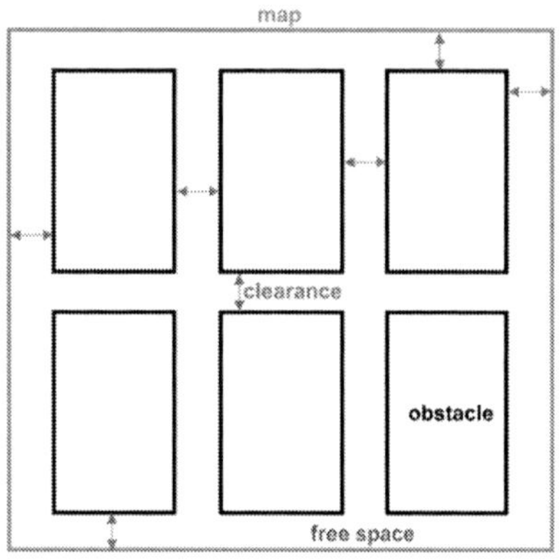

Figure. 1. Clearance graphically explained

they are algorithms that discretize the map to be traversed and create a graph on which they develop the search. All algorithms use a resolution of 1, that is, each node corresponds to a square on the grid map.

Among the deterministic algorithms is the group of (*) that use a heuristic to guide the search for the destination node. Probabilistic algorithms differ in the way they take the sample nodes or process the final path.

In Section II, a literature review is made showing a generality of each of the algorithms used, related previous works and the techniques for the evaluation of the works that were used. In the Section III, the construction of the scenarios is discussed in detail, namely, how the maps are constructed by making variations in the number of obstacles and clearance dimensions and the considerations taken into account when making changes in the position of the obstacles. The metrics used to perform the sensitivity analysis of the constraints chosen on the proposed scenarios are also defined. In Section IV, the results are shown using strip plots with the seaborn library in Python. These show the response of each algorithm to variations in the constraint's clearance and number of obstacles. The results are discussed, and a conclusion is given in Section V.

II. LITERATURE REVIEW

Among the path planning algorithms used in robotics there are algorithms that use a discretization of the map and convert this information into a graph that can then be traversed using different strategies to find the path between the starting node and the destination node. In this work, several of these algorithms are used that base their solution on graphs. The A* algorithm is one of the most used path planning algorithms in robotics. This algorithm was developed by Peter E. Hart et al. [8]. It combines the breadth first search technique with a heuristic to simplify the search and improve convergence times without being greedy. The Dijkstra algorithm was developed by Edsger Dijkstra [6] and is a complete algorithm that traverses the entire search space until the solution is found. Regarding the Bidirectional algorithm A* [14], it is based on A* with the variation that the route of the nodes is made in two directions, one from the start node to the goal node and one from the goal node to the initial node and ends when these two semi solutions are found. This algorithm manages to reduce the execution time to a value less than half the time used by A*. The BFS algorithm [13] [21] makes a search that goes down the levels, starting with the levels closest to the start node and moving up to the levels towards the destination node. Contrary to BFS, the Depth First Search (DFS) algorithm, as shown in [5] and [19], does the search by going through the tree branch by branch, that is, it advances through a branch and when it finishes it returns to the start node and goes through the neighboring branch, and so on until the tree is finished. Greedy Best First Search [7] uses a heuristic that tries to always predict which is the node that takes it closer to the destination node. As the last algorithm evaluated from the group of deterministic algorithms, we have the Visibility Road Map [10] [15], which is based on creating a graph, putting as nodes all the points or corners of the obstacles present on the map that are visible to the start node, goal node and among them. This created graph is much smaller than if the created graph with all the nodes of the free space is used and, therefore, it will be easier to solve. Then, to find the shortest path between the start and end nodes of this graph, any algorithm can be applied to traverse graphs, for example, Dijkstra, A*, etc.

Four probabilistic algorithms were considered, one of which is Rapidly Exploring Random Tree (RRT) [12] and the others are some variants of it. This algorithm does not go through all the nodes of the free space, but rather randomly takes a few that meet the condition of being within the defined circumference with the current node as the center and radius a number less than or equal to the expansion distance parameter. The points that coincide in the obstacle space are discarded and another random number is generated to replace it. This continues until eventually the destination node is found within the generating circle. With this methodology, by not completely covering the free space, it is possible to reduce the number of nodes traveled and, with this, the execution time. On the other hand, the price that compensates for this greater speed is that the generated path is not the smoothest possible and the length of the path obtained is not as good as what is obtained with deterministic algorithms, but it is quite close, which for many applications makes it more attractive. The other variant used, RRT Path Smoothing [3], applies the same original RRT to get the set of nodes between the start node and the goal node. Then runs a smoothing process to smooth the resulting path. This process is based on generating the least number of direct straight lines towards the destination node and eliminating the intersections that occur with obstacles. The RRT Sobol Sampler variant [11] [20], for its part, differs in the way it generates each random point in the search process for the destination node, for which it uses a technique called Sobol filter. Finally, the applied RRT* algorithm [16] uses a combination of the original RRT algorithm and a heuristic such as that of the A* algorithm, to guide the algorithm towards the destination node. This succeeds in eliminating unnecessary branches in other directions that are usually seen in the original

RRT.

Some works in the literature that involve data analytics and robotics have been done in IoT or in robotics applied to medicine [1] [17]. These approaches use data analytics to make predictions with the data and improve their processes. The most used tools in data analytics are presented in [2] where the authors make an analysis of the leading tools in data analytics and locate the Python language in second place with a growth in terms of use in this area of more than 15% from 2015 to 2016. It also refers to the libraries used in data analytics such as pandas, scipy, matplotlib that we have also used in this work. Regarding the evaluation of path planning algorithms in robotics, we can find works that evaluate several algorithms and compare the performance between them, as in [9] where the authors make an evaluation of the performance of 5 algorithms from the literature, focusing on the length of the generated path and processing time, ranking the algorithms that obtained the best balance between both metrics as the best. In [4], the authors also analyze 5 path planning algorithms, 4 of them from the literature and one that they present in the same work. They show an analysis of the performance of these algorithms taking as metrics the length of the path obtained and the processing time. They evaluate the response of these algorithms to the variation in the size of the navigation map in terms of grid units. At the end, they implement their algorithm in ROS (Robot Operating System) [23] and make a comparison of their execution time there. In [22], the authors make an evaluation of the trajectory produced by 5 algorithms from the literature, in which they also combine the path length, processing time and curvature metrics. One of the five algorithms shown in the proposal is introduced by the authors in this work. Works that combine data analytics with the study of performance or constraints in path planning algorithms were not found and in this work an attempt is made to make that contribution to the state of the art.

III. Methodology

Prior to introducing the scenarios and the methodology used in this study, we want to give the reader a first impression of how different the selected algorithms are in terms of their processing time. A comparison among them is shown in Figure 2. The Figure 2(a) shows the test scenario for the algorithms. The scenario is a map with two obstacles, with the start point in the lower left corner with coordinates (0,0) and the goal point in the upper right corner with coordinates (200,200). The Figure 2(b) shows the processing time of each algorithm, measured in seconds. The simulation was run on a laptop with an Intel Core i9 processor and 32GB of RAM running the Microsoft Windows 10 operating system.

A. Scenarios

Several scenarios were built in which different number of obstacles are placed on a map of 200x200 units. These units (U) represent a way of generalizing the dimensions of the maps and can be changed to any measurement units, for example, cm, inches, feet, meters, km, etc. Maps were built with options

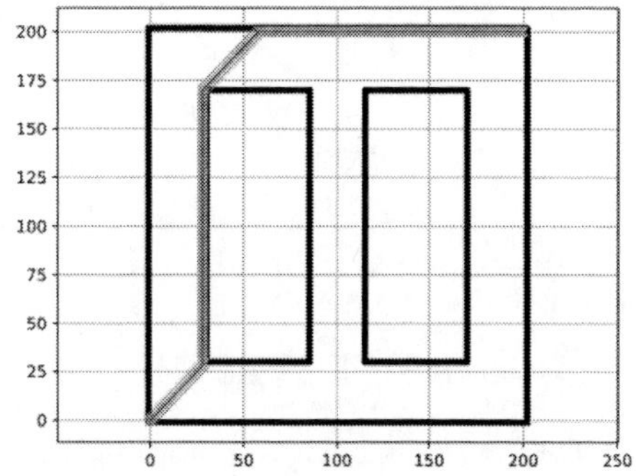

(a) Simple scenario to test algorithms.

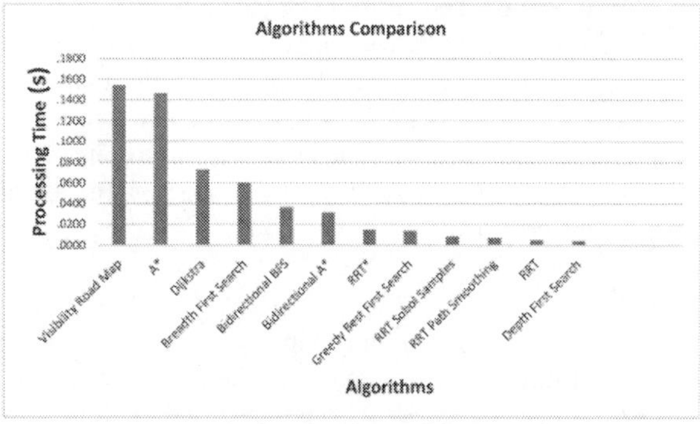

(b) Processing time for algorithms under test.

Figure. 2. Processing time comparison among algorithms under study.

TABLE I
VARIANTS OF SCENARIOS BY NUMBER OF OBSTACLES

# Obstacles	Variants Scenarios
1	1
2	2
3	4
4	1
5	4
6	2
7	4
8	2

from one to eight obstacles, all of them maintaining clearance throughout the configuration space. The obstacles were moved from their position, when possible, to study if the position of the obstacles has any influence on the evaluated metrics. Thus, for the scenario with one obstacle, there are no variants since moving the obstacle from position maintaining the same clearance means rotating it and at any feasible angle of rotation it will always give the same square. Based on this criterion, in the Table I is shows the number of variants generated with the number of obstacles and their rotations.

To evaluate the effect of clearance on the metrics, the simulations were run by varying clearance values in intervals of 5 units, within the interval [5, 30].

The starting point is the origin of coordinates (0, 0) and the goal is the upper right corner with coordinates (200,

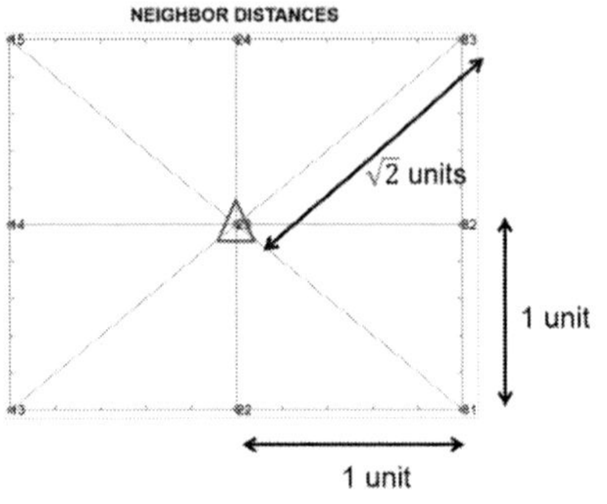

Figure. 3. Neighbor node concept illustrated

200). Obstacles are convex figures (squares and rectangles) distributed on the map in such a way that there is the same clearance throughout the map. In the resulting graph, each node is connected to its close neighbors. Close neighbors of a node are defined as those nodes that have a distance of 1 or $\sqrt{2}$ U from the original node. Figure 3 illustrates the neighbor node concept graphically.

B. Metrics

The metrics used were the length of the path generated by the algorithm and the number of iterations made by an algorithm in each scenario. The number of iterations in this work refers to the number of times that the studied algorithm accesses a node to operate on it. This metric is used since all the evaluated algorithms solve the path planning problem on a node-based map. On the other hand, this avoids using the convergence time of the algorithms, which is dependent on various factors such as the hardware, operating system or processes that run in the background on a computational platform and, therefore, makes the reproducibility of the results difficult.

C. Simulation

From the combination of 20 maps constructed by combining obstacles and clearance values according to those discussed in sub-section III-A, plus the 12 algorithms mentioned in Section I, 1440 scenarios were built on which the simulation was run to obtain the data from the Path_length and Iteration metrics that will later be used for the analysis. The simulations and data processing were done using the Python language. For the simulations, PythonRobotics [18] was used and, for the data processing, the pandas library [24] was used in the dataframe preprocessing and profiling analysis and the seaborn library [25] was used to graph the results.

IV. Results and Discussion

Once the data has been processed, we can observe from the resulting graphs some behaviors of the algorithms with the chosen constraints. We will start by analyzing the effects of the clearance constraint on the Path_length metric.

Figure 4 illustrates the effect of the clearance value on the length of the path produced by each algorithm. For

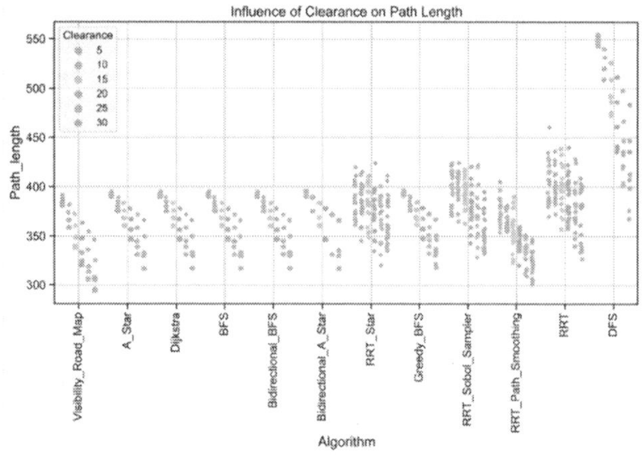

Figure. 4. Effects of the clearance over Path_length

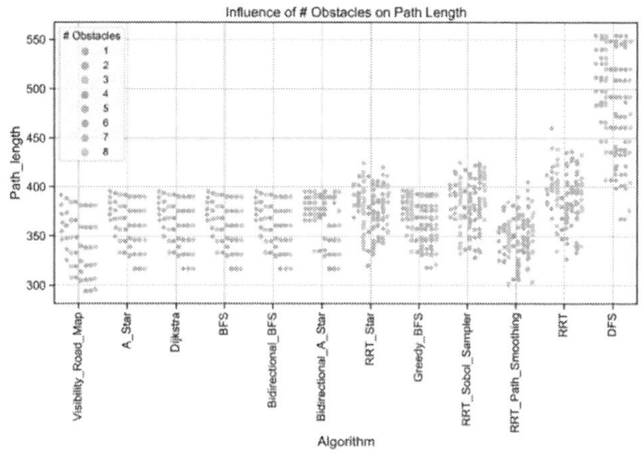

Figure. 5. Effects of the # Obstacles over Path_length

all algorithms, there is an inverse relationship between the clearance size and the length of the generated path, that is, as we increase the value of the clearance, the generated path is smaller in length. This occurs because, when we increase the clearance or, in other words, we increase the size of the free space within the configuration space, each algorithm has more options to search and establish better resulting path values.

In Figure 5, we can see that, for the algorithms A*, bidirectional A*, Bidirectional BFS, BFS, Dijkstra and Visibility Road Map, they do not show dependence on where the obstacles are located, but only on the number of obstacles and the clearance value between them. On the other hand, for the algorithms DFS, Greedy Best First Search and the group of probabilistic algorithms, there is influence of the position in which the obstacles are placed.

Reviewing Figure 6, we can see that, for the algorithms A*, Bidirectional A*, Bidirectional BFS, BFS and Dijkstra, the number of iterations increases as we increase the clearance value. This is because these algorithms, to a lesser or greater extent, sweep the available nodes when they apply their strategy to find the solution. By increasing clearance, we are

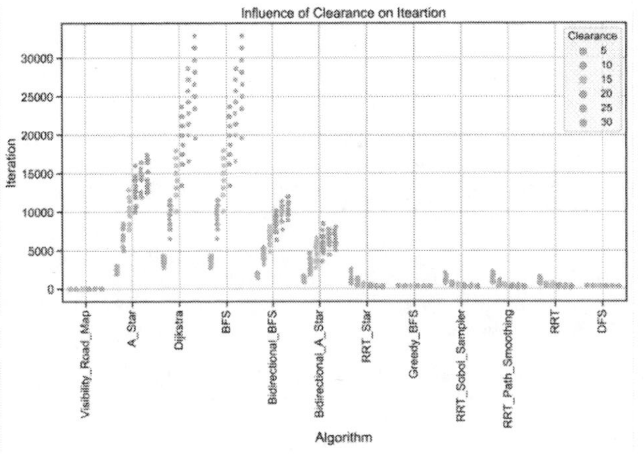

Figure. 6. Effects of the clearance over Iteration

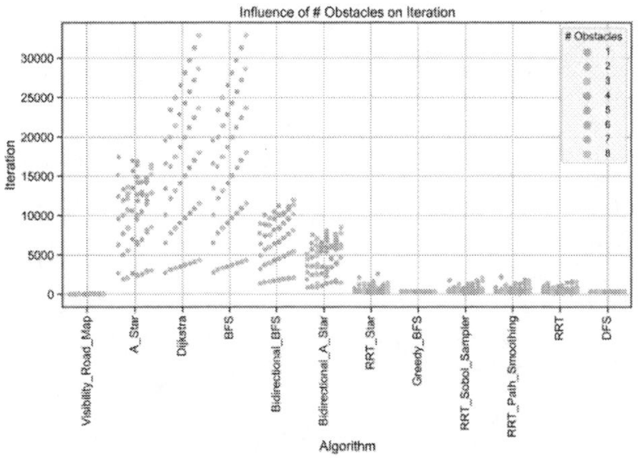

Figure. 7. Effects of the # Obstacles over Iteration

increasing the number of nodes in free space, therefore, we are increasing the number of nodes that these algorithms must evaluate. The DFS algorithm, for its part, uses a strategy that keeps the number of iterations independent of the clearance value, but pays the price by generating path lengths with values well above the rest of the algorithms evaluated. The Greedy BFS algorithm, due to its greedy nature, uses very few iterations since it only needs to have one path available between the start node and the target node. The Visibility Road Map algorithm keeps the number of iterations almost constant because, to find the solution, it creates a graph based on the number of visible points of the obstacles present and does not consider the number of nodes in the free space that we are varying with clearance.

With the probabilistic algorithms, we can notice instead that, as the clearance value increases, it becomes easier to find the solution, that is, they use fewer iterations. This is because, the narrower the corridor through which the samples must be taken, the more likely that the samples taken will overlap with the obstacle space. This sample must be discarded and a new one must be taken that matches the free space. This will make it necessary to do more iterations to be able to go through narrower paths. As can be seen, clearance has inverse effects on the number of iterations used between deterministic and probabilistic algorithms.

Regarding the effect of the number of obstacles on the metric of the number of iterations shown in Figure 7, it is well defined for the Bidirectional BFS, BFS and Dijkstra algorithms that there is no relationship with the position of the obstacles, but only the number of obstacles and the clearance value between them. On the other hand, probabilistic algorithms do show a dependency with the position of the obstacles. In case of the Visibility Road Map, when the number of obstacles increases, the number of iterations also increases. This is because of its nature of using the information of the obstacles to create the graph where the search will be done. However, there is no dependency of the clearance value on the number of iterations.

TABLE II
SUMMARY OF ALGORITHM IMMUNITY WITH THE CONSTRAINTS

	Clearance Immunity		# Obstacles Immunity	
Algorithm	**Path Length**	**Iteration**	**Path Length**	**Iteration**
Visibility Road Map	no	yes	no	no
A*	no	no	no	no
Dijkstra	no	no	no	no
BFS	no	no	no	no
Bidir BFS	no	no	no	no
Bidir A*	no	no	no	no
RRT*	no	no	no	no
Greedy Best First Search	no	no	no	no
RRT Sobol Sampler	no	no	no	no
RRT Path Smoothing	no	no	no	no
RRT	no	no	no	no
DFS	no	no	no	no

In Table II, based on the information from the four graphs in Figures 4, 5, 6 and 7, the immunity presented by the algorithms to the constraints evaluated has been summarized. As a result, we can see that Visibility Road Map is the only algorithm that really presents immunity with respect to the number of iterations versus the clearance value. This is because, regardless of where the obstacles are located or how distant they are from each other, this algorithm will create a graph with the same number of nodes and edges for the same group of obstacles if their shapes are maintained and, therefore, solving the search will always have the same number of nodes.

Table III shows a summary of the type of correlation among the constraints clearance and number of obstacles with the metrics path_length and iteration. The minus sign "-" represents a negative correlation, i.e., while one variable increase the other variable decrease. In this case, when clearance or number of obstacles increase, path_length or iteration decrease. Similarly, the plus sign "+" indicates a positive correlation, in other words, when the constraint variable increases, the metric variable also increases. The sign "x" means no correlation between variables can be defined.

V. CONCLUSION AND FUTURE WORK

In this work, the influence exerted by the clearance value and number of obstacles constraints on the generated path

TABLE III
TYPE OF CORRELATION AMONG (CLEARANCE, PATH_LENGTH, ITERATION) AND (# OBSTACLES, PATH_LENGTH, ITERATION). SIGN - IS NEGATIVE, + IS POSITIVE AND X NO CORRELATION

	Clearance		# Obstacles	
Algorithm	**Path Length**	**Iteration**	**Path Length**	**Iteration**
Visibility Road Map	-	x	-	+
A*	-	+	-	x
Dijkstra	-	+	-	+
BFS	-	+	-	+
Bidir BFS	-	+	-	+
Bidir A*	-	+	x	x
RRT*	-	-	x	x
Greedy Best First Search	-	-	-	-
RRT Sobol Sampler	-	-	x	x
RRT Path Smoothing	-	-	x	x
RRT	-	-	x	x
DFS	-	-	-	-

length and number of iterations metrics on a group of robotics path planning algorithms was explored. From the simulations carried out, and the analysis made to the data, it was possible to establish relationships between the metrics, the algorithms, and the restrictions. These results are shown qualitatively and were obtained using data analysis tools in Python language.

As an extension of this work, we intend to develop statistically validated indices that allow a quantitative approach and allow to generalize a prediction model of the behavior of the algorithms under different types of constraints.

VI. ACKNOWLEDGMENT

This project has received funding from the European Union's Horizon 2020 research and innovation programme under grant agreement No 101007134. Also this work was in part funded by National Secretariat of Higher Education, Science, Technology and Innovation of Ecuador (SENESCYT).

REFERENCES

[1] A. Banerjee, C. Chakraborty, A. Kumar, and D. Biswas, "Emerging trends in iot and big data analytics for biomedical and health care technologies," In Handbook of data science approaches for biomedical engineering, pp. 121–152, 2020.

[2] S. Bonthu and K. H. Bindu, "Review of leading data analytics tools," International Journal of Engineering & Technology, vol. 7, no.3, pp. 10–15, 2017.

[3] X. Cao, X. Zou, C. Jia, M. Chen, and Z. Zeng, "Rrt-based path planning for an intelligent litchi-picking manipulator," Computers and electronics in agriculture, vol. 156, pp. 105–118, 2019.

[4] I. Chaari, A. Koubaa, H. Bennaceur, A. Ammar, M. Alajlan, and H. Youssef, "Design and performance analysis of global path planning techniques for autonomous mobile robots in grid environments," International Journal of Advanced Robotic Systems, vol. 14, no.2, pp. 1–15, 2017.

[5] T. H. Cormen, C. E. Leiserson, R. L. Rivest, and C. Stein, "Introduction to algorithms," MIT press, 2009.

[6] E. W. Dijkstra, "A note on two problems in connexion with graphs," Numerische mathematik, vol. 1, no.1, pp. 269–271, 1959.

[7] C. Frăsinaru and B. Răschip, "Greedy best-first search for the optimal-size sorting network problem," Procedia Computer Science, vol. 159, pp. 447–454, 2019.

[8] P. E. Hart, N. J. Nilsson, and B. Raphael, "A formal basis for the heuristic determination of minimum cost paths," IEEE transactions on Systems Science and Cybernetics, vol. 4, no. 2, pp. 100–107, 1968.

[9] M. Korkmaz and A. Durdu, "Comparison of optimal path planning algorithms," In 2018 14th International Conference on Advanced Trends in Radioelecrtronics, Telecommunications and Computer Engineering (TCSET), pp. 255–258, IEEE, 2018.

[10] J. C. Latombe, "Robot motion planning," Springer Science & Business Media, vol. 124, 2012.

[11] S. LaValle, "Planning algorithms," Cambridge university press, 2006.

[12] S. M. LaValle, "Rapidly-exploring random trees: A new tool for path planning," Computer Science Dept. Oct., vol. 98, no. 11, 1988

[13] E. F. Moore, "The shortest path through a maze," In Proc. Int. Symp. Switching Theory, pp. 285–292, 1959.

[14] G. Nannicini, D. Delling, D. Schultes, and L. Liberti, "Bidirectional a* search on time-dependent road networks," Networks, vol. 59, no. 2, pp. 240–251, 2012.

[15] C. Nissoux, T. Simeon, and J.-P. Laumond, "Visibility based probabilistic roadmaps," In Proceedings 1999 IEEE/RSJ International Conference on Intelligent Robots and Systems. Human and Environment Friendly Robots with High Intelligence and Emotional Quotients, vol. 3, pp. 1316–1321, IEEE, 1999.

[16] I. Noreen, A. Khan, and Z. Habib, "Optimal path planning using rrt* based approaches: a survey and future directions," Int. J. Adv. Comput. Sci. Appl, vol. 7, no. 11, pp. 97–107, 2016.

[17] S. Panicucci et al., "A cloud-to-edge approach to support predictive analytics in robotics industry," Electronics, vol. 9, no. 3, pp. 492, 2020.

[18] A. Sakai, D. Ingram, J. Dinius, K. Chawla, A. Raffin, and A. Paques, "Pythonrobotics: a python code collection of robotics algorithms," arXiv preprint arXiv:1808.10703, 2018

[19] A. Shojaie, A. Jauhiainen, M. Kallitsis, and G. Michailidis, "Inferring regulatory networks by combining perturbation screens and steady state gene," Plos One, vol. 9, no. 2, pp. 1–16, February 2014.

[20] I. M. Sobol, "On the distribution of points in a cube and the approximate evaluation of integrals," Zhurnal Vychislitel'noi Matematiki i Matematicheskoi Fiziki, vol. 7, no. 4, pp. 784–802, 1967.

[21] K. Ueno, T. Suzumura, N. Maruyama, K. Fujisawa, and S. Matsuoka, "Efficient breadth-first search on massively parallel and distributed memory machines," Data Science and Engineering, vol. 2, no. 1, pp. 22–35, 2017.

[22] S. Zaheer, M. Jayaraju, and T. Gulrez, "Performance analysis of path planning techniques for autonomous mobile robots," In 2015 IEEE international conference on electrical, computer and communication technologies (ICECCT), pp. 1–5, IEEE, 2015.

[23] M. Quigley et al., "ROS: an open-source Robot Operating System," ICRA workshop on open source software, vol. 3, no. 3.2 pp. 5, Kobe, Japan, 2009.

[24] W. McKinney, "pandas: a foundational Python library for data analysis and statistics," Python for high performance and scientific computing, vol. 14, no. 9, pp. 1–9, 2011.

[25] M. L. Waskom, "Seaborn: statistical data visualization," Journal of Open Source Software, vol. 6, no. 60, pp. 3021, 2021.

Detection of Concept Drift in Manufacturing Data with SHAP Values to Improve Error Prediction

Christian Seiffer
Business Informatics
Furtwangen University
Furtwangen, Germany
sech@hs-furtwangen.de

Holger Ziekow
Business Informatics
Furtwangen University
Furtwangen, Germany
zie@hs-furtwangen.de

Ulf Schreier
Business Informatics
Furtwangen University
Furtwangen, Germany
schu@hs-furtwangen.de

Alexander Gerling
Business Informatics
Furtwangen University
Furtwangen, Germany
gera@hs-furtwangen.de

Abstract—**Production processes are inherently subject to dynamic change. This makes the extraction of error causes and the prediction of errors from manufacturing data by machine learning (ML) a difficult challenge, but at the same time it is the key to improve product quality and thus to economic profit. As part of the PREFERML research project (Proactive Error Avoidance in Production through Machine Learning), we present a method for detecting concept drift using clustering based on SHAP values (SHapley Additive exPlanations) and propose strategies to handle concept drift. Evaluation based on real manufacturing data shows that the cluster specific approach improves concept drift detection and can yield economic benefits.**

Index Terms—**AI in manufacturing, error prediction, concept drift detection, clustering, SHAP values**

I. Introduction

The support provided by machine learning in the context of manufacturing processes is finding more and more application, as optimized error avoidance is a key competitive advantage. Among other things, these models can be used to predict in real time during the production process whether the examined piece of production will yield a production error at a later stage or not. A reliable prediction offers the possibility to remove individual product components from the production process that would later turn out to be defective. This leads to the avoidance of follow-up costs. However, there is a risk of incorrectly classifying error-free parts as defective, which means that future profits are not realized. A ML classification model tries to learn the underlying error-cause correlations. Yet, even if the model represents reality almost perfectly, the application can be problematic as production processes are subject to constant change. Previously learned error-cause correlations may no longer be valid in the future, which is known as concept drift. Using outdated concepts can be misleading and reduces the quality of the classification. Hence, concept drift must be recognized and the models adapted accordingly. The error-cause relationships are usually highly complex, so that there are several concepts that can be affected by concept drift to varying degrees. A blanket analysis of the entire data (without separating these concepts) does not distinguish between the individual correlations and may therefore be insufficient. SHAP values [1] allow us to subdivide the data into subsets that correspond to different concepts each. This is part of our approach by which the specific concepts can be individually examined for drift and targeted options for optimizing individual clusters can be derived. Our strategy is to monitor the quality of predictions on a cluster specific basis and to disregard predictions of errors if the expected costs exceed the expected gains.

Our work is organized as follows. Section II introduces the realities and problems of classification and concept drift in manufacturing. Section III introduces methods relevant to understanding our approach. Section IV gives an overview of the project in which this work is embedded and Section V deals with related work. Section VI describes the approach we developed. The description of the experiments in Section VII is followed by the presentation of the results in Section VIII. The paper is concluded with a brief summary and further research aspects in Section IX.

II. Domain

For a better understanding of the problem, the production environment, the application of ML as well as the problem and the handling of concept drift are explained in more detail below.

A. *Manufacturing setup*

A typical production setup consists of several production lines. An example of one is given in Fig. 1. It consists of a number of test stations that serve as quality gate for recent production steps. The arrangement of the test stations can be simply sequential, but also more complex. Workpieces pass through the individual test stations and are forwarded if they remain error-free. Each test station checks incoming workpieces for certain characteristics. The measurements of the individual parts are stored in the *Product Quality Management System* (PQM), that supports the monitoring of production.

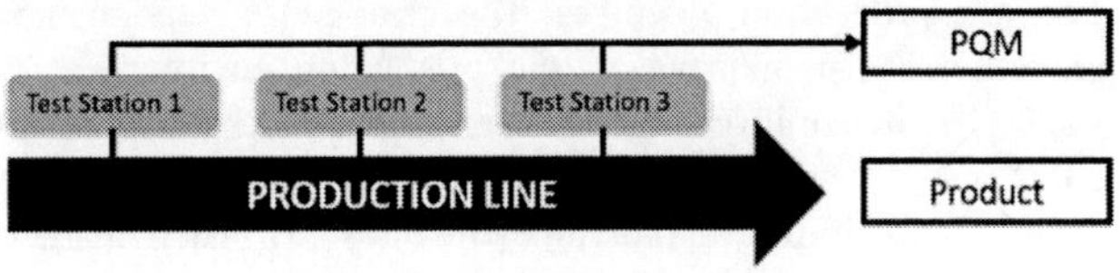

Fig. 1: Typical production setup [2]

If tolerance limits are exceeded during a measurement, a workpiece is labeled defective and it is removed from the production process. Products that leave the production process free of defects lead to economic profits. Early fault detection in the production process through correct error predictions therefore ensures economic savings. Defects in production can usually be traced back to causes. However, these are often complex or difficult to identify due to the large amounts of data that are generated in the PQM System.

B. Classification and prediction in manufacturing

Artificial intelligence, such as binary classification models, can be used here to work out the error-cause relationships on the one hand, and on the other hand to provide forecasts for future measurements about future susceptibility to errors. Due to the described economic implications, this has great potential. The measurement features of the individual test stations form the set of input variables for classification. The occurrence of a defective workpiece at a particular test station is stored as a binary variable, which is the target variable for classification. Its recording takes place chronologically after the measurements of input variables.

When correlations are learned through artificial intelligence, the classification models created can be used to make predictions about defects. As soon as all measured values of a certain model are acquired for a workpiece, a prediction is created. We refer to the state of a production process without support of ML as the *status quo*. Here, the workpieces pass through all production steps and are only removed from the process when an error has occurred. Alternatively, we can trust predictions of an existing ML model and remove the corresponding workpiece from the production process. Subsequent costs in production are then saved. Although the remaining production steps and test stations will not be passed, there might be possibilities to check in a separate step whether the workpiece is actually defective or not. At the same time, incorrect predictions result in missed profits when the products would actually have been error-free. It is therefore obvious to evaluate predictions in the context of manufacturing from an economic point of view. Classifications within a production line can be done in many ways. From the set of different errors that occur at a certain test station, a specific error can be selected, or a subset of all errors can be combined and treated as one fault. Any subset of the set of measurement features can be selected, provided that the measurements were made before the selected error occurred.

C. Concept drift in manufacturing

The time factor plays a major role in handling data derived from the production processes. The error-cause relationships are often not permanent, as the production environment is subject to dynamic change. For example, mechanical properties of tools used at the test stations can change and affect the tolerance limits of individual features [3]. Then learned correlations of the classification models no longer hold and there is a risk that increasingly wrong predictions are given, which is called concept drift. This effect can be detected by monitoring the quality of the positive predictions, e.g., using precision, see Section III. Each significant drift signals a change in the underlying relationships that the ML model used has not learned. If workpieces are mistakenly removed from the production process in case of a positive prediction, this yields a deterioration of the economic profit. Quality managers can provide information to determine a critical threshold at which further deterioration leads to economic losses. This state equals the *status quo* where no predictions are made. Since the quality of the predictions can only be monitored retrospectively, the decision to trust the prediction model must already be made at the previous instance. This means that a deterioration in performance can only be reacted to with a delay. Concept drift might also occur due to the increase of errors without them being correctly predicted. In this case, classification does not yield worse results than in the *status quo* and has no negative effect in comparison.

III. FUNDAMENTALS

The following sections require the knowledge of some methodological basics, which will now be presented.

A. Evaluating classification results in manufacturing

We consider the case of a binary classification model that tries to predict whether a workpiece will later be defective (class 1) or not (class 0), based on measured values in production. We evaluate results of a ML mechanism compared to the *status quo* without ML support. Not making a prediction (*status quo*) corresponds to a negative prediction of a ML mechanism. Since the positive predictions make the difference, we focus on these and neglect negative predictions.

Domingos [4] defines a cost matrix C, where $c(i, j)$ represents costs of a piece of class j that is predicted to be class i. Quality managers can assess the benefits of correct failure prediction $c(1, 1)$ and the costs of incorrect failure prediction $c(0, 1)$. They depend on the specific product, test station and error and must be determined individually. Note that $c(1, 1) > 0$, while $c(0, 1) < 0$, as there are savings when a faulty part is correctly predicted as. We define *total savings* TS as sum of savings due to the number of true positive instances TP and costs due to the number of false positive instances FP:

$$TS = TP * c(1, 1) + FP * c(0, 1) \quad (1)$$

To simplify, we set $c(0, 1) = -1$, $c(1, 1)$ can be determined as any multiple thereof:

$$TS = TP * c(1, 1) - FP \quad (2)$$

Total savings represent a metric with which the results of a classification can be evaluated from an economic point of view. As mentioned, the *status quo* does not use artificial intelligence. No errors are detected, but no workpieces are mistakenly removed from the process either, which yields $TS = 0$.

If the focus of the evaluation is on the quality of the positive predictions, then precision is a suitable metric:

$$precision = \frac{TP}{TP + FP} \quad (3)$$

In this respect, a threshold τ can be derived below which the classification leads to negative *total savings* and is therefore uneconomical.

$$TS = 0 = TP * c(1,1) - FP \rightarrow FP = TP * c(1,1) \quad (4)$$

Using (3), this gets:

$$\tau = \frac{TP}{TP + TP * c(1,1)} = \frac{1}{1 + c(1,1)} \quad (5)$$

As the precision of a single instance is a binary output, it makes sense to evaluate precision with the help of a sliding window over the last instances. In the following we call the number of instances within a sliding window n_{win}.

B. Concept drift and detecting drift in data streams

Given the quality measurements X, a ML classification model M predicts the conditional probability $P_t(Y|X)$ at time t, where Y represents a production error. We call the occurrence of the true label Y due to certain common properties of a subset of input data X *concept*. If the underlying relationships change over time, $P_t(Y|X) \neq P_{t+1}(Y|X)$ may hold after some time, which is known as concept drift. Independently of this, $P_t(X) \neq P_{t+1}(X)$ might occur as well. If there is no drift of the nature $P_t(Y|X) \neq P_{t+1}(Y|X)$, this is called virtual drift [5]. In the context of model predictions this is of smaller interest, as it does not affect the performance of classification. As the nature of the underlying classification problem is often not trivial, there might be several concepts $P_t^i(Y|X)$ that can be affected by concept drift to different degrees. This affects established performance measures of classification, such as precision or recall [5]. There are several methods for analyzing data streams for drift [6]. They have in common that they signal a deviation in data streams when it is significant, depending on various criteria. Different types of drift can be detected, such as sudden or incremental drift [5]. This complicates the quality of correct drift detection. For example, an outlier should not trigger a drift detection if there are no significant trends apart from it [6]. One of the well-known drift detectors is the Page-Hinkley test (PHT) [7].

C. State of the art drift detection in manufacturing

In order to describe the use of ML in manufacturing, we consider a point in time from which a certain amount of data is already known (Window $W1$) and from which further data can be expected in the future (Window $W2$). A typical application based on total data is shown in Fig. 2. During an initialization phase (red) a classifier model M is created based on already available data, which provides predictions for future data. This is part of the ongoing process (blue) as well as the assessment and handling of concept drift that considers all available data

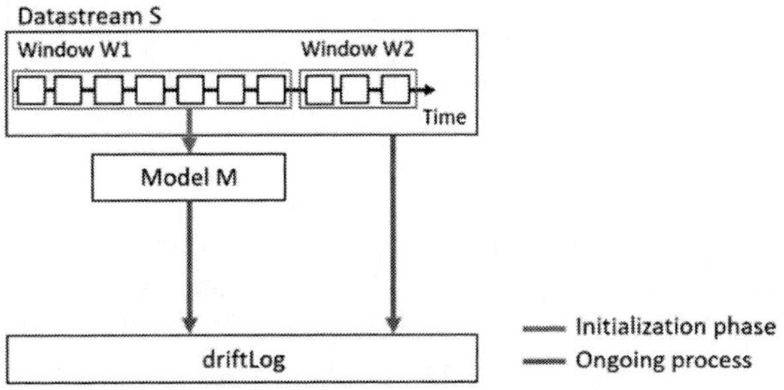

Fig. 2: Basic ML approach.

as a whole. All relevant information is stored within $driftLog$. Since concept drift is usually accompanied by a deterioration in prediction quality, the *status quo* with $TS = 0$ should always be considered as an alternative with regard to economic evaluation.

Algorithm 1 describes the procedure in detail. We define tuple t as instance of datastream S that includes the set of features X and the corresponding labels Y. Features X are derived from S by the attribute $S.X$, labels Y accordingly by $S.Y$. Model M predicts a label y for instance t. t and y are added to previous data collection $driftLog$. If y is positive, a possible concept drift needs to be investigated. The evaluation of whether a possible positive prediction of the next instance should be considered or not (boolean $ignore$) is calculated by the function $handle\_drift()$. The idea behind this is to remove workpieces when the current predictions seem reliable and not to trust them when the prediction quality is too low in order to improve the economic balance compared to the status quo. In Section VI, we propose two strategies for doing so.

D. SHAP values and their clustering

The idea of Shapley values has its origins in game theory [8]. However, the concept can be extended for the interpretation of model predictions [1]. The basis is a learned model that gives a prediction for a target variable based on a set of features for each instance. The values of each feature can influence the prediction. Depending on its value each feature contributes to the model output value of a single instance. The contribution of a feature, given that all other features remain constant, is called SHAP value. The transformation

Algorithm 1: Basic ML approach.

Input : tuple $t \in S$
classifier model M
dataframe $driftLog$
Output: dataframe $driftLog$
$y \longleftarrow M.predict(t.X)$
if y *is positive* **then**
 $ignore \longleftarrow handle\_drift(driftLog, t.X, y, args)$
$driftLog.add(t, y, ignore)$

of the original values X to the SHAP values SV will in the following be referred to as function $SHAP()$:

$$SV = SHAP(M, X) \tag{6}$$

For illustration, we trained a model with synthetic data consisting of two features A and B and 10000 instances. Feature values were generated from the standard normal distribution. 1000 randomly drawn instances were given the label *1*, which is supposed to represent an error. This adds some noise to the data. In addition, all instances with $A < -0.6$ or $B > 2.3$ received the label *1*. This created a region with significantly higher error probability. Using the model that has learned this relationship, we can create the SHAP values of an independent dataset also drawn from the standard normal distribution. Table I shows eight selected instances and the predicted error probability $\hat{y}$ calculated by the model. Values are rounded to two decimal places. The labels Y are assigned according to the learned correlations.

The prediction of the model can be understood as follows: The values of the features of Instance 1 are both outside the range with high error probability. Both features contribute to the low prediction. Instance 3 is in the critical range for A, but not for B. The model has learned that all instances in the described range are faulty. Therefore, the prediction is understandable, the value of A contributes significantly. Conversely, for Instance 5 and Instance 6, B leads to a high error probability. Both features A and B contribute to the high predictions of Instance 7 and Instance 8.

The SHAP values map this contribution of the individual features to the prediction. Table I includes the SHAP values for the named instances. Negative values signal a tendency to low error probability, positive values contribute to a high prediction. The described similarities regarding the contribution to the prediction become apparent.

Fig. 3 illustrates the SHAP values of Instance 5: The probability space $[0, 1]$ is transformed according to the logit function and forms the axis. The model output value is the prediction of Instance 5. The base value corresponds to the expected value of model output. The red arrow symbolizes feature A that contributes to an increased prediction, while the blue arrow relates to feature B that leads to a decreased prediction. The length of the arrows is the quantitative contribution and corresponds to the respective SHAP value. The value 2.61

TABLE I: EXEMPLARY INPUT DATA, CORRESPONDING SHAP VALUES, PREDICTIONS AND LABELS.

ID	A	B	$SHAP(M, A)$	$SHAP(M, B)$	$\hat{y}$	Y
1	0.39	-2.21	-1.34	-0.33	0.08	0
2	1.07	0.87	-1.28	-0.11	0.10	0
3	-0.63	-0.51	8.36	-0.02	1.00	1
4	-1.47	-0.85	8.33	-0.08	1.00	1
5	0.55	2.61	-0.74	5.56	0.98	1
6	1.16	2.34	-0.69	5.57	0.98	1
7	-0.87	2.43	6.00	2.69	1.00	1
8	-0.62	2.6	6.00	2.69	1.00	1

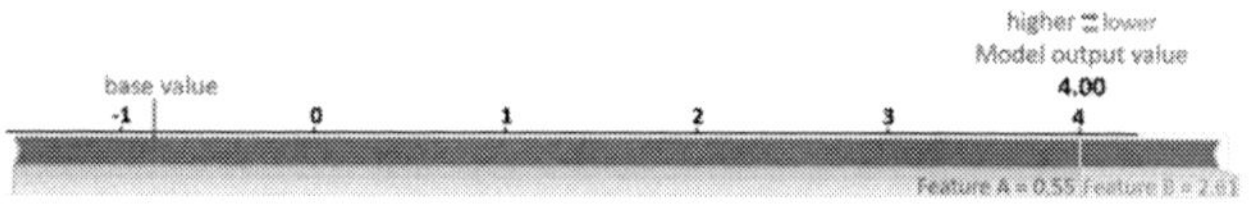

Fig. 3: SHAP values of Instance 5.

for feature B provides a significant increase of the error probability, while 0.55 for feature A speaks against an error.

If the examined instances are clustered, corresponding groups are formed which are similar with respect to their contribution to the prediction. Therefore, the assumption is that each concept $P(Y|X)$ goes along with a cluster. Since the computation of SHAP values requires a supervised learning model, the clustering of SHAP values is also called supervised clustering [9]. All SHAP values have the same unit, that of the model output. This does usually not apply to the original values of an input dataset. Thus, clustering can be done without further normalization and instances are collected whose features have a similar effect on the prediction, i.e., they are similar in terms of explanation [10]. The predictions of the instances within a cluster are always similar, but instances with similar or the same prediction can belong to different clusters. Fig. 4 shows the distribution of SHAP values from Table I. Slight jitter is added for visibility and the points are marked depending on the label of the corresponding instance. Four different clusters are clearly visible. The cluster near the origin belongs to instances where both SHAP values for A and B speak against an error. The bottom right cluster contains instances where only B tends to increase the probability of error, and the top left cluster contains instances where B is the only reason for a high probability of error. In the middle of these two clusters are instances where both A and B make an error likely.

As the number of instances increases, the main characteristics of Fig. 4 are preserved. Since the data is drawn from the standard normal distribution, clustering the input data does not provide any insights. The contributions of the features to the prediction would not be visible.

The example shows that the influence of the feature on the predictions of the individual instances is not revealed either by

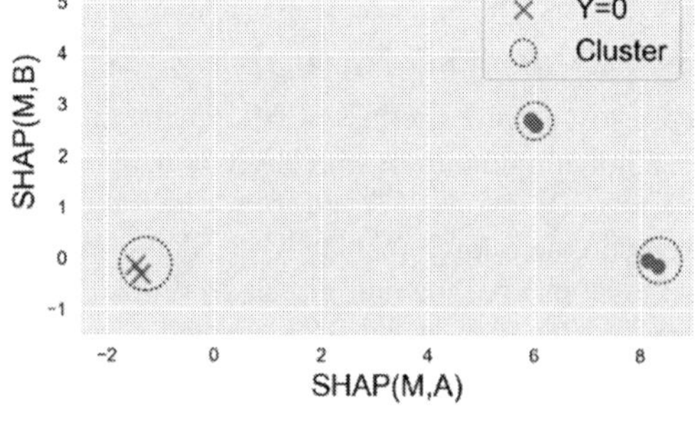

Fig. 4: Distribution of SHAP values of input data.

clustering the original data or by clustering instances according to their predictions.

IV. The PREFERML Concept

Avoiding errors at an early stage during production is the goal of the PREFERML project (Proactive Error Avoidance in Production through Machine Learning). The system is intended to achieve economic advantages through improved prediction quality of errors and to increase the quality of the manufactured products. To this end, the areas of machine learning processes, big data technologies and knowledge modeling are closely interlinked (see Fig. 5). The scalable application is based on the automated creation of a large number of models and their automated maintenance to reduce manual effort. The ML models generated within the framework of PREFERML serve, on the one hand, to retrospectively provide the learned error-cause correlations for quality managers. On the other hand, they provide a prediction about the defectiveness of future instances through classification. Economic benefits can only be achieved if the prediction models are of sufficient quality in the long term. To ensure this, the detection and handling of concept drift is hence a central part of PREFERML.

V. Related Work

In the following, previously published ideas and approaches related to fault detection in manufacturing and concept drift research are presented.

A. Fault detection and monitoring product quality in manufacturing

The approaches to fault diagnosis and product quality prediction include both unsupervised learning [12] and supervised learning [13]. Neural networks or decision tree-based approaches are used as classifiers in diverse applications [14], [15]. Hirsch, Reimann and Mitschang [14] compare a variety of classifiers for fault diagnosis using industrial data. They focus on the occurrence of defects in the last production step of a production line and evaluate random forests as the most suitable classifier. There are alternative ways to monitor the quality of products and workpieces during production processes. Wuest, Irgens and Thoben [16], for example, check the quality of products by monitoring the state of a product during the production process.

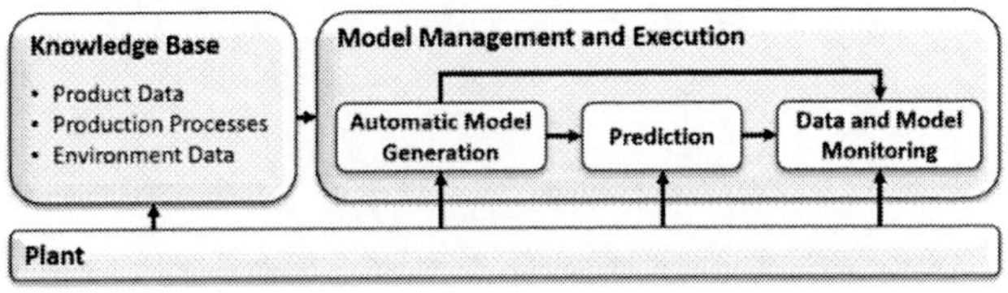

Fig. 5: Conception overview of PREFERML [11]. Arrows represent data flow between two components.

B. Concept drift research and applications

Gama, Žliobaitė, Bifet, Pechenizkiy and Bouchachia [5] shed a light on different aspects of handling concept drift and refer to state of the art methods. They discuss the various possibilities for drift detection. Besides the sequential analysis, where the Page-Hinkley test is a variant, distributions of two different time windows can be examined for statistically significant differences. With the availability of the label of incoming data, they see two alternatives: retraining or adaptation of an existing model. They define online adaptive learning as a sequence of the steps *predict*, *diagnose*, and *update*. For the evaluation of the used model the authors suggest, among others, precision and emphasize the consideration of baseline approaches. Lu et al. [17] add to this work and propose a framework for handling concept drift in the context of stream data, including *training and learning*, *prediction*, *concept drift detection*, *concept drift understanding* and *concept drift adaptation*. Accordingly, besides the time and lasting of drift occurrence, *concept drift understanding* concerns the aspects of *severity of drift* and *region of drift* (with respect to the feature space). They also see training new models and adapting existing models as consequences for dealing with drift, and propose precision as an evaluation metric, among others. They note a lack of *concept drift understanding* for existing drift detection methods, in the sense that apart from the time at which drift occurs, little information can be derived.

Adams et al. [18] try to fill this gap by expanding concept drift detection with an explainability level. Their approach introduces a cause-effect relationship to explain drifts.

Wang and Abraham [19] present an alternative approach to previously established mechanisms for detecting concept drift, which they call *Linear Four Rate (LFR)*. This method aims to identify data points that are part of the new concept to provide an updated basis for retraining. The authors show significantly better performance in terms of proven evaluation metrics compared to other methods for drift detection.

Baier, Hofmann, Kühl, Mohr and Satzger [20] present a method for handling concept drift in the context of regression problems, which they call *intersection approach*. During a period of drift predictions are derived from a simple model and a more complex model is trusted in ordinary situations.

Regression problems are also part of the work of Zenisek, Holzinger and Affenzeller [21]. They detect concept drift in industrial streaming data. However, their focus is on predictive maintenance and they look at the functionality of machines rather than a manufacturing process. They present a method in which the prediction quality is calculated within a sliding window. On this basis, a predefined threshold is used to decide whether drift is present. In a further approach, they provide a concept drift forecast on which drift detection is performed.

Just like our work, Sakamoto et al. [22] deal with concept drift detection and clustering. However, they aim to detect changes in clustering results. In our work, however, changes in classification results are the subject of investigation.

Demšar and Bosnić [23] study concept drift in streaming data using model explanation. They monitor the contributions of attributes to the predictions over time. The idea is similar to our approach of using SHAP values. In contrast, we separate the individual concepts into clusters and monitor the performance of the predictions per cluster.

C. *SHAP values in machine learning*

Mokhtari, Higdon and Başar [24] use SHAP values in the context of financial data to obtain important features for predicting commentaries. They also show that, in their case, predictions based on SHAP values are better than predictions based on the orginal data. As part of a seismic classification task, Meng, Yang, Qian and Zhang [25] use SHAP values to determine the most important attributes. They investigate the effects of the most important attributes on the model output using SHAP plots. Lundberg, Erion and Lee [9] use an example to show the benefit of supervised clustering with SHAP values. In the context of income prediction, they identify groups with common factors relevant to income.

VI. HANDLING CONCEPT DRIFT IN MANUFACTURING DATA

For each prediction, the question arises whether it makes economic sense to act according to it. If defects are predicted, a workpiece can be removed from the production process or it can be further processed. This decision inevitably has economic consequences: either a workpiece is correctly identified as defective and costs are saved, or the prediction is wrong and economic revenue is foregone. Our goal is to develop an approach that, based on an incoming data stream of production data, can be used to

- specifically detect concept drifts,
- efficiently derive measures and thus to
- maximize economic savings.

The decision for the upcoming workpiece has to be made on the basis of the information of all previous instances. For this purpose, we have developed a method that extends the basic use of ML in manufacturing (see Fig. 2). While the *Basic ML approach* considers all available data as a whole, our proposed method (see Fig. 6) involves dividing the same data into clusters based on their SHAP values. The initialization phase (red) remains the same, the ongoing process (blue) additionally includes the assignment of the instances to the most suitable cluster before the handling of drift.

In Subsection III-D, we showed how concepts $P(Y|X)$ can be derived on the basis of SHAP values and how the corresponding instances are distributed to clusters. We continue the example and generate 100 instances from the standard normal distribution according to those of Table I. However, we now assign the labels in such a way that a different correlation applies, namely an increased error probability if $A < -1$ (instead of $A < -0.6$ or $B > 2.3$). Adding SHAP values of these instances to Fig. 4 yields Fig. 7. Now, the actual labels are distributed differently in some clusters. The cluster near the origin with negative predictions now contains some faulty instances. For our application, these changes are less important, because they occur exactly the same with *status quo*. Of greater interest are the other clusters. Here, there are now some instances that are error-free, although faults are predicted based on certain values for A and B. In the context of manufacturing, these developments lead to consequential costs and it would be good if the error-free instances were not removed from the production process according to their prediction.

By monitoring cluster specific data we want to detect such changes of the nature $P_t(Y|X) \neq P_{t+1}(Y|X)$ and handle drift individually for each cluster. This includes a decision based on the prediction quality as to whether or not the next workpiece with a positive prediction will be removed from the production process. The detailed procedure is as follows. In a first step, all clusters are derived from the past data (here: data of $W1$), which is described in Algorithm 2. As mentioned in Subsection III-D, $SHAP(M, X)$ transforms measurements X to SHAP values according to the learned classifier M. The function $clustering()$ represents a common cluster algorithm such as k-means [26], that returns $centers$, the coordinates of the derived clusters. Each instance t of a dataframe is allocated to the closest center c of $centers$. The set $clusters$ is returned that includes all previous of these tuples. In a second step, each instance of past and future data is evaluated with regard to concept drift (see Algorithm 3). The function $handle\_drift()$ determines whether to ignore a possible positive prediction of the upcoming instance due to poor current prediction performance. We propose the following

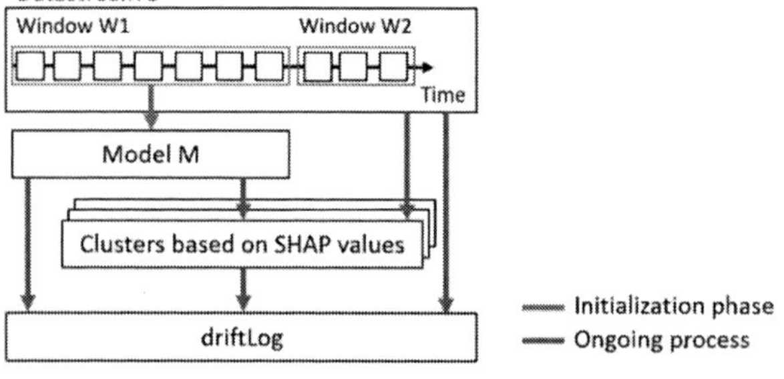

Fig. 6: Handling drift based on clustering of SHAP values.

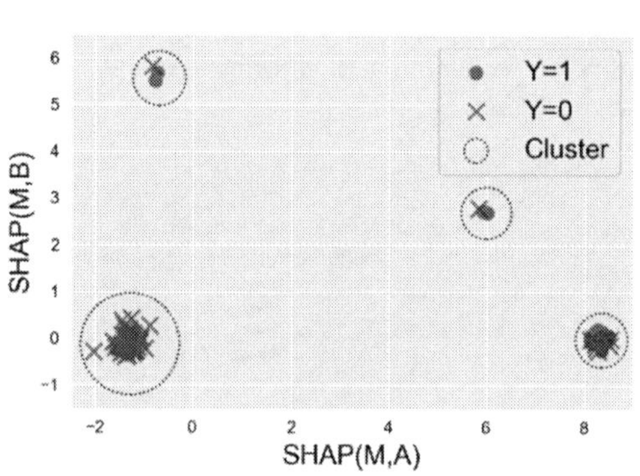

Fig. 7: Evolution of clusters based on SHAP values.

Algorithm 2: Derive clusters

Input : dataframe D
classifier model M
Output: dataframe $clusters$
$clusters \longleftarrow \emptyset$
$centers \longleftarrow clustering(SHAP(M, D.X))$
for $t \in D$ **do**
  $c \longleftarrow get\_center(SHAP(M, t.X), centers)$
  $clusters.add(t, c)$

two strategies for doing so. The variant *handle drift based on current precision only* makes this decision based on the current precision. In this case, $args$ includes the precision threshold τ and the size n_{win} of the sliding window for precision. With the actual labels Y of the input data $driftLog$ the precision of the last n_{win} positive predictions is calculated. If this is below the precision threshold τ, $true$ is returned, otherwise $false$. Due to little available data, n_{win} may exceed the number of instances so far. In this case, precision cannot be calculated and $false$ is output. This strategy is inspired by the procedure of a drift detection mechanism described by Zenisek, Holzinger and Affenzeller [21].

The alternative approach *handle drift based on current precision and established drift detection mechanisms like Page-Hinkley* extends the condition for output $true$. It requires the stream of precision values of all previous sliding windows. If the current precision is below the precision threshold τ and additionally a significant negative drift is detected for the precision stream at the current instance, $true$ is returned. This is done by established drift detectors with the help of a sensitivity parameter $sens$. $False$ is returned again, when precision is above the precision threshold τ. The second strategy is more reluctant compared to the first one, but continues to trust the prediction (possibly rightly) if the precision only briefly falls below the precision threshold τ. For this purpose, first the SHAP values of the measured values of the respective instance t are calculated and assigned to the closest cluster c via the existing cluster centers $centers$. At the same time, a binary prediction y is created on the basis of the measured values. If this is positive, all instances of the relevant cluster c are assigned to the dataframe $clusterLog$. The function $handle\_drift()$ evaluates this data with respect to concept drift and returns a boolean value $ignore$ that decides whether or not to ignore the next positive prediction. $args$ includes parameters for drift detection to be set in advance, which is described below. $driftLog$ stores the decision $ignore$ and the predicted label y of instance t.

Algorithm 3: Evaluate incoming data

Input : tuple $t \in D$
dataframe $clusters$
set of cluster centers $centers$
classifier model M
set of parameters $args$
dataframe $driftLog$
Output: boolean $ignore$
dataframe $clusters$
dataframe $driftLog$
$y \longleftarrow M.predict(t.X)$
$c \longleftarrow get\_center(SHAP(M, t.X), centers)$
$clusters.add(t, c)$
if y *is positive* **then**
  $clusterLog \longleftarrow$
    $get\_log\_of\_cluster(clusters, c, log)$
  $ignore \longleftarrow$
    $handle\_drift(clusterLog, t.X, y, args)$
$driftLog.add(t, y, ignore)$

VII. EXPERIMENTS

We carried out the approach described in Fig. 6 based on real manufacturing data of our industry partner SICK AG and compared the two strategies of the function $handle\_drift$ designed in Section VI. The data used come from a total of six production lines and cover similar periods of about one year. For each experiment, a test station of a specific production line was selected. The different types of errors occurring there were combined, so that for classification an error Y always represents any type of error. All measurements recorded at previous test stations served as feature set X. This resulted in 30 experiments. These were conducted retrospectively and simulated the described methods under real-time conditions. Metadata on the data used is given in Table II.

The ML model shown in Fig. 6 resulted from the first part of the chronologically sorted data which contains 67% of the total number of errors. The remaining instances were part of window $W2$. XGBoost [27] with tree booster was used to create classification models, Page-Hinkley test served as the drift detector. Clustering was done using k-means algorithm, with the number of clusters determined by the elbow heuristic. After consulting with quality engineers, we set $c(1,1) = 10$ and got $\tau = \frac{1}{11}$. In a pretest, a sensitivity analysis was performed on the parameters n_{win} and $sens$ (in the case of Page-Hinkley test it is called λ). A parameter setting of $n_{win} = 100$ and $\lambda = 0.1$ was considered suitable, which was chosen to conduct the experiments. For comparison, the procedure based on clustering was also performed on total data (see Subsection II-C). Note, that this resembles the state of the art of applying concept drift detection without our clustering based approach. The evaluation of an experiment is based on *total savings* TS. In the case of several clusters, these

TABLE II: METADATA ON EXPERIMENTAL DATA.

Characteristic	mean	min	max
Instances	~ 76746	10721	194932
Errors	~ 1531	139	4284
Features	~ 93	17	1105

are calculated by the sum of *total savings* over all clusters. Baseline for all experiments is $TS = 0$, which corresponds to the result of the *status quo*.

VIII. RESULTS

In the following, an evaluation on the basis of a selected experiment is shown first. Afterwards, the approaches developed are evaluated on the basis of all experiments carried out.

A. *Use case*

The clustering in the selected case resulted in four clusters. Fig. 8 shows the occurrence of the corresponding instances over time. It includes jitter for visibility of data density. The colored area marks the corresponding time period. A vertical black line indicates the end of Window $W1$. The temporal distributions of the data of Clusters 1 and 4 are similar, as are those of Clusters 2 and 3. Noticeable are periods in which the density of the instances of Clusters 2 and 3 decreases and at the same time those in Clusters 1 and 4 increase, so that for Clusters 2 and 3 there is a longer period in which no data are assigned to them. Data of $W2$ are distributed mainly in Cluster 2. Especially in Cluster 1 it is noticeable that the density of data in $W2$ is significantly lower than in $W1$.

Since model M was created with data of $W1$ the evaluation of classification results focuses on data of $W2$. Table III summarizes the results of the classification for the clusters and total data. Especially for Cluster 2 and Cluster 3 there are negative *total savings*, which indicates concept drift.
Applying *handle drift based on current precision only* yields the results shown in Table IV. Due to the small number of positive predictions Cluster 1 and Cluster 4 are not affected. However, *total savings* for Cluster 2 and Cluster 3 can be increased clearly. Improvements are similar for total data, but slightly smaller.

This is confirmed by Fig. 9, which shows precision over time for the different clusters and total data. It illustrates precision threshold τ as black dotted horizontal line and drift detected by Page-Hinkley (λ=0.1) test as vertical red line. A vertical black line indicates the end of $W1$, y-range goes from 0 to 1 in each case. As there are too few predictions in the sliding window, no data points are available for cluster

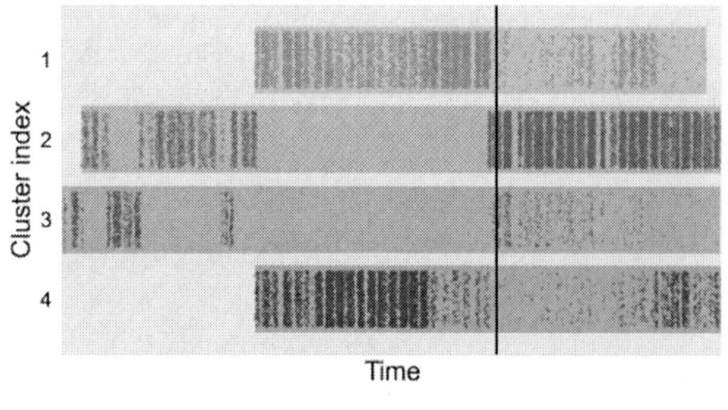

Fig. 8: Use case - time distribution of cluster instances.

TABLE III: USE CASE: CLASSIFICATION RESULTS FOR $W2$ - BASIC ML WITHOUT HANDLING DRIFT.

Data	Instances	Errors	TP	FP	TS
Cluster 1	778	16	1	0	10
Cluster 2	11094	301	139	3994	-2604
Cluster 3	479	15	15	463	-313
Cluster 4	993	34	6	0	60
$\sum_{clusters}$	13344	366	161	4457	-2847
Total data	13344	366	161	4457	-2847

1. While the precision of Cluster 2 is permanently low in $W2$, a strong deterioration of the prediction can be seen for Cluster 3 at the beginning of $W2$. In both cases, there is no lasting improvement. Cluster 2 shows the potential of a mechanism that ignores the positive predictions in case of poor performance: Once the precision is below τ, it stays there.

The strategy *handle drift based on current precision and established drift detection mechanisms like Page-Hinkley* leads to similar results for the clusters (see Table V). However, *total savings* for total data are considerably lower. With regard to the *status quo* with *total savings* $TS = 0$, it can be seen that both approaches perform better for the clusters, but the latter shows no improvement in the case of total data.

B. *General view*

Looking at the nature of clusters over all experiments, it turns out that some clusters have unique characteristics. For example, there are clusters whose instances are all free of errors or at least whose predicted labels are negative. Some clusters contain only instances of $W1$, so these concepts were unnecessarily learned by the model and are not used later. Yet, it may happen that only very few instances of a cluster belong to $W1$. Then only little data was available for the model to learn the corresponding concept. Accordingly, the prediction quality deteriorates in the later course. In the experiments conducted, drift occurs mostly in the form of a sudden drift, a reoccurring drift occurs only in a few cases.
The performance of the different strategies for handling drift can be determined for the individual experiments based on *total savings* of the examined case. The cluster-specific strategy *handle drift based on current precision only* ($TS = 94$) proved to be the best in the use case examined in Section VIII-A. We

TABLE IV: USE CASE: CLASSIFICATION RESULTS FOR $W2$ - HANDLE DRIFT BASED ON CURRENT PRECISION ONLY.

Data	Instances	Errors	TP	FP	TS
Cluster 1	778	16	1	0	10
Cluster 2	11094	301	22	195	25
Cluster 3	479	15	9	91	-1
Cluster 4	993	34	6	0	60
$\sum_{clusters}$	13344	366	38	286	94
Total Data	13344	366	31	307	3

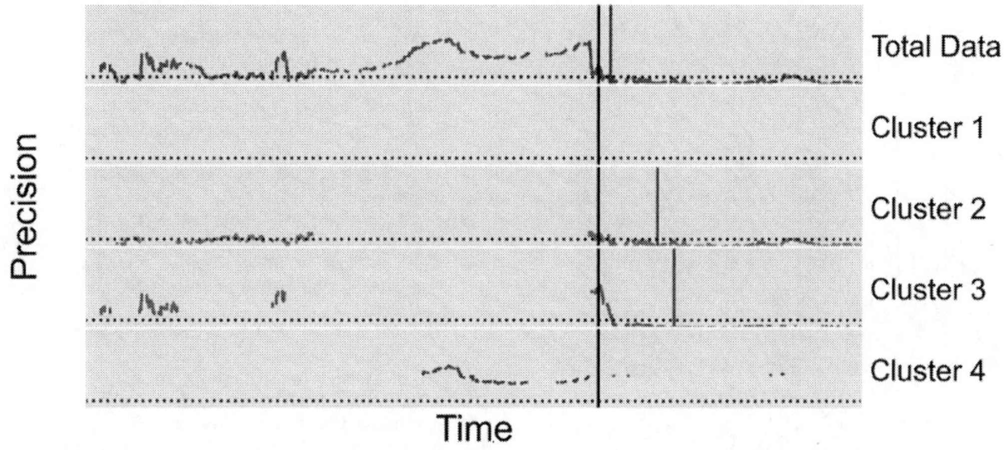

Fig. 9: Use case - cluster specific precision within a sliding window (n=100) over positive predictions.

did this evaluation for each of the 30 experiments. Summing up the *total savings* of the respective approaches across all experiments, we obtain the results shown in Fig 10.

A similar picture emerges as in the use case described: it makes more economic sense to handle drift on the basis of individual clusters. As a criterion for deciding whether a workpiece should be taken out of the production process according to a positive prediction, the current precision seems to be the most suitable. Since the *status quo* goes along with *total savings* $TS = 0$, this also applies to the totality of experiments. For a deeper analysis, the individual strategies are compared in pairs using all experiments. For each approach, we counted how often it performs best in each pairwise comparisons with all other approaches. Fig. 11 illustrates the most important pairwise comparisons.

Again, it becomes apparent that the best results are achieved with the cluster specific approaches. In a direct comparison of clustering based approaches, the strategy that handles drift on the basis of current precision only performs best. It can be concluded that precision in this application is a good metric to monitor the quality of model predictions.

IX. CONCLUSION

The detection of concept drift in complex relations is often difficult or does not allow detailed conclusions to be drawn.

TABLE V: USE CASE: CLASSIFICATION RESULTS FOR $W2$ - HANDLE DRIFT BASED ON CURRENT PRECISION AND DRIFT DETECTION MECHANISMS.

Data	Instances	Errors	TP	FP	TS
Cluster 1	778	16	1	0	10
Cluster 2	11094	301	29	272	18
Cluster 3	479	15	10	99	1
Cluster 4	993	34	6	0	60
$\sum_{clusters}$	13344	366	46	372	89
Total Data	13344	366	47	560	-113

Yet, detecting concept drift is important to ensure benefits of applying a model. We have examined this challenge in the context of a manufacturing use case, where model performance impacts economic savings. We have developed and tested a method that uses SHAP values to assign the learned concepts to clusters so that they can be examined individually. Our evaluation demonstrates the benefits of the proposed clustering based approach with real manufacturing data. Here, we tested our approach for cluster specific assessment in combination with two strategies for handling drift. Our tests show better performance of drift detection using only precision values than for using the Page-Hinkley test additionally. However, in both cases our approach of clustering based assessment outperformed approaches without clustering. Note, that the

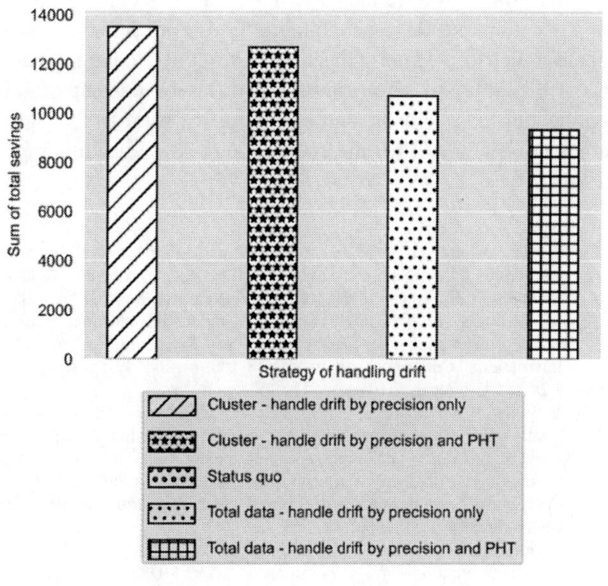

Fig. 10: Sum of *total savings* over all experiments.

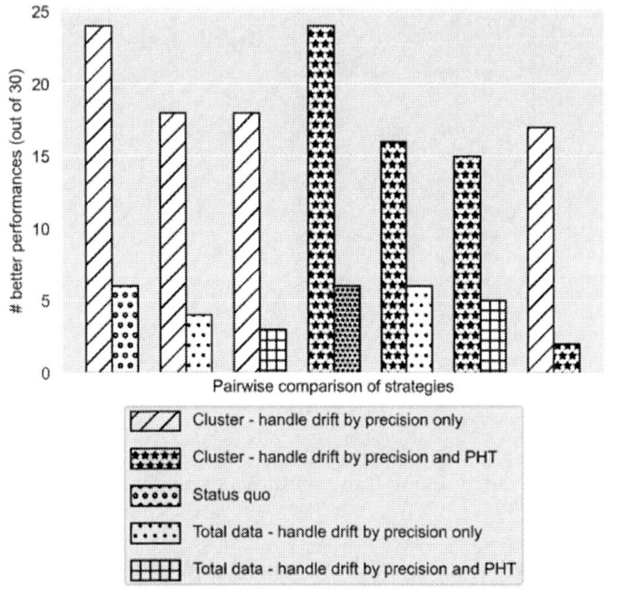

Fig. 11: Pairwise comparison of strategies to handle drift.

focus of our work is on the drift detection mechanism using clusters. Hence, we used a simple strategy for drift handling (i.e., ignoring predictions for a given cluster or total data). However, future work will address different measures such as retraining the models. The same applies to the number of the derived clusters. According to our approach, the clusters are initially inferred. It is possible that new concepts will emerge over time that actually require their own cluster. The quality of the clustering could be monitored and adjusted if necessary.

ACKNOWLEDGMENT

This project was funded by the German Federal Ministry of Education and Research, funding line "Forschung an Fachhochschulen mit Unternehmen (FHProfUnt)", contract number 13FH249PX6. The responsibility for the content of this publication lies with the authors. Also, we want to thank the company SICK AG for the cooperation and partial funding.

REFERENCES

[1] S. M. Lundberg and S.-I. Lee, "A unified approach to interpreting model predictions," in *Advances in Neural Information Processing Systems*, I. Guyon *et al.*, Eds., vol. 30. Curran Associates, Inc., 2017.

[2] A. Gerling *et al.*, "A reference process model for machine learning aided production quality management," ser. Proceedings of the 22nd International Conference on Enterprise Information Systems, May 5-7,2020 : Volume 1, 2020, pp. 515 – 523.

[3] Y. Wilhelm, U. Schreier, P. Reimann, B. Mitschang, and H. Ziekow, "Data science approaches to quality control in manufacturing: A review of problems, challenges and architecture," ser. Service-Oriented Computing : 14th Symposium and Summer School on Service-Oriented Computing, SummerSOC 2020, Crete, Greece, September 13-19, 2020. Cham: Springer, 2020, pp. 45 – 65.

[4] P. Domingos, "Metacost: A general method for making classifiers cost-sensitive," in *Proceedings of the fifth ACM SIGKDD international conference on Knowledge discovery and data mining*, 1999, pp. 155–164.

[5] J. Gama, I. Žliobaitė, A. Bifet, M. Pechenizkiy, and A. Bouchachia, "A survey on concept drift adaptation," *ACM computing surveys (CSUR)*, vol. 46, no. 4, pp. 1–37, 2014.

[6] Y. Kadwe and V. Suryawanshi, "A review on concept drift," *IOSR Journal of Computer Engineering*, vol. 17, pp. 20–26, 01 2015.

[7] E. S. Page, "Continuous inspection schemes," *Biometrika*, vol. 41, no. 1/2, pp. 100–115, 1954.

[8] L. S. Shapley, *17. A value for n-person games*. Princeton University Press, 2016.

[9] S. M. Lundberg, G. Erion, and S.-I. Lee, "Consistent individualized feature attribution for tree ensembles," *ArXiv*, vol. abs/1802.03888, 2018.

[10] C. Molnar, *Interpretable Machine Learning*, 2019, https://christophm.github.io/interpretable-ml-book/, retrieved on 08/26/2021.

[11] H. Ziekow *et al.*, "Proactive error prevention in manufacturing based on an adaptable machine learning environment," ser. Artificial Intelligence: From Research to Application: The UR-AI Symposium 2019, March 13th, 2019, Offenburg, Germany. Karlsruhe: Hochschule Karlsruhe - Technik und Wirtschaft, 2019, pp. 113 – 117.

[12] N. Kolokas, T. Vafeiadis, D. Ioannidis, and D. Tzovaras, "A generic fault prognostics algorithm for manufacturing industries using unsupervised machine learning classifiers," *Simulation Modelling Practice and Theory*, vol. 103, p. 102109, 2020.

[13] T. Zhou, L. He, J. Wu, F. Du, and Z. Zou, "Prediction of surface roughness of 304 stainless steel and multi-objective optimization of cutting parameters based on ga-gbrt," *Applied Sciences*, vol. 9, p. 3684, 09 2019.

[14] V. Hirsch, P. Reimann, and B. Mitschang, "Data-driven fault diagnosis in end-of-line testing of complex products," in *2019 IEEE International Conference on Data Science and Advanced Analytics (DSAA)*, 2019, pp. 492–503.

[15] K. B. Lee, S. Cheon, and C. O. Kim, "A convolutional neural network for fault classification and diagnosis in semiconductor manufacturing processes," *IEEE Transactions on Semiconductor Manufacturing*, vol. 30, no. 2, pp. 135–142, 2017.

[16] W. Thorsten, D. Weimer, C. Irgens, and K.-D. Thoben, "Machine learning in manufacturing: advantages, challenges, and applications," *Production & Manufacturing Research*, vol. 4, no. 1, pp. 23–45, 2016.

[17] J. Lu *et al.*, "Learning under concept drift: A review," *IEEE Transactions on Knowledge and Data Engineering*, vol. 31, no. 12, pp. 2346–2363, 2019.

[18] J. N. Adams *et al.*, "A framework for explainable concept drift detection in process mining," *ArXiv*, vol. abs/2105.13155, 2021.

[19] H. Wang and Z. Abraham, "Concept drift detection for streaming data," in *2015 international joint conference on neural networks (IJCNN)*. IEEE, 2015, pp. 1–9.

[20] L. Baier, M. Hofmann, N. Kühl, M. Mohr, and G. Satzger, "Handling concept drifts in regression problems–the error intersection approach," *arXiv preprint arXiv:2004.00438*, 2020.

[21] J. Zenisek, F. Holzinger, and M. Affenzeller, "Machine learning based concept drift detection for predictive maintenance," *Computers & Industrial Engineering*, vol. 137, p. 106031, 2019.

[22] Y. Sakamoto *et al.*, "Concept drift detection with clustering via statistical change detection methods," in *2015 Seventh International Conference on Knowledge and Systems Engineering (KSE)*. IEEE, 2015, pp. 37–42.

[23] J. Demšar and Z. Bosnić, "Detecting concept drift in data streams using model explanation," *Expert Systems with Applications*, vol. 92, pp. 546–559, 2018.

[24] K. E. Mokhtari, B. P. Higdon, and A. Başar, "Interpreting financial time series with shap values," in *Proceedings of the 29th Annual International Conference on Computer Science and Software Engineering*, ser. CASCON '19. USA: IBM Corp., 2019, p. 166–172.

[25] Y. Meng, N. Yang, Z. Qian, and G. Zhang, "What makes an online review more helpful: an interpretation framework using xgboost and shap values," *Journal of Theoretical and Applied Electronic Commerce Research*, vol. 16, no. 3, pp. 466–490, 2021.

[26] D. Arthur and S. Vassilvitskii, "k-means++: the advantages of careful seeding," in *SODA '07: Proceedings of the eighteenth annual ACM-SIAM symposium on Discrete algorithms*. Philadelphia, PA, USA: Society for Industrial and Applied Mathematics, 2007, pp. 1027–1035.

[27] T. Chen and C. Guestrin, "Xgboost: A scalable tree boosting system," ser. KDD '16. New York, NY, USA: Association for Computing Machinery, 2016, p. 785–794.

Discovering DataOps: A Comprehensive Review of Definitions, Use Cases, and Tools

Kiran Mainali
KTH Royal Institute of Technology
Stockholm, Sweden
e-mail: mainali@kth.se

Lisa Ehrlinger
Software Competence Center Hagenberg GmbH
Hagenberg, Austria,
Johannes Kepler University Linz
Linz, Austria
e-mail: lisa.ehrlinger@scch.at,

Johannes Himmelbauer
Software Competence Center Hagenberg GmbH
Hagenberg, Austria
e-mail: johannes.himmelbauer@scch.at

Mihhail Matskin
KTH Royal Institute of Technology
Stockholm, Sweden
e-mail: misha@kth.se

***Abstract*—Data management approaches have changed drastically in the past few years due to improved data availability and increasing interest in data analysis (e.g., artificial intelligence). The volume, velocity, and variety of data requires novel and automated ways to "operate" this data. In accordance with software development, where DevOps is the de-facto standard to operate code, DataOps is an emerging approach advocated by practitioners to tackle data management challenges for analytics. In this paper, we uncover DataOps from the scientific perspective with a rigorous review of research and tools. As a result, we make the following three-fold contribution: we (1) outline definitions of DataOps and their ambiguities, (2) identify the extent to which DataOps covers different stages of the data lifecycle, and (3) provide a comprehensive overview on tools and their suitability for different stages of DataOps.**

***Keywords*—DataOps; Data lifecycle management; Data analytics.**

I. Introduction

The increasing volume, velocity, and variety of data in recent years opened the possibility for enhanced analytics, e.g., in artificial intelligence applications [1]. Along with these possibilities, companies are putting higher effort into data analytics projects, which are becoming increasingly complex due to data characteristics, sophisticated tools, changing business needs, varied interests among stakeholders, and a lack of a standardized process [2]. While data analytics projects are still struggling with a standardized process, software development has successfully employed DevOps [3], which is an efficient and practical approach for delivering software applications at a higher pace using a combinations of cultural philosophies, practices, and tools [4][5]. There is a recent trend to adopt DevOps practices for data analytics projects [6].While collecting data, DevOps can reduce the effort and time for data retrieval [7]. Furthermore, in the data transformation and analysis, DevOps can maintain and update scripts and manage tools and technologies effectively and collaboratively using a Continuous Integration (CI) server and a central code repository. However, data analytics projects differ from software development in many aspects (e.g., the data and analytics pipeline, stateful data stores, and process controls) and therefore bear more similarities with data integration and business analysis projects [8]. The significant difference is the creation of an analytics pipeline, which copies operational data from business, performs business-rule-based data transformations, and populates the data in a central storage from which analysts can extract business information. This challenge cannot be simply solved by exploiting DevOps practices, but requires a more adjusted approach: DataOps.

In the process of establishing DataOps as a data analytics methodology, people and organizations supporting the concept derived 18 principles of DataOps in the manifesto [9]. The DataOps principle summarizes the best practices, goals, philosophies, mission, and values for DataOps practitioners. The manifesto puts team communication over tools and the process. Experimentation, iteration, and feedback are more important than designing and developing the whole pipeline upfront. Sense of responsibility and cross-functional collaboration is advocated to increase the project efficiency reducing individual soiled responsibilities and heroism.

DataOps is a method to automatically manage the entire data life cycle from data identification, cleaning, integration to analysis and reporting [10]. Its primary goal is business value maximization of data. It borrows proven practices from DevOps in the software development lifecycle. While DevOps is a mature field in software development, DataOps is still in its infancy stage. However, there is very little research to establish DataOps as a methodology.

In 2018, Ereth et al. [11] contributed with a working definition of DataOps. The authors conclude that further research is required to elaborate on this new discipline by investigating the process, related technologies, and tools, as well as the value

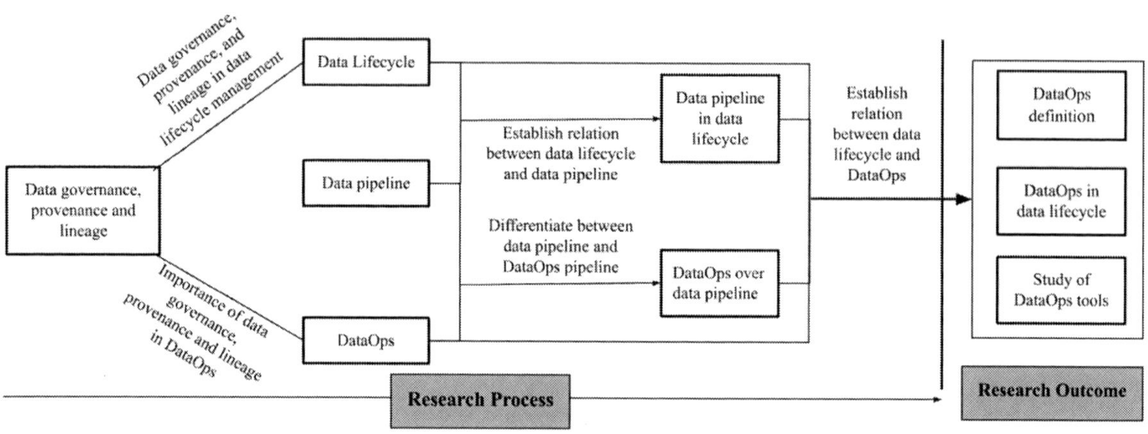

Figure 1. Illustration of the Exploratory Research Method.

proposition DataOps brings to business [11].

In 2020, Raj et al. [12] performed an extensive literature review of DataOps with a focus on the usability. Their paper presents a case study of a large telecommunication company and how their processes evolved by supporting DataOps [12].

Despite the few scientific papers, numerous resources from practitioners are available. Several companies strongly advocate DataOps and deliver a product to support the DataOps principles, e.g., IBM [13], DataKitchen [14], iCEDQ [15], and Eckerson [16]. IBM is a pioneer of the term DataOps and offers numbers of products for different data lifecycle stages (e.g., data collecting, analysis, storage, organization, and publishing) under the umbrella of their cloud service. DataKitchen is one of the leading solution providers for DataOps and is continuously working on establishing DataOps as a methodology with industrial research, e.g., the DataOps manifesto [9] and DataOps implementation guidelines [17]. iCEDQ provides a data monitoring platform and several whitepapers [18] and blogs [19] to help in understanding the implementation of DataOps in practice. Eckerson is a global research and consulting firm and published several reports to define DataOps [20], exploring the use of DataOps [21], and selection criteria for DataOps tools [22], amongst others.

In this paper, we contribute to the discipline of DataOps with a rigorous review of research as well as tools to bridge the gap between theory and practice. The results of the study can be divided into the following three contribution: (1) a summary of DataOps definitions and their ambiguities, (2) an investigation on how DataOps covers the stages of the data lifecycle, and (3) a comprehensive overview on tools and their suitability for different stages of DataOps.

The rest of the paper is organized as follows. Section II presents the research method used, while Section III presents the result. Finally Section IV concludes the paper and discusses possible future work.

II. Research Method

In this work, we investigate DataOps with explorative qualitative research using literature review and online research, illustrated in Figure 1. We started with collecting scientific articles from Google [23], Google scholar [24], ResearchGate [25], IEEE [26], KTH Library [27], KTH-Diva [28], and Semantic Scholar [29], as well as whitepapers and reports from several companies practicing DataOps. In total, we used 71 out of 157 analyzed research articles and 39 out of 112 accessed online resources.

Figure 1 shows the detailed process of research and the outcome of the study. The plain rectangle box represents topics covered, and the line denotes tasks performed to get the result.

III. Results

This section presents the result of our work to (1) define DataOps and point-out ambiguities, (2) investigate DataOps in data lifecycle management and (3) explore state-of-the-art tools for different stages of the data lifecycle.

A. *DataOps Definition – What is DataOps?*

DataOps is a consequence of three emerging trends: process automation, digital-native companies pressure on traditional industry, and the essence of data visualization and representation of results [30]. There is no commonly agreed definition of DataOps till now. The first time the term DataOps was used in [31] where the importance of executing data analytics task rapidly with ease of collaboration and assured quality outcome in diverse big data and cloud computing environment is discussed. However, the term DataOps gained its popularity only after Andy Palmer's contribution [32], where he describes DataOps as communication, collaboration, integration, and automation enabler practiced with cooperation between data engineers, data scientists and other stakeholders. [33] considers DataOps goal as taking data from the source and delivering to the person, application or system where it produces business value. Some other definitions describe DataOps as "analytic process which spans from data collection to delivery of information after data processing" [34], "develop and deliver data analytics projects in a better way" [43], "is combination of value and innovation pipeline" [35] or "data management approach to improve communication and integration between previously inefficient teams, system and data" [36].

Our analysis shows that different perspectives inspired DataOps definitions. Some definitions are more goal oriented [37]–[39] while some are activities oriented [38][40] and furthermore some are process and team oriented [6][41][42]. From a goal oriented approach, DataOps is viewed as a process to eliminate errors and inefficiency in data management, reducing the risk of data quality degradation and exposure of sensitive data using interconnected and secure data analytics models. From a process and team-oriented perspective, DataOps is a way of managing activities of data lifecycle with a high level of data governance, collaborating data creators and consumers using digital innovations.

From application perspective, DataOps is a set of practices in the data analytics field that takes proven practices from other industries [43]. It is the combination of proven methodologies that helped to grow other industries: DevOps and Agile methodology from the software industry and lean manufacturing from the automotive/manufacturing industry [10]. DataOps combines the speed and flexibility of Agile and DevOps and quality control of Statistical Process Control (SPC). Agile helps to deliver analytics results in faster ways, DevOps automates the process of analysis and SPC from lean manufacturing tests and monitors the data flow quality in the entire data analytics lifecycle.

DataOps has its own approaches on top of derived processes from other methodologies to tackle the challenges in the field due to the heterogeneity of data analysis projects. Separating the production environment from development gives room for data workers to experiment with the changes and altogether remove the fear of failure. With two different environments, product quality can be assured by continuous testing and cross-environment monitoring. Including customers and other stakeholders in data analytics project sets communication and feedback loop to minimum iteration. With this, changes and improvements in the pipeline can deliver faster results without affecting current pipeline production. Also, role-based task distribution fosters the responsibility of everyone while maintaining the coalition of a team effort.

DataOps pipeline (shown in Figure 2a) starts with gathering data and business requirements. Active involvement of managers, data providers, and analysts creates the baseline for pipeline development. Once business requirements and data are finalized, the development of the data pipeline starts. The developed data pipeline is orchestrated by orchestration tools and tested before deploying to the production environment. There could be multiple development environments for each involved data worker. However, the deployment will not be done without assembling all individual work to make the whole pipeline fulfilling all test requirements. Testing and orchestrating of data pipeline will be supported by Continuous Integration (CI) tools and deployment is done through Continuous Development (CD) tools. Deployment task automation reduces the workload of reconfiguration and reworks on the pipeline in another environment. With a combination of CI and CD, data pipeline moves swiftly from the innovation stage to the production stage. In the production phase, pipeline runs in an orchestrated environment as in a development environment. Continuous monitoring follows the pipeline input, performance, and output and cross-validates the monitoring outcomes with test results from the development environment and business requirements. The production team and monitoring teams are responsible for carrying out tasks in a production environment. Teams are composed of people with a different areas of expertise and interests to deliver quality performance. Finally, results will be shared with customers and stakeholders with the expectation of feedback and comments.

Figure 2b illustrates the DataOps ecosystem where various categories of tools aligned in order with people to match the process of converting input to generate insights as output through series of data lifecycle movement in between. Depending on project goal and level of automation, tools and technologies from the stacks are chosen. It is not always necessary to apply all the tools categories listed above. DataOps' primary objective is to deliver quality results in improved time and low cost. If that can be fulfilled by using one or a few tools from the list above, then the project can be delivered with those tools. DataOps is also about continuous improvement, so people working in the project should never give up on experimenting with new technologies and delivering better project results.

1) Ambiguities in DataOps Practices: DataOps is an emerging concept. In recent years information collection and work contributions are progressing in the DataOps through the involvement of DataOps practitioners and enthusiasts. But, there are some prevalent misconceptions in DataOps, which are listed and explained below by observing the industry implementation use cases and scenarios [21][22][35][44] provided by DataOps practitioners:

- **DataOps is just DevOps applied in data analytics.** DataOps is not DevOps for data. It takes best practices from DevOps and Agile methodology and combines with lean manufacturing's SPC and data analytics specific tasks to streamline data lifecycle and provide quality results. Data analytics projects and software development projects have significant differences.
- **DataOps is all about using tools and technology in the data pipeline.** DataOps is not about automating everything using tools and technologies and keeping human involvement away. DataOps advocates a balanced involvement of people along with tools and technology. Communication and collaboration are highly focused on DataOps to turn data into value for all involved parties.
- **DataOps is an expensive methodology.** Acquiring and running different tool always comes with a price. Data analytics projects will cost to an organization, whether they follow DataOps or not. One should compare their investment with the value going to receive in the near future. Furthermore, proper research on tools and technology before implementing on data pipeline can help make informed decision to cut the cost to a minimal.

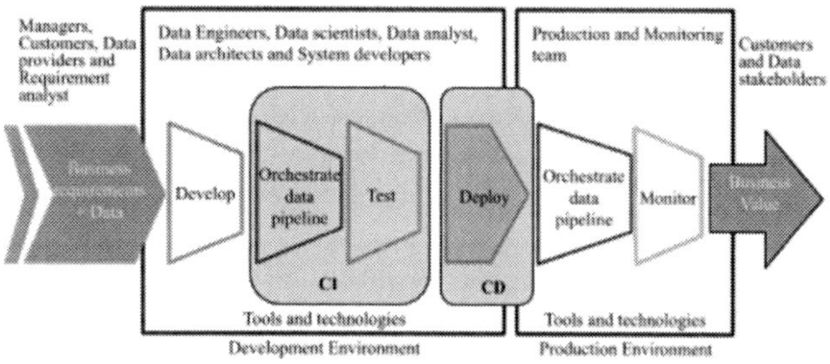

(a) DataOps pipeline.

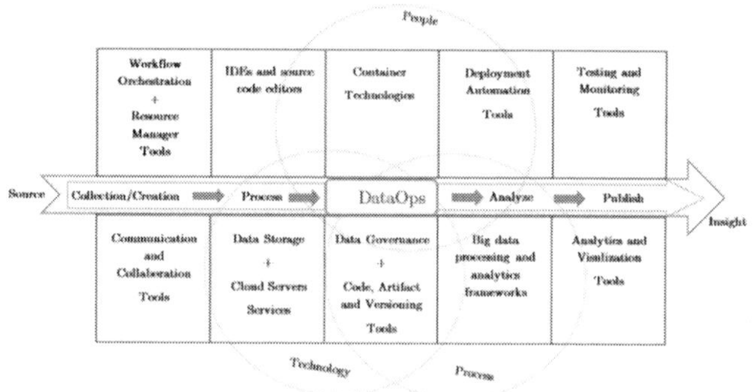

(b) DataOps framework.

Figure 2. Illustration of DataOps Pipeline and Framework.

- **With DataOps, there is no need for coding.** Without writing code data pipeline task cannot be formed at all. So coding is always a baseline of data analytics projects. With DataOps, even the coding process can be reduced to minimal by reusing and versioning of codes, algorithms and configuration. IDEs and source code editors provide easy writing and debugging of codes.
- **DataOps can only use on data analysis tasks.** DataOps is not just generating reports and delivering fancy charts, templates, bars, and figures. It is about covering the whole data lifecycle from the collection of data to disposal. Moreover, it is not just about covering the data lifecycle; it is also about creating a data-driven organization culture that emphasizes collaboration, communication, transparency, and quality on organizational tasks.
- **DataOps and data pipeline are two different ways of data analytics task propagation.** DataOps is an approach to implement a data pipeline. We apply the DataOps principle and practices while developing and executing data pipelines. Data pipeline with DataOps methodologies is also called DataOps pipeline. DataOps is not an entirely new way of performing data analytics tasks; rather, it redesigns the data pipeline to deliver quality results in a short time with minimal cost and effort.

2) Challenges in DataOps implementation: For an organization to succeed with DataOps, there is a need to consider potential issues. Challenges that need to be considered when implementing DataOps practices are listed below.

- **Changing the organization's culture:** DataOps is all about delivering analytics result faster, and the only way to make it happen is to encourage communication and collaboration across all departments. Data scientists, data engineers, managers, data analysts, system architects, system developers, customers and other data stakeholders all need to come together to break the status quo. DataOps can bring significant change, and for its success, everyone needs to be on board. This includes top executives, IT and business managers, data workers and everyone involved in data analytics project.
- **Innovation with low risk:** DataOps advocates continuous improvement in the product and cycle time, which means lesser time for development, test, and deployment. Teams need to move quickly without compromising quality. Not just quality but also complying with company policies and standards. Automation gives extra space to reduce cycle time by reducing the manual task of testing, monitoring and deployment. With automation on the deployment cycle, there is little time for reviews increasing the risk of missing out details and pieces of information. So initially, it will take time to implement for total confidence in ensuring data and process quality.
- **Cost of DataOps:** The initial cost of introducing new tools and technology, employee training and moving from the old system can be substantial, and it is easy to get discouraged at the beginning when there are no immediate benefits to realize. Nevertheless, in the long run, DataOps will pay off by reducing cycle time and standardizing the analytics product and process quality.
- **Transition from expertise-based team to cross-functional teams:** DataOps succeeds with cross-functional team collaboration and communication. Creating integrated data analytics teams will bring employees together from different departments and with varied expertise to solve a specific problem. Nevertheless, the challenge of structural change is enormous. One should include all related and required members in the team with proper authorities and responsibilities. There should always be a trust-based environment among team members and between analytics teams, management, and customers.
- **Managing multiple environments:** DataOps, with multiple environments, provides freedom of innovation and improvement but also creates the necessity of proper management of those environments. Without an appropriate system management plan, it can quickly go out of hand and create cost and performance exhaustion instead of

benefits.

- **Sharing knowledge:** Tribal knowledge creates a big problem, and DataOps can make it even worst: new tools and technologies, change in processes and execution of data analytics projects in different platforms than before. Without useful documentation or creation of knowledge base, teamwork can be a challenging task to accomplish.
- **Tools and technology diversity:** In DataOps, several tools and technologies are used to accomplish the required tasks. This brings the challenges of maintaining and matching the performances of tools individually and collectively. One tool should not impact and restrict the performance of others. So careful selection of tools is always emphasized.
- **Security and quality:** With multiple environments and team players in project, security and quality is crucial to maintain. Data privacy, system security, data codes and insights quality, data workers and stakeholder's authority should be well described and implemented in DataOps from the beginning. Otherwise, it will be hard to enforce when things go out of hand.

B. DataOps in the Data Lifecycle

DataOps minimizes the analytics cycle time by covering the entire stages of data analysis. The data lifecycle relies on people and tools [10], and DataOps collaborates with people and tools to better manage the data lifecycle. Data analytics pipeline alters data through a series of tasks. Whether it is the ETL (Extraxt, Transform, Load) / ELT (Extract, Load, Transform) pipeline or analysis pipeline, the output will always be different from the input. In data pipelines, one of the challenging tasks is to track data. Data goes through a series of transformations while going from one stage to another. In DataOps, data lifecycle management is unavoidable because of the need to monitor the quality of processes and products. Data governance and data lineage are part of DataOps to assure process and product quality. Quality assurance and the DataOps principle of reproducible and reuse are highly dependent on managing and maintaining data lifecycle change events. Data governance and data lineage is not an easy task to address; it starts with managerial level planning and flourishes with the tools and approach we use to implement our plans.

DataOps applies to the entire data lifecycle [45], from data collection to publishing the result, all data preparation and analysis stages can implement DataOps methodology. It provides the significant advantage of easy management of data lifecycle by applying the intrinsic approach to handle data throughout the analytics cycle. Data pipeline transports data from one stage of the lifecycle to another. DataOps restructures data pipelines and take them out of the black box making them measurable, maintainable through collaboration, communication, integration, and automation. As a result of the restructuring , data lifecycle management becomes more straightforward. DataOps support all stages in the data lifecycle; with the right people and technology in use, data will flow from one stage to another seemingly. With DataOps, a

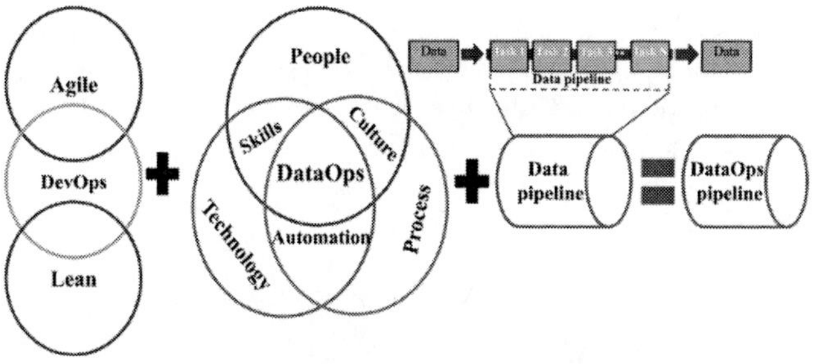

Figure 3. Data Pipeline to DataOps.

published result from the analysis can be trackback to a raw data source, decomposing each transformation task performed over them. DataOps acknowledges the interconnected nature of data engineering, data integration, data quality, and data security [32] and combines all these aspects of data analytics to form an interspace of data movement between data lifecycle stages.

Figure 3 illustrates the DataOps pipeline advancement from data pipeline by adding Agile, DevOps and Lean functionalities with inclusion of people, process, and technology for a designated task. In DataOps, there is no necessity of creating separate pipelines for different stages. Preferably, DataOps utilizes the technical modularity of orchestration, workflow management, and automation tools to provide flexible and customized transformation process when needed.

In the following Section C, the coverage of different stages of data lifecycle in data analytics projects is compared. The comparison is done whether tools used in DataOps can be used in data lifecycle stages: Creation/ Collection, Process, Analyze, Storage, and Publish. These stages of lifecycle are identified by doing extensive literature review of CRUD lifecycle [46], IBM lifecycle [38], USGS lifecycle [39] and DataOne lifecycle [40].

C. Evaluation of DataOps Tools and Technologies

This section provides an overview on the most popular DataOps tools as baseline for further research and to support practitioners in the selection of proper tools for DataOps tasks. Since there are numerous tools with the same features and functionality, it is hard to cover every tool in detail. We picked some of the popular tools and compared them categorically based on the evaluation criteria. Selecting tools and technology in DataOps is a rigorous process and needs detailed research and planning before selecting a particular tool for the designated task [22]. Tools presented in Tables 2-8 are based on their mass user base, relevant features to support the given functionality and popularity of the product in data analytics project execution. Tools presented in the feature-based comparison table are picked after extensive online research by listing and comparing other tools from the same functional categories.

Evaluation Criteria: The criteria for the DataOps tool evaluation and comparison are detailed in Table I and their selection is based on installation easiness, operation simplicity, integration support to other technologies, and general applicability of the tools. Criteria present a general overview of tools and technologies to non-technical data workers and decision-makers to give a general idea and a starting point to research tools before using them in the project.

TABLE I. EVALUATION CRITERIA

Criteria	Measures
Complexity	Measures how complex is the installation and implementation process of the presented tool. Evaluation is based on the code complexity and dependencies that need to be setup **-HIGH**: Need a high level of coding and configuration to install the product. **-MEDIUM**: Moderate level of coding and configuration required. **-LOW**: Easy to install with no line of code or a few lines of code.
Usability	Measures how simple the tool is to use after the installation, especially for nontechnical data workers. **-HIGH**: Easy to use with little or no technical, coding, or system-related knowledge. **-MEDIUM**: Moderate knowledge of the system, code architecture, or technical detail is required. **-LOW**: High level of technical expertise and/or coding knowledge is required.
Compatibility	Measures the integration capacity of the tool with different operation environments, other tools, databases, data types and/or programming languages. **-HIGH**: Supports a wide range of tools, operation environment, database, data types, and programming languages. **-MEDIUM**: Have some level of support either explicit (in the number of specific tools, languages, databases, data types and/or programming languages declared officially) or have implicit partial support provided through unofficial projects. **-LOW**: Little or no support available.
Application	Provides the information related to the tools' applicability to arrays of projects, data analysis use cases, and industries. **-GENERIC**: Can be used in a variety of projects based on the nature of tools. **-SPECIFIC**: Industry/project-specific usage.
Lifecycle	Lists in which data lifecycle stage the tool can mostly be used.
License	Describes whether the tool is commercial, opensource, freemium, free + commercial and other pricing forms.

We use the following abbreviations in the comparison tables.

Abbreviations for data lifecycle stages: C - Creation/collection; P - Process; A - Analyze; S - Storage; Pu - Publish.

Abbreviations for pricing modules: O - Open-source; Co - Commercial; F - Free; N - Non-profit; Fm - Freemium; U - User based pricing.

1) Categorization of tools and technologies: Tools used in DataOps are categorized in the following functional categories and presented categorically from Table 2 to Table 8 (all references to the tools presented in comparison Tables can be found in the external Dropbox hosted file [47]). The categorization is based on the tools' purpose in the data pipeline. Some tools are uncategorized and kept under "Other tools and technologies" because they do not fall under the first seven categories listed below.

Workflow orchestration tools: Workflow orchestration or pipeline orchestration defines the logical flow of tasks from start to end in the data pipeline. In DataOps, orchestration tools create a logical flow of data analytics task and assemble other tools and technologies, infrastructures, and people to accomplish the job. Several orchestration tools are available with similar design principles targeted to various users and use cases. Choosing them for pipeline workflow management is a thorough job. Orchestration tools include resource provisioning, data movement, data provenance, workflow scheduling, fault tolerance, data storage, and platform integration in the data pipeline [48]. However, all orchestration tools do not have all features inbuilt to support every task in a data pipeline. So, choosing the right orchestration tool is essential to manage tasks in the data pipeline. There has been a practice of developing custom-built workflow orchestration tools for a specific project [49]–[51]. In Table II, comparison of some of the existing popular pipeline orchestration tools is presented by using the comparison criteria presented in Table I.

Testing and monitoring tools: Continuous testing and monitoring are the principal mission of DataOps. With these, performance, quality of input and result, code, and toolchain performance throughout of data pipeline is ensured. Testing and monitoring applies in entire stage of the data lifecycle. In DataOps, testing and monitoring start from the top management by setting the criteria of project quality, and test cases are developed according to the proposed criteria. After the development of test cases and monitoring criteria, suitable existing tools or custom-built test and monitoring framework can be integrated into the data pipeline. Some of the testing and monitoring tools are presented in Table III.

Deployment automation tools: DataOps continuously moves code and configurations from the development environment to the production environment after test cases are satisfied. The deployment automation applied through the process of continuous integration and continuous deployment. Representative tools widely used in deployment automation are presented in Table IV.

Data governance tools: Testing and monitoring are keeping a record of the principles of data governance. Where testing and monitoring are more focused on tracking the whole DataOps pipeline performance measures, data governance is related to data change management and data lineage tracking. Some Tools used in data governance are presented in Table V.

Code, artifact, and data versioning tools: Code, artifacts, and data versioning tools (some presented in Table VI) provide a platform to store different versions of codes, data sets, docker images, and other related documents like logs, user manuals, system manuals, and configurations. With the use of the right tool, accessing and reusing different versions of stored artifacts becomes easier.

Analytics and visualization tools: The importance of visual presentation is always high while demonstrating results. Customers and non-data workers always relish on fined tuned

TABLE II. WORKFLOW ORCHESTRATION TOOLS

Tools	Lifecycles	Complexity	Usability	Compatibility	Applications	License
Airflow	C, P, A	HIGH	MEDIUM	HIGH	GENERIC	O
Apache Oozie	C, P, A	HIGH	MEDIUM	LOW	GENERIC	O
Reflow	P, A	HIGH	LOW	LOW	SPECIFIC	O
Data Kitchen	P, A	LOW	HIGH	HIGH	GENERIC	Co
BMC Control-M	P, A	MEDIUM	MEDIUM	HIGH	GENERIC	Co
Argo Workflows	P, A	HIGH	LOW	LOW	GENERIC	O
Apache NIFI	C, P, A	MEDIUM	MEDIUM	MEDIUM	SPECIFIC	O

TABLE III. TESTING AND MONITORING TOOLS

Tools	Lifecycles	Complexity	Usability	Compatibility	Applications	License
iCEDQ	C, P, A	LOW	HIGH	HIGH	GENERIC	Co
Data Band	P	HIGH	LOW	MEDIUM	GENERIC	O, Co
RightData	S, A, P	MEDIUM	MEDIUM	HIGH	GENERIC	Co
Naveego	C, P, S	HIGH	HIGH	LOW	SPECIFIC	Co
DataKitchen	C, P, S	HIGH	MEDIUM	HIGH	GENERIC	Co
Enterprise Data Foundation	S, A, P	HIGH	LOW	LOW	SPECIFIC	F, N

TABLE IV. DEPLOYMENT AUTOMATION TOOLS

Tools	Lifecycles	Complexity	Usability	Compatibility	Applications	License
Jenkins	C, P, A, S, Pu	MEDIUM	HIGH	HIGH	GENERIC	O
DataKitchen	C, P, A, S, Pu	HIGH	MEDIUM	HIGH	GENERIC	Co
Circle CI	C, P, A, S, Pu	MEDIUM	MEDIUM	MEDIUM	GENERIC	F, Co
GitLab	C, P, A, S, Pu	MEDIUM	MEDIUM	HIGH	GENERIC	O, Co
Travis CI	C, P, A, S, Pu	MEDIUM	HIGH	HIGH	GENERIC	F, Co
Atlassian Bamboo	C, P, A, S, Pu	LOW	HIGH	HIGH	GENERIC	Co

TABLE V. DATA GOVERNANCE TOOLS

Tools	Lifecycles	Complexity	Usability	Compatibility	Applications	License
Apache Atlas	C, P, A, S, Pu	HIGH	MEDIUM	MEDIUM	GENERIC	O
Talend	C, P, A, S, Pu	MEDIUM	MEDIUM	MEDIUM	SPECIFIC	O, Co
Collibra	C, P, A, S, Pu	LOW	LOW	LOW	SPECIFIC	Co
IBM	C, P, A, S, Pu	MEDIUM	HIGH	MEDIUM	GENERIC	Co
OvalEdge	C, P, A, S, Pu	LOW	HIGH	HIGH	GENERIC	Co

TABLE VI. CODE, ARTIFACT AND DATA VERSIONING TOOLS

Tools	Lifecycles	Complexity	Usability	Compatibility	Applications	License
GitLab	C, P, A, S, Pu	MEDIUM	HIGH	MEDIUM	GENERIC	F, Co
Github	C, P, A, S, Pu	MEDIUM	HIGH	MEDIUM	GENERIC	F, Co
DVC	C, P, A, S, Pu	MEDIUM	HIGH	MEDIUM	GENERIC	O
DockerHub	C, P, A, S, Pu	MEDIUM	HIGH	MEDIUM	GENERIC	F, Co

TABLE VII. ANALYTICS AND VISUALIZATION TOOLS

Tools	Lifecycles	Complexity	Usability	Compatibility	Applications	License
Tableau	A	LOW	MEDIUM	HIGH	GENERIC	Co
Power BI	A	LOW	MEDIUM	MEDIUM	GENERIC	Co
QlikView	A	LOW	MEDIUM	LOW	GENERIC	Co

TABLE VIII. COLLABORATION AND COMMUNICATION TOOLS

Tools	Lifecycles	Complexity	Usability	Compatibility	Applications	License
Slack	C, P, A, S, Pu	LOW	HIGH	HIGH	GENERIC	Fm, U
Jira	C, P, A, S, Pu	LOW	HIGH	HIGH	GENERIC	Fm, U
Trello	C, P, A, S, Pu	LOW	HIGH	HIGH	GENERIC	Fm, U

quality results. Data visualization and analytics tools play a big part in understandably presenting results with assured quality. With the support of analytics and visualization tools presented in Table VII, data workers can better communicate results.

Collaboration and communication tools: To better coordinate among team members, communication and collaboration tools (some presented in Table VIII) are necessary. Tools can be simple, from email applications to advance communication tools that have fancy features to automate and record most of the routine tasks.

Other tools and technologies: Other tools and technology include containers technology, resource managers, data storage services, IDEs and source code editors, cloud servers and Big data processing and analytics frameworks. All tools and technologies are integrated among or with above presented tools where as Big data and analysis framework can also be used independently. In [47], popular tools and services under the other tool and technologies section are listed by categorically dividing them to present general use of such tools and technologies in DataOps.

IV. Conclusion

Since the rise of the term DataOps, significant contribution to its definition and practical applications can be observed. DataOps enthusiasts collaborate to create a common principle for uniformly applying the methodology in the heterogeneous data operation environments. Despite all these efforts, still certain ambiguities remain in the applicability of DataOps due to the diverse nature of the data analysis process. Data analysis itself is a broad field, where numerous tools, approaches, and technologies can lead to the same result. However, DataOps advocates collaboration, quality control, and fast delivery of analysis tasks by extending proven DevOps methodology from SDLC as well as Agile and Lean Manufacturing's SPC. With these three reference methodologies and the advantage of existing tools and technologies, DataOps is continuously evolving to an efficient and reliable methodology for data management.

When implementing DataOps principles, it is key to select the right tool for a given use case. DataOps tools and technologies can be used in several stages of the data lifecycle based on their functionalities. Some tools are particularly useful for certain stages, e.g., analysis and visualization tools. Others, like communication and collaboration tools, are independent of the data lifecycle. Deployment automation tools, data governance tools, code, artifact, and data versioning tools, containers, resource manager, IDE and source codes editors, and cloud servers are used across all stages of the data lifecycle. However, workflow orchestration and testing and monitoring tool support over data lifecycle stage depends on their features. Some tools can provide support to the entire pipeline process, whereas others are specifically tailored to certain tasks. Furthermore, big data processing and analysis frameworks provide a complete solution even though the focus is more on data processing and analysis.

In summary, there are numerous tools available on the market with similar features and functionalities. This paper compares their features with respect to the data analysis lifecycle and therefore supports a practitioner in selecting the proper tool for a given use case. Using suitable tools allows to cover all stages of the data lifecycle with the DataOps methodolgy. Eventually, every stage of the data lifecycle (i.e., from data collection, processing and analyzing, to publishing) can be covered by one or a combination of tools and technologies. It is up the the DataOps engineer and to the respective use case which combination of tools are most suitable for which tasks.

This paper focuses on the exploration of existing concepts in DataOps and aims at sheding light to the large variety of tools and technologies. Thus, it acts as starting point for further research on the successful implementation of the DataOps methodology. For future work, we plan to experiment with DataOps by implementing it in different data analysis projects and to validate (1) on the one hand the efficacy of the methodology itself, and (2) on the other hand the performance of different tools for different use cases. The second step can be achieved by implementing tools for the same functionality and to test their performance on a specific industry use case. We also claim that a compatibility rating (based on combined performance when used together in data analytics tasks) of one tool from one functional group to other functional groups would help DataOps practitioners make informed decisions.

Acknowledgement

The research in this paper has been funded by BMK, BMDW, and the Province of Upper Austria in the frame of the COMET Programme managed by FFG and is further supported by the EC H2020 project *"DataCloud: Enabling the Big Data Pipeline Lifecycle on the Computing Continuum"* (Grant nr. 101016835).

References

[1] A. Gandomi and M. Haider, "Beyond the hype: Big data concepts, methods, and analytics," *International Journal of Information Management*, vol. 35, no. 2, pp. 137–144, 2015.

[2] H. Baars and J. Ereth, "From data warehouses to analytical atoms - The internet of things as a centrifugal force in business intelligence and analytics," in *24th ECIS 2016*. Association for Information Systems, 2016.

[3] L. Fischer *et al.*, "AI System Engineering—Key Challenges and Lessons Learned," *Machine Learning and Knowledge Extraction*, vol. 3, pp. 56–83, 2021.

[4] M. Artac, T. Borovssak, E. Di Nitto, M. Guerriero, and D. A. Tamburri, "DevOps: Introducing infrastructure-as-code," in *Proceedings - 2017 IEEE/ACM 39th ICSE-C 2017*. IEEE, jun 2017, pp. 497–498.

[5] L. E. Lwakatare *et al.*, "DevOps in practice: A multiple case study of five companies," *Information and Software Technology*, vol. 114, pp. 217–230, oct 2019.

[6] Z. Zhang, "DevOps for Data Science System," Master's thesis, KTH, 2020.

[7] K. Kontostathis. (2017) Collecting Data, The DevOps Way. [Retrieved: 2021-07-30]. [Online]. Available: https://insights.sei.cmu.edu/devops/2017/11/collecting-data-the-devops-way.html

[8] S. Ward-Riggs, "The Difference Between DevOps and DataOps – Altis Consulting," [Retrieved: 2021-08-22]. [Online]. Available: https://altis.com.au/the-difference-between-devops-and-dataops/

[9] The DataOps Manifesto, "The DataOps Manifesto ," [Retrieved: 2021-08-19]. [Online]. Available: https://www.dataopsmanifesto.org/

[10] C. Bergh, G. Benghiat, and S. Eran, *The DataOps Cookbook*, 2nd ed., 2019.

[11] J. Ereth, "DataOps – Towards a Definition," in *LWDA*, 2018, pp. 104–112.

[12] A. Raj, D. I. Mattos, J. Bosch, H. H. Olsson, and A. Dakkak, "From Ad-Hoc data analytics to DataOps," in *Proceedings - 2020 IEEE/ICSSP*, 2020, pp. 165–174.

[13] "Dataops — ibm," [Retrieved: 2021-08-19]. [Online]. Available: https://www.ibm.com/analytics/dataops

[14] "Datakitchen — the complete enterprise dataops platform," [Retrieved: 2021-08-19]. [Online]. Available: https://datakitchen.io/

[15] "Dataops platform — etl testing and monitoring — icedq," [Retrieved: 2021-08-19]. [Online]. Available: https://icedq.com/

[16] "Eckerson group - data analytics consulting research," [Retrieved: 2021-08-19]. [Online]. Available: https://www.eckerson.com/

[17] DataKitchen, "DataOps in Seven Steps," 2017, [Retrieved: 2021-08-23]. [Online]. Available: https://medium.com/data-ops/dataops-in-7-steps-f72ff2b37812

[18] H. Crocket, "Fundamental Review of the Trading Book: Data Management Implications," iCEDQ, Tech. Rep., 2018.

[19] S. Gawande, "DataOps Implementation Guide," iCEDQ, Tech. Rep., 2019.

[20] J. Ereth and W. Eckerson, "DataOps: Industrializing Data and Analytics Strategies for Streamlining the Delivery of Insights," Eckerson Group, Tech. Rep., 2018.

[21] W. Eckerson, "Best Practices in DataOps: How to Create Robust, Automated Data Pipelines," Eckerson Group, Tech. Rep. June, 2019.

[22] W. W. Eckerson, "The Ultimate Guide to DataOps: Product Evaluation and Selection Criteria," Eckerson Group, Tech. Rep., 2019.

[23] "Google," [Retrieved: 2021-04-03]. [Online]. Available: https://www.google.com/

[24] "Google Scholar," [Retrieved: 2021-04-03]. [Online]. Available: https://scholar.google.com/

[25] "ResearchGate," [Retrieved: 2021-04-03]. [Online]. Available: https://www.researchgate.net/

[26] "IEEE," [Retrieved: 2021-04-03]. [Online]. Available: https://ieeexplore.ieee.org/Xplore/home.jsp

[27] "KTH Library," [Retrieved: 2021-04-03]. [Online]. Available: https://www.kth.se/en/biblioteket

[28] "KTH-Diva," [Retrieved: 2021-04-03]. [Online]. Available: https://kth.diva-portal.org

[29] "Semantic Scholar," [Retrieved: 2021-04-03]. [Online]. Available: https://www.semanticscholar.org/

[30] M. Stonebraker, N. Bates-Haus, L. Cleary, and L. Simmons, *Getting Data Operations Right*, 1st ed., R. Roumeliotis and J. Bleie, Eds. O'Reilly Media, Inc., 2018.

[31] L. Lenny, "3 reasons why DataOps is essential for big data success — IBM Big Data and Analytics Hub," jun 2014, [Retrieved: 2021-08-12]. [Online]. Available: https://www.ibmbigdatahub.com/blog/3-reasons-why-dataops-essential-big-data-success

[32] A. Palmer, "From DevOps to DataOps - DataOps Tools Transformation — Tamr," may 2015, [Retrieved: 2021-08-24]. [Online]. Available: https://www.tamr.com/blog/from-devops-to-dataops-by-andy-palmer/

[33] E. Jarah, "What is DataOps? — Platform for the Machine Learning Age — Nexla," [Retrieved: 2021-08-01]. [Online]. Available: https://www.nexla.com/define-dataops/

[34] "DataOps and the DataOps Manifesto — by ODSC - Open Data Science — Medium," 2019, [Retrieved: 2021-07-30]. [Online]. Available: https://medium.com/@ODSC/dataops-and-the-dataops-manifesto-fc6169c02398

[35] DataKitchen, "DataOps is NOT just DevOps for data," 2018, [Retrieved: 2021-08-25]. [Online]. Available: https://medium.com/data-ops/dataops-is-not-just-devops-for-data-6e03083157b7

[36] G. Anadiotis, "DataOps: Changing the world one organization at a time — ZDNet," 2017, [Retrieved: 2021-08-18]. [Online]. Available: https://www.zdnet.com/article/dataops-changing-the-world-one-organization-at-a-time/

[37] A. Wahaballa, O. Wahballa, M. Abdellatief, H. Xiong, and Z. Qin, "Toward unified DevOps model," in *Proceedings of the IEEE ICSESS*. IEEE Computer Society, nov 2015, pp. 211–214.

[38] IBM, "Wrangling big data: Fundamentals of data lifecycle management," *IBM Managing data lifecycle*, 2013.

[39] J. L. Faundeen *et al.*, "The United States Geological Survey Science Data Lifecycle Model: U.S. Geological Survey Open-File Report 2013–1265," Tech. Rep., 2013.

[40] S. Allard, "DataONE: Facilitating eScience through Collaboration," *Journal of eScience Librarianship*, vol. 1, no. 1, pp. 4–17, 2012.

[41] J. Densmore, *Data Pipelines Pocket Reference*, 1st ed., 2020.

[42] B. Plale and I. Kouper, "The Centrality of Data: Data Lifecycle and Data Pipelines," in *Data Analytics for Intelligent Transportation Systems*. Elsevier Inc., apr 2017, pp. 91–111.

[43] S. Gibson, "Exploring DataOps in the Brave New World of Agile and Cloud Delivery," Tech. Rep., 2020.

[44] A. Palmer, M. Stonebraker, N. Bates-Haus, L. Cleary, and M. Marinelli, *Getting DataOps Right*, 1st ed. O'Reilly Media, Inc., 2019.

[45] Margaret Rouse, "What is DataOps (data operations)? - Definition from WhatIs.com," 2019, [Retrieved: 2021-08-25]. [Online]. Available: https://searchdatamanagement.techtarget.com/definition/DataOps

[46] X. Yu and Q. Wen, "A view about cloud data security from data life cycle," in *2010 International Conference on Computational Intelligence and Software Engineering, CiSE 2010*, 2010.

[47] M. Kiran, E. Lisa, H. Johannes, and M. Matskin, "Comparison of dataops tools and technologies," [Retrieved: 2021-08-21]. [Online]. Available: https://www.dropbox.com/s/9nqo3r72ce7nix5/DataOps_tools_ComparisonKiran.pdf

[48] M. Barika, S. Garg, A. Y. Zomaya, L. Wang, A. V. Moorsel, R. Ranjan, S. Garg, L. Wang, and A. Van Moorsel, "Orchestrating big data analysis workflows in the cloud: Research challenges, survey, and future directions," *ACM Computing Surveys*, vol. 52, no. 5, 2019.

[49] Y. D. Dessalk, "Big Data Workflows: DSL-based Specification and Software Containers for Scalable Executions," Master's thesis, KTH, 2020.

[50] H. Chen, J. Wen, W. Pedrycz, and G. Wu, "Big Data Processing Workflows Oriented Real-Time Scheduling Algorithm using Task-Duplication in Geo-Distributed Clouds," *IEEE Transactions on Big Data*, vol. 6, no. 1, pp. 131–144, oct 2018.

[51] H. Hu, Y. Wen, T. S. Chua, and X. Li, "Toward scalable systems for big data analytics: A technology tutorial," *IEEE Access*, vol. 2, pp. 652–687, 2014.

Feature Engineering vs Feature Selection vs Hyperparameter Optimization in the Spotify Song Popularity Dataset

Alan Cueva Mora
School of Computer Science
Technological University Dublin
Dublin, Ireland
e-mail: d20125565@mytudublin.ie

Brendan Tierney
School of Computer Science
Technological University Dublin
Dublin, Ireland
e-mail: brendan.tierney@tudublin.ie

***Abstract*—Research in Featuring Engineering has been part of the data pre-processing phase of machine learning projects for many years, but we sometimes forget its importance. It can be challenging for new people working with machine learning to understand its importance along with various approaches to find an optimized model. This work uses the Spotify Song Popularity dataset to compare and evaluate Feature Engineering, Feature Selection and Hyperparameter Optimization. The result of this work will demonstrate that Feature Engineering has a greater effect on model efficiency when compared to the alternative approaches.**

Keywords-feature engineering; language identification; feature selection; hyperparameter optimization; cross-validation.

I. INTRODUCTION

Feature selection and hyperparameter optimization are two sophisticated machine learning techniques with a strong research background. For an early-stage data scientist, it is very easy to think that they are the best alternatives for a machine learning task.

Feature engineering is an important, but labour-intensive take on machine learning [1]. Most machine learning performance is heavily dependent on the representation of the feature vector. As a result, much of the actual effort in deploying machine learning algorithms goes into the design of pre-processing pipelines, data transformations, domain and metadata knowledge [1].

Kaggle competitions and the Knowledge Discovery and DataMining (KDD) Cup have seen feature engineering play a very important part in several winning submissions [2]. Additionally, the Kaggle Algorithmic Trading Challenge was won with an ensemble of models and feature engineering. The features engineered for these competitions were created manually by the data scientist, utilizing their domain knowledge.

This paper is structured as follows. Section 2 shows a brief exploration of related work. Sections 3, 4 and 5 step through using feature engineering, feature selection and hyperparameter optimization of a regression machine learning task over the Spotify Song Popularity dataset [3]. The influence of each step over the machine learning task is measured using a Cross-Validation (CV) [4] and the Root Mean Square Error (RMSE) loss function. Finally, Section 6 presents the conclusions and future work.

II. RELATED RESEARCH

There are some common research topics in machine learning literature. One of them is about comparing different machine learning methods to solve specific tasks [5] [6] and identify the best scenario for a method.

Another common machine learning research topic is to compare similar techniques, as is the case of feature selection and feature extraction [7]. The objective of both methods is to reduce the feature space to improve data analysis. Feature selection performs the reduction by selecting a subset of features without transforming them, while feature extraction reduces dimensionality by computing a transformation of the original features to create other features that should be more significant.

In featuring engineering research, it is common to find comparisons between combinations of different engineered features and methods to identify which methods generally benefit from the same set of engineered features [8].

Considering that in every machine learning task the objective is to reduce the error, there is no reason not to compare completely different techniques, such as those proposed in this work.

III. FEATURE ENGINEERING

Feature engineering involves calculating new features, based on the values of the other features, and it is primarily a manual, time consuming task [8].

The Spotify Song Popularity dataset [3] consists of 129 thousand rows and 17 independent variables of which three are strings and cannot be used in the machine learning task. For this type of data, feature engineering focuses on generating numerical variables from these.

Every new variable was evaluated with a correlation (spearman) test to validate its relationship with the target and its criterion could be very weak (0.0-0.19), weak (0.2-0.39), moderate (0.4-0.59), strong (0.6-0.79), and very strong (0.8-1.0). Some variables could be generated in different ways, or their values were similar to those of another variable. In these cases, the correlation test was used to compare all variants and the best one was used. All statistics generated for this step were statistically significant (p-value < 0.05).

A. Numerical Release Date

This variable is the numerical representation of the 'release_date' variable (YYYY-MM-DD or YYYY if the data is incomplete). The integer part is the year and the float part is the elapsed percentage of the year:

$$year\_rd = year(release\_date) + (day\_of\_year(release\_date)/365)$$

This new variable is similar to the variable 'year'; both variables are moderately correlated with the target variable, but 'year' (r=0.5386) is a better option than 'year_rd' (r=0.5391). This is why this variable was discarded.

B. Number of Artists

This variable was created from the 'artists' variable which is a string formatted as a Python list. Each value was transformed to a list object, and its length is the value for this new variable. Its test shows a very weak negative correlation (r=-0.1968). This fits in with an observed pattern where songs with many artists tend to be unpopular

C. Artists' Mean Popularity Value

This variable was calculated from the 'artists' and 'popularity' variables. First, a dictionary of artist's popularity was created. Each song's popularity is used to calculate the artists' mean popularity value.

There is a risk here. When evaluating a new song and one artist is not present in the dictionary, his/her popularity is zero. Considering the influence of this variable on the final result, an imputation should be made to avoid overfitting. The imputation used is the mean value of the artist's popularity. Its test shows a strong correlation (r=0.911).

D. Name Length

The length of the 'name' of the song produces a weak negative correlation (r=-0.2941). This fits with the observed pattern where songs with long names tend to be unpopular.

E. Name Language

Worldwide, English songs are more popular than other languages and recently thanks to Reggaeton, Spanish songs are popular too, but this information is not available in the dataset. One easy way to get the language is to detect the language in the title (name) of the song.

There are some libraries available in Python to detect language, some of them based on neural networks. For this new variable, five libraries were taken into consideration.

- LangDetect [9] is a direct port of Google's language-detection library from Java to Python.
- TextBlob [10] uses Google Translate API for language detection. It requires internet connection.
- FastText [11] is a text classifier that works with pretrained models.
- LangId [12] works with transductive learning and transfer learning techniques.
- CLD3 [13] uses a trained neural network model.

Five language detection tasks were performed using each library. LangDetect identified 46 languages, TextBlob 88, FastText 120, LangId 79 and CLD3 97, so there were five new high cardinality variables.

Some encoders were taken into consideration to evaluate the best way to represent these new variables.

- Label Encoder encodes a categorical variable with value between 0 and n_categories-1.
- Target Encoder [14] replaces features with a blend of the expected value of the target given a particular categorical value and the expected value of the target over all the training data.
- Leave One Out Encoder [14] is similar to target encoder, but excludes the current row's target when calculating the mean target for a level to reduce the effect of outliers.
- Min Hash Function [15] is inspired by the document indexation literature, and in particular the idea of Locality-Sensitive Hashing (LSH).

A correlation test was performed in every combination of library-encoder to identify the best one (see Figure 1). The results show that Text Blob with Target Encoder is the best option.

Between the libraries for language detection, TextBlob gives the best results. When performing a manual inspection of the results, it was evident other libraries confused Spanish and Italian, and this perception was supported by its statistics where TextBlob was the best, regardless of the encoder.

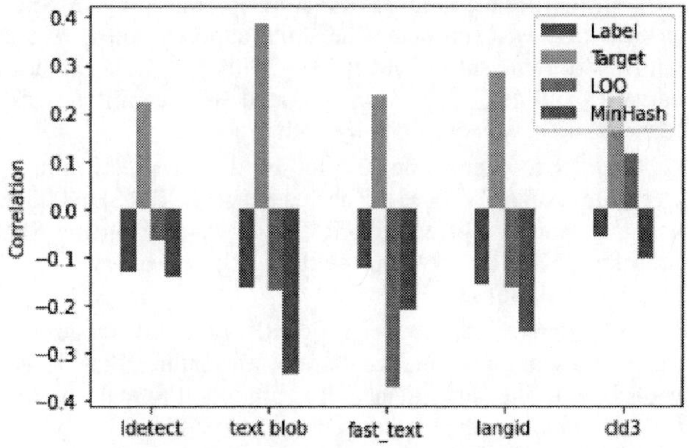

Figure 1. Libraries and Encoders Correlation Comparison

Finally, a Cross-Validation [4] (k=5) shows the result of the feature engineering process was a RMSE reduction from 17.1624, using only the original non-string features, to 8.9846 including the new variables.

IV. FEATURE SELECTION

In machine learning, feature selection entails selecting a subset of the available features in a dataset to use for model development. Among its advantages are generating better models and reducing computations cost [16]. The techniques considered in this section are Least Absolute Shrinkage and Selection Operator (LASSO) and Sequential Forward Selection (SFS).

First, an SFS task was executed using all features to detect any negative performance contribution to the model. Figure 2 shows there are no clear negative contributions to the model, but approximately 5 features seem to have a neutral contribution to the performance.

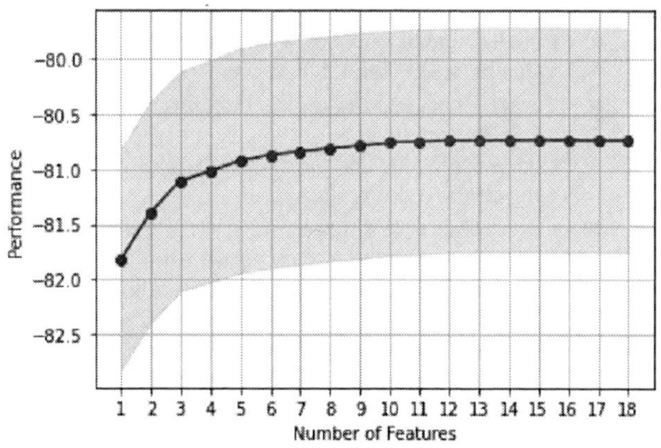

Figure 2. Sequential Forward Selection using all features

In order to get the number of features to consider based on evidence, a LASSO task was run using different regularization parameter values. The recommended values are 0.1, 0.01 and 0.001 and the one that includes more variables (regularization=0.01) reduces the number of features from 18 to 14, excluding 'danceability', 'energy', 'liveness' and 'speechiness'.

Considering the number of features proposed by LASSO, an SFS task was run using the same number, and it results with a different subset of features. The SFS task excludes variables 'mode', 'key', 'explicit' and 'danceability'. Only 'danceability' was excluded by both processes.

In order to choose the best subset, three regression tasks were run using CV (k=5). The results were RMSE=8.9846 using all non-string features, RMSE=8.9845 using the SFS subset and RMSE=8.9984 using the LASSO subset with SFS being the best subset.

The improvement is insignificant, so the advantage is to reduce the computational cost and omit features that do not contribute to the performance. It is important to mention that no new features were excluded by any methods.

V. Hyperparameter Optimization

Hyperparameter optimization consists of testing a set of hyperparameters of a model and identifying the optimal values for them. In this section, five methods were taken into consideration. They can be divided in two groups: linear (1 and 2) and tree methods (3, 4 and 5).

1) Linear Regression (LR): creates a linear relationship between features and target.
2) Ridge Regression (RR): is a variant of LR where the loss function is the linear least squares.
3) Decision Tree Regressor (DTR): is the regression version of the decision tree method.
4) Extra Tree Regressor (ETR): is similar to DTR, but this method changes the way of splitting the nodes.
5) Random Forest Regressor (RFR): is an ensemble of a multitude of decision trees. It uses averaging to improve accuracy and control overfitting.

The hyperparameter optimization task was performed using a CV grid search (K=3). Unfortunately, there are no hyperparameters for the Linear Regression, for the Ridge Regression there is one, the regularization strength, but this only improves the RMSE by 0.000004, so this step focused on the tree methods.

In the tree methods, one parameter directly influences the results. This parameter is the max depth parameter, which specifies how many levels of nodes the tree could have. When this parameter is set to none, the tree will expand the nodes until all leaves are pure or until all leaves contain less than two samples.

Limiting the tree was clearly a good option, not only because the train for the entire tree takes too much time, but the results are better. After an exhaustive evaluation, the best values of max depth were 11 for DTR and 15 for ETR and RFR. Another parameter was the criterion which measures the quality of a split where the only options that worked were mean square error and mean squared error with Friedman's improvement score for potential splits, but the results prove that this parameter does not affect the metrics.

In the specific case of DTR and ETR, there was an option to add Bagging Regression (BR). The BR is an optimization to improve the stability and accuracy of the method. The Bagging splits the data and uses it in different decision trees and ensembles the result. In both cases the BR was the best option.

In order to compare the RMSE metrics with the previous section of this work, five CV tasks (K=5) were run using the best parameters for each method. Figure 3 shows that the RFR model gets the best metrics.

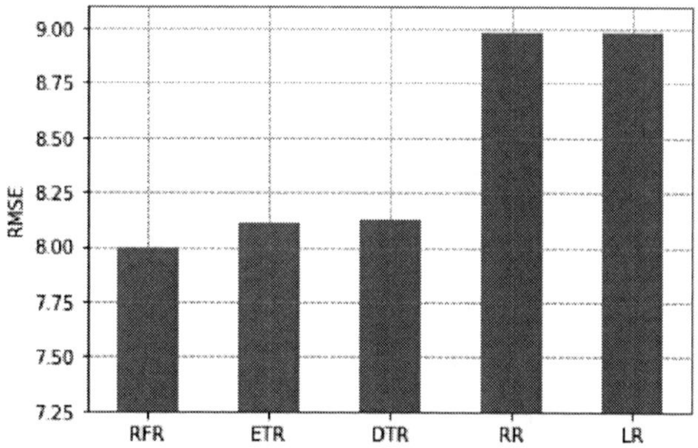

Figure 3. Model Comparison

The result of the hyperparameter optimization and the model comparison was a RMSE reduction from 8.98 to 7.99. Although the grid search task is automatic, it takes a lot of execution time, which requires monitoring because it can easily crash when computer resources are depleted.

VI. CONCLUSIONS AND FUTURE WORK

The analysis performed over the Spotify Song Popularity dataset involves feature engineering, feature selection, hyperparameter optimization and model selection using CV to validate each step.

Feature engineering was by far the technique that generated the best reduction of the RMSE metric. Figure 4 shows how this technique reduced the error to almost half, while the improvements produced by Feature Selection and Hyperparameter Optimization/Model Selection was not significant.

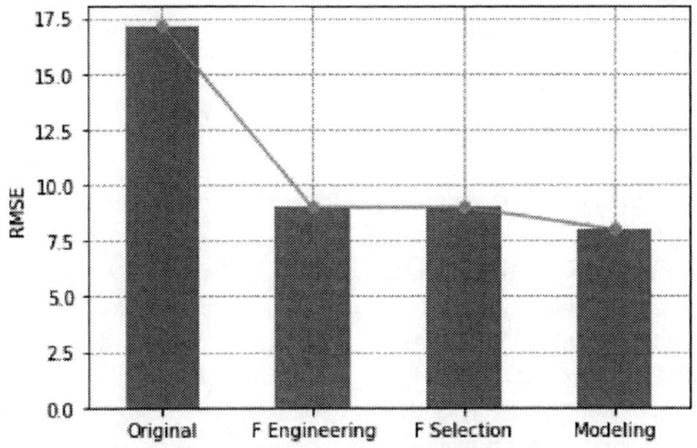

Figure 4. Sections Improvement Comparison

For this dataset, it can be concluded that a well performed feature engineering task has a greater impact on the model performance than more sophisticated machine learning techniques. Even when each step takes approximately the same time and resources, its value is not the same.

This experiment focused on using one particular dataset. Future work will look to expand to include more datasets from a variety of domains. This will be done to evaluate the effect of these tasks and to see if similar outcomes can be achieved.

REFERENCES

[1] Y. Bengio, A. Courville, and P. Vincent, "Representation learning: A review and new perspectives," IEEE Transactions on Pattern Analysis and Machine Intelligence, vol. 35, no. 8, pp. 1798–1828, 2013.

[2] W. Zhou, T. D. Roy, and I. Skrypnyk, "The KDD Cup 2019 Report," SIGKDD Explor. Newsl. 22, Jun 2020, pp. 8-17, doi: 10.1145/3400051.3400056

[3] Kaggle.com, Spotify Popularity Prediction. Retrieved: Aug, 2021. [Online]. Available from: https://www.kaggle.com/c/spotify-popularity-prediction/ 2021.03.22

[4] D. Berrar, "Cross-Validation," Encyclopedia of Bioinformatics and Computational Biology, Vol 1, pp. 542–545, Elsevier, 2019, doi: 10.1016/B978-0-12-809633-8.20349-X

[5] S. Abu-Nimeh, D. Nappa, X. Wang, and S. Nair, "A comparison of machine learning techniques for phishing detection," Proceedings of the anti-phishing working groups 2nd annual eCrime researchers summit on - eCrime '07, 2007, pp 60-69, doi: 10.1145/1299015.1299021.

[6] S. Pouriyeh et al., "A comprehensive investigation and comparison of Machine learning Techniques in the domain of heart disease," 2017 IEEE Symposium on Computers and Communications (ISCC), Jul 2017, pp. 204-207, doi: 10.1109/iscc.2017.8024530.

[7] S. Khalid, T. Khalil, and S. Nasreen, "A survey of feature selection and feature extraction techniques in machine learning," 2014 Science and Information Conference, 2014, pp. 372-378, doi: 10.1109/SAI.2014.6918213.

[8] J. Heaton, "An empirical analysis of feature engineering for predictive modeling", SoutheastCon 2016, 2016, pp. 1-6, doi: 10.1109/SECON.2016.7506650

[9] Pypi.org. langdetect. Retrieved: Aug, 2021. [Online]. Available from: https://pypi.org/project/langdetect/

[10] Readthedocs.io. TextBlob: Simplified Text Processing documentation. Retrieved: Aug, 2021. [Online]. Available from: https://textblob.readthedocs.io/en/dev/ 2020

[11] A. Joulin, E. Grave, P. Bojanowski, and T. Mikolov. Bag of Tricks for Efficient Text Classification Retrieved: Aug, 2021. [Online]. Available from: https://arxiv.org/abs/1607.01759 2016

[12] M. Lui and T. Baldwin. "Cross-domain Feature Selection for Language Identification" Proceedings of the Fifth International Joint Conference on Natural Language Processing, pp. 553-561, Nov. 2011. Available from http://www.aclweb.org/anthology/I11-1062

[13] Pypi.org. pycld3. Retrieved: Aug, 2021. [Online]. Available from: https://pypi.org/project/pycld3/

[14] W. D. McGinnis, C. Siu, A. S, and H. Huang. "Category Encoders: a scikit-learn-contrib package of transformers for encoding categorical data" The Journal of Open Source Software, vol 3, pp. 501, Jan. 2018, doi: 10.21105/joss.00501

[15] P. Cerda and G. Varoquaux. Encoding high-cardinality string categorical variables. Retrieved: Aug, 2021. [Online]. Available from: https://arxiv.org/abs/1907.01860 2020

[16] P. Cunningham, B. Kathirgamanathan, and S. J. Delany. Feature Selection Tutorial with Python Examples. Retrieved: Aug, 2021. [Online]. Available from: https://arxiv.org/abs/2106.06437 2021

A Concept for a Comprehensive Understanding of Communication in Mobile Forensics

Jian Xi*†, Michael Spranger† and Dirk Labudde†‡

†University of Applied Sciences Mittweida
Forensic Science Investigation Lab (FoSIL), Germany
Email: {xi, spranger}@hs-mittweida.de
‡Fraunhofer
Cyber Security
Darmstadt, Germany
Email: labudde@hs-mittweida.de

***Abstract*—Nowadays, mobile devices play a crucial role in our daily life. In practice, criminals also use mobile devices to communicate. Therefore, they have been becoming an important resource for evidence for law enforcement agencies. Especially, the communication between criminals may provide information that could be important for a criminal investigation. Furthermore, the extensive use of mobile devices every day leads to a huge amount of data. Often, it would take too much time to analyze and sort through all the data manually and in some cases it is not even possible. Additionally, investigators are faced with a heterogeneity in the data. Not only are different messengers used to communicate, yet communication is no longer restricted to textual communication and might also include videos or pictures. For this reason, this paper proposes a novel concept that takes different types of media and communication channels in a joint semantic analysis of the content into account. Additionally, a communication network can be derived in terms of topics discussed between users that communicated via smartphone.**

***Index Terms*—Semantic Analysis; Mobile Forensics; Multimodal Machine Learning.**

I. Introduction

In recent years, the emergence of mobile devices changed our life completely. It became the most essential communication medium for acquiring and exchanging information in our daily life. However, it also enables criminals to commit crimes in a very effective manner. Especially, in a well-organized criminal offense, various mobile devices are used for different purposes like locating the targeting places and the victims, organizing the actions or even taking photos for confirming the activities after a crime was committed. Usually, mobile communication is neither limited to one specific medium or communication channel, e.g., email, social networks like Facebook, Telegram, WhatsApp etc. nor to a single data modality like text, image, audio and video etc. Consequently, it inevitably leads to not only isolated and segmented information but also to heterogeneity in the data. In order to support the investigators to understand such communication data in an investigation process, we propose a concept for a joint semantic analysis, which provides comprehensive understanding of communication data for reconstructing an overall view of the data.

The paper is organized as follows: in Section II, we conduct a brief review of related work of semantic analysis in the forensic field. Then we explain the proposed concept of the joint semantic analysis in Section III. Finally, a short discussion is given and some outlooks of future work are discussed in Section IV.

II. Related Work

Most of the existing work in the area of forensic analysis handles the single modalities separately for each case. As shown in [1], Machine Learning-based approaches are reported to detect sexual predatory chats in online text conversations. Focusing on crime scene investigation, [2] presented an Convolution Network-based approach that utilizes feature engineering to improve the image retrieval performance. Similarly, based on feature engineering, video data is examined for detecting illicit content, e.g., pornographic material [3], where periodic patterns and salient regions are respectively analyzed at first in audio-frames and visual-frames. Subsequently, the multi-modal co-occurrence semantics is described by a multi-model fusion approach. Recently, deep learning approaches have also been considered in the forensic filed e.g., detecting drug dealing via social media [4] and detecting video manipulation [5].

As shown the existing methods are not able to jointly process the data in multi-modality. Yet, the semantic context of a mobile conversation is embodied coherently by the data in diverse modalities [6] [7]. In addition, all the data can be transferred via different channels, which in fact inevitably lead to segmented information in data understanding. Furthermore, the amount of mobile messages grows tremendously. Analyzing such a big amount of heterogeneous data manually is overwhelming. As so far, no system reported analyzes all the data modalities in a joint manner in the forensic field. Yet a critical question needs to be answered in such case:

how to understand data consistently whose semantic content is represented by different modalities?

III. Concept of Joint Semantic Analysis

In order to address the aforementioned issues, a feasible and stable solution for a joint semantic analysis in mobile forensics is proposed, as shown conceptually in Figure 1. By means of this joint semantic analysis, the communication data can be analyzed jointly and consistently in an investigation process.

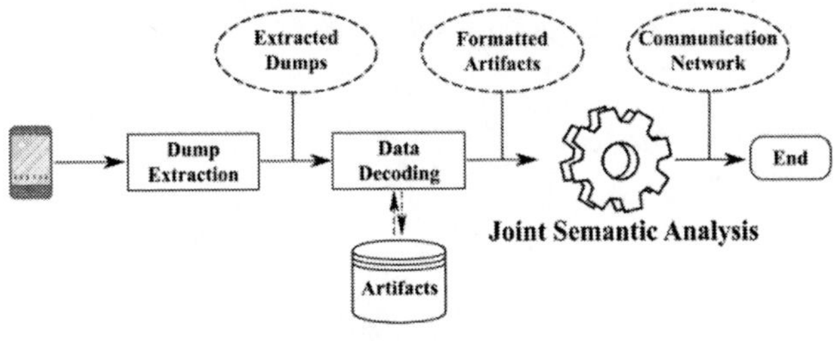

Figure 1. Illustration of the concept for the joint semantic analysis of communication on mobile devices.

The different components are as follows:
Dump Extraction: Extracting data from targeted suspicious mobile devices is a critical step in forensic analysis since there are various different operating systems, hardware, and software. Furthermore, criminals often delete files, which contain information that may be used against them in a criminal investigation. The dump should be extracted in compliance with the chain of custody.
Data Decoding: The foundation of jointly analyzing communication covering all communication channels is a common understanding of the data. For this purpose, extracted dumps need to be restructured in a pre-defined artifact format that includes the necessary information like communication channel, whether a message was send or received and deleted as well, the information about sender, receiver as well caller. The storage information is also necessary for multimedia data. Note that the artifacts can be extracted from multiple dumps (devices).
Joint Semantic Analysis: Aiming at explaining the coherent semantic content and hidden connections in a mobile communication consistently, we formally formulate the joint semantic analysis as follows:

$$\tilde{e} = \text{argmax}_{\boldsymbol{\theta}} \tilde{P}(e|d_{cm}; \boldsymbol{\theta}) \quad (1)$$

where e is the semantic context in the conversation data D, which is mostly presented by a topic and possibly connected to a concrete crime, $d_{cm} \in D$ stands for a single artifact message spread via the communication channel $c \in D_c$ {WhatsApp, Telegram, Facebook Messenge, email etc.} and represented in the modality $m \in D_m$ {Text, Image, Audio, Video etc.}. D is time- and semantically-coherent and organized chronologically. $\boldsymbol{\theta}$ is the parameter set that captures the latent semantic topics in the data and it could be inferred in the topic modeling.

The critical work at this step focuses on finding an intermodal relation that implies a semantic concept between different modalities and channels. For this reason, the individual elements of the respective modalities need to be derived first. Meanwhile, these semantic elements need to be searchable in investigation. Subsequently, the semantic connection (intermodal correspondence) can be determined by considering the whole context in communication. For this purpose, we need at first to map the content of all multimedia data into a textual semantic space to extract semantic topics. For image data, the traditional classification approach [8] or image captioning [9] can be used, where the former delivers only discrete labels like *people* or *car*, etc., while the latter describes the coherent information of image as a whole scene with a natural sentence, e.g., *a man is holding a gun in a bank*. The performance of semantic image captioning can be evaluated by standard evaluation approaches [10]. Instead of merely focusing on describing semantic content of an image, the semantic interpretations and the relations between image and text can be determined as shown in [11]. Meanwhile, a scene graph is planed to be extracted in order to determine how a scene graph contributes to understanding a conversation [12]. Similar, a video can also be translated to a textual representation, i.e., a natural sentence with respect to the content [13]. The audio data can be transcribed into text form by means of Automatic Speech Recognition (ASR) [14]. Note that based on the proposed approaches, the multimedia data is semantically represented in textual form, which can be used for retrieving the forensic information, as well as extracting the coherent semantic topics of the data by using Latent Dirichlet Allocation (LDA) [15]. After topic modeling, each artifact will get a label that has the highest probability with respect to extracted topics. The semantic meaning of this label can be explained by the most important features selected according to the posterior probability of the extracted topics. Finally, a communication in given suspicious data can be represented by these extracted semantic topics. This semantic representation can be used as evidentiary information for clarifying the forensic facts and avoiding misinterpretations of the communication.

IV. Conclusion and Future Work

In this paper, we proposed a concept for a joint semantic analysis in mobile forensics that aims to support investigators when examining the content of an entire communication by taking the multi-modality, as well as multi-channels into account simultaneously. As a result, the investigators are able to capture the overall information of the data in terms of the semantic concepts, which could be related to specific cases. This semantic connection in data is a key information that helps investigators to completely reconstruct the whole criminal scenario. Meanwhile, multiple devices can also be analyzed jointly in this process. In future work, we need to integrate some case-related words, in other words *prior knowledge* from investigators in this pipeline. Furthermore, an alias matching strategy needs to be developed for matching the people who have different names in different communication channels as well as devices.

ACKNOWLEDGMENT

This paper has been funded by the EU-project FORMOBILE. This project has received funding from the European Union's Horizon 2020 research and innovation programme under grant agreement No 832800. Any dissemination of results must indicate that it reflects only the author's view and that the Agency is not responsible for any use that may be made of the information it contains.

REFERENCES

[1] C. Ngejane, J. Eloff, T. Sefara, and V. Marivate, "Digital forensics supported by machine learning for the detection of online sexual predatory chats," *Forensic Science International: Digital Investigation*, vol. 36, p. 301109, 2021.

[2] Y. Liu, Y. Peng, D. Hu, D. Li, K.-P. Lim, and N. Ling, "Image retrieval using cnn and low-level feature fusion for crime scene investigation image database," in *2018 Asia-Pacific Signal and Information Processing Association Annual Summit and Conference (APSIPA ASC)*, 2018, pp. 1208–1214.

[3] Y. Liu, X. Gu, L. Huang, J. Ouyang, M. Liao, and L. Wu, "Analyzing periodicity and saliency for adult video detection," *Multimedia Tools and Applications*, vol. 79, 02 2020.

[4] J. Li, Q. Xu, N. Shah, and T. Mackey, "A machine learning approach for the detection and characterization of illicit drug dealers on instagram: Model evaluation study," *Journal of Medical Internet Research*, vol. 21, p. e13803, 06 2019.

[5] A. L. Sandoval Orozco, C. Quinto Huamàn, D. Povedano Àlvarez, and L. J. Garcìa Villalba, "A machine learning forensics technique to detect post-processing in digital videos," *Future Generation Computer Systems*, vol. 111, pp. 199–212, 2020.

[6] H.-J. Bucher, "Multimodal understanding or reception as interaction theoretical and empirical foundations of a systematic analysis of multimodality," *Visual linguistics. Theory-method case studies (Bildlinguistik. Theorien-Methoden-Fallbeispiele)*, pp. 123–156, January 2011.

[7] J. R. Hobbs, "Why is discourse coherent?" *SRI International*, November 1978.

[8] X. Zhai, A. Kolesnikov, N. Houlsby, and L. Beyer, "Scaling vision transformers," *CoRR*, 2021.

[9] A. Karpathy and F.-F. Li, "Deep visual-semantic alignments for generating image descriptions," in *Proceedings of the IEEE Conference on Computer Vision and Pattern Recognition(CVPR)*, June 2015, pp. 3128–3137.

[10] P. Anderson, B. Fernando, M. Johnson, and S. Gould, "Spice: Semantic propositional image caption evaluation," in *ECCV*, 2016.

[11] C. Otto, M. Springstein, A. Anand, and R. Ewerth, "Understanding, categorizing and predicting semantic image-text relations," in *Proceedings of the 2019 on International Conference on Multimedia Retrieval*, 2019, pp. 168–176.

[12] D. Xu, Y. Zhu, C. B. Choy, and L. Fei-Fei, "Scene graph generation by iterative message passing," in *2017 IEEE Conference on Computer Vision and Pattern Recognition (CVPR)*, 2017, pp. 3097–3106.

[13] V. Iashin and E. Rahtu, "Multi-modal dense video captioning," *arXiv e-prints*, Mar. 2020.

[14] A. Baevski, Y. Zhou, A. Mohamed, and M. Auli, "wav2vec 2.0: A framework for self-supervised learning of speech representations," in *Advances in Neural Information Processing Systems 33: Annual Conference on Neural Information Processing Systems 2020, NeurIPS 2020, December 6-12, 2020, virtual*, H. Larochelle, M. Ranzato, R. Hadsell, M. Balcan, and H. Lin, Eds., 2020.

[15] D. M. Blei, A. Y. Ng, and M. I. Jordan, "Latent dirichlet allocation," *Journal of Machine Learning Research*, pp. 993–1022, March 2003.

Classification of Bots and Gender using Topic Unigrams

Astrid Fleig, Lisa Geyersbach, Melissa Göhler, Patricia Kurz, Paul Limburg, Dirk Labudde and Michael Spranger
University of Applied Sciences Mittweida
Mittweida, Germany
Email: spranger@hs-mittweida.de

***Abstract*—In social networks such as Twitter, author profiling plays a big role. It is especially interesting to differentiate between accounts from humans and bots and to make a prediction about the age and the gender of human users. The information can be helpful to analyze possible manipulations, networks and crimes. This paper presents an approach to differentiate between bots and humans, as well as the gender for the human accounts using Tweets. For each sub-problem, a linear Support-Vector Machine (SVM) was used and different feature and featuresets were tested. The analysis showed that the topic model is the best feature for all categories. For this feature, the term frequencies of the most important terms of the topics were used. In comparison to other approaches, this approach could increase the performance. More precisely, only with this feature it was possible to reach accuracies between 99.7% and 100%.**

***Index Terms*— Author Profiling; Bot Detection; Gender Detection; Twitter; Spanish; English.**

I. Introduction

In social networks like Twitter, accounts run by bots are common [1] [2]. Some can be recognized at first sight, others stay undiscovered [3]. Depending on their use, bots can be a positive and helpful extension to the Twitter experience or can be harmful and deceptive [4]. Positive examples are weather bots that regularly post the weather, like @EmojiWeatherUSA, temperature in a certain area, like @EVER_WEATHER or tsunami warnings, like @NWS_PTWC. However, negative examples are bots that try to deceive people, use spam or harm users with malicious links [5] [6]. So called social bots use their platform to react to real peoples' tweets and spread commercial, political or ideological opinions. Using good deception methods, like being able to interact in conversations, those bots stay undetected by common Twitter users and can influence large groups of people. For example, they can bring users to believe in certain misinformation or vote for a specific politician in the next election [7]. By identifying bots automatically, a lot of those negative influences can be prevented.

Another interesting task is knowing the gender of Twitter users. This is being explored for several reasons. A Twitter user's gender can be used for forensic, criminological, political or phenomenological analysis [8]. For example, the amount of Tweets about an upcoming election can be analyzed regarding the author's gender or the members of a criminal network can be inspected further. Getting this information about the author's gender can be challenging because it does not need to be disclosed on the user profile. Thus, finding a way to accurately guess the gender of a user would be helpful. In this paper the focus is on the genders female and male.

The field of author profiling is well studied and even a competition regarding the described classification tasks was held with good results in 2019 by PAN [9].

In this paper, a new feature set is tested to identify whether a Twitter user is a bot or human and, afterwards, whether the human users are female or male. This feature set consists of a combination of extracted topics, bigrams and other surface-level features. Especially, the topics have not yet been used before. In addition to that the transferability of the system from one language to another is explored. Merely the content of each author's tweets will be used for these tasks.

In Section II, other approaches are discussed. Afterwards, in Section III an overview of the data used is given. In Section IV the different pre-processing steps are described, as well as the the feature extraction and the classification process. Finally, in Section V the results are presented and discussed, while in Section VI a brief conclusion is given and possible future work discussed.

II. Literature

The differentiation of bots and humans, as well as women and men, is an important problem, which is addressed often. There are many ways to approach this topic.

Different literature uses different classifiers for this task, e.g. Naive Bayes (NB) [2], Random Forest [2] [10] or logistic regression [11] [12] [13]. The best results are obtained by using a support-vector machine [4] [14] [15]. To solve the multi class problem a combination of multiple SVMs was used [4].

Using a combination of a Convolutional Neural Network (CNN) and a Recurrent Neural Networks (RNN) [16] is a different approach but obtains slightly worse results.

Popular features for those kinds of classification problems are word- and character n-grams, especially, word unigrams and word bigrams as well as character-3-to-5-grams [4] [16] [11] [12] [14] [15]. Partly, a TF-IDF-weighting with sublinear term frequency was used [14]. The latter has been proven to be useful especially for the gender differentiation.

Profile data like follower ratio and tweet frequency can be used for the differentiation if available [2] [10]. This data obtained good results for classifying authors in humans, bots and cyborgs [2]. It was also shown, that humans tweet more irregular and in undetermined time intervals, which results in entropy being a helpful feature for detecting humans. Tweet length was also already used for this task [10].

Furthermore, hashtags and user-mentions were proven to be relevant features [4]. Also, to detect typical bot behavior especially hashtag- and user-mention count as well as the number of retweets and hyperlinks can be helpful [13] [17].

Literature shows a connection between bots and spam [2]. Spam can be understood as the lack of topic variance or extreme persistence of one topic. This can be shown by repeatedly tweeting the same tweet or merely posting tweets containing only one or few specific topics. Because most bots are focusing on specific topics and are recognizable by that behavior, topics can possibly be used as a feature. Finding and defining topics in tweets is an interesting subject, e.g. to filter tweets by factual relevant tweets. Approaches for this problem are topic detection using Latent Dirichlet Allocation (LDA) [18] or unigram clustering resulting in network-graphs with relations [19]. Using LDA can also show how intensely authors focus on one topic by using certain words frequently [17]. In connection to this, sentiment analysis can be used as well [17].

Differentiating between the two examined genders obtained the best results by using emoji lists, punctuation trigrams, Part-Of-Speech (POS)-trigrams, document sentiment or different wordlists as features [11]. In addition to that POS-sequence-patterns, the differentiation of writing styles and the consideration of word endings obtained good results for gender detection in texts [20].

Based on the described literature, in this paper linear SVMs and a feature set containing hashtag-, user-mention- and retweet count, document length, punctuation marks and word unigrams as well as bigrams is being used. Special attention is given to the topics of the tweets.

III. Data Set Description

The data used was originally provided for the author profiling task of the PAN competition in 2019. Overall, data sets for two languages, English and Spanish, were provided. Each of the data sets includes 100 tweets per author, as well as the ground truth. [9] The data was split into training and validation data as suggested by the PAN organizers [9].

The data sets are balanced in terms of their class distribution, as shown in Table I. Additionally, the original test data set was used to test the model developed in this work under the same conditions as in PAN 2019. The test data have the same characteristics and class distribution as the training data set.

IV. Methods

In this paper, an SVM based classification approach is chosen for both, the classification of bots and humans, as well as females and males. The approach is based on successful approaches discussed in the literature.

The overall procedure is shown in Figure 1 and consists of several consecutive and parallel sub-tasks, which are necessary for extracting the different feature sets.

Each task shall be explained in more detail below.

TABLE I
Overview of the class distribution of all data sets

	Spanish				English			
	b	h	f	m	b	h	f	m
train	1040	1040	520	520	1440	1440	720	720
	$\sum$ 2080				$\sum$ 2880			
val	460	460	230	230	620	620	310	310
	$\sum$ 920				$\sum$ 1240			
test	900	900	450	450	1320	1320	660	660
	$\sum$ 1800				$\sum$ 2640			

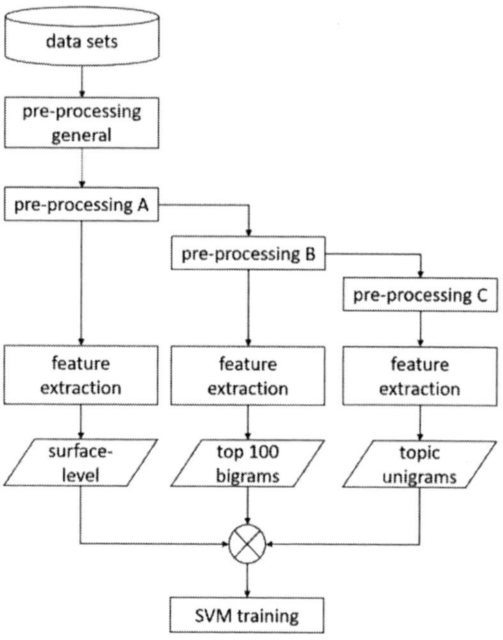

Fig. 1. General procedure for the classification tasks.

A. Pre-processing

The general pre-processing task is independent of the type of feature to be extracted. It consists of several steps, which were partly taken from [4]. In particular, every word was converted to lowercase and numbers, digits and isolated letters were erased. During the feature extraction process it was found that links are not useful for the classification, because there are no significant differences between the tweets of the different categories in regards to their number and content. Therefore, they were deleted. Furthermore, stop words for the respective languages were removed. However, for the Spanish data English stop words were removed as well because some English words or phrases are in the data. Finally, all spaces, resulting from the general pre-processing step were deleted.

For the extraction of certain feature sets special pre-processing was necessary. For the extraction of the bi-grams all special characters and punctuation marks, but hashtags and user-mentions were deleted (pre-processing B). They were included because the relation between hashtag or user-mention and an additional word can be important, e.g. the term 'Trump' is often used with the hashtag '#politics'. The same pre-processing steps were used for the extraction of surface level features, however, exclamation marks, question marks and ellipses were not deleted (pre-processing A). Lastly, pre-processing step C deletes # and @ symbols. For the extraction of topic unigrams, pre-processing steps A and C were combined. Hashtags and user-mentions were deleted for the extraction of topic-unigrams as it is irrelevant whether a term is used inside or outside a hashtag or user-mention, since only the frequency of each term is counted.

B. Extracting Surface-Level Features

After pre-processing step B some surface-level features were extracted. First, the number of words of all tweets an author has written was analyzed. This proved to be useful in combination with other surface-level features.

Further, the number of retweets, user-mentions, and hashtags per author were considered as features, as well as the number of punctuation marks. During the feature extraction it became apparent that bots in this data set use more user-mentions than humans. In addition bots use twice as many hashtags. In the same way, retweets were helpful when differentiating between bots and humans. The opposite seems to be true for the gender classification. Here, these features show very similar usage in both gender categories.

As a stand-alone feature ellipses were not helpful for the tasks. However, in combination with other features the number of support vectors can be lowered by using them as a feature. Overall, humans use exclamation and question marks more often than bots. Furthermore, female and male authors are predominantly different in their use of ellipses.

C. Extracting Topical Terms and Bigrams

As it turned out, the most efficient feature can be created by using unigram topic models.The feature creation process is shown in Figure 2.

After pre-processing B, a Document-Term-Matrix (DTM) was created with a minimum Term Frequency (minTF) and minimum Document Frequency (minDF) of two. An LDA was executed on these DTMs. After running multiple tests and adjusting the topic count, with an amount of seven topics the best result were achieved on the given training data. For further steps and to prevent overfitting, only the top 20 words of each of the extracted topics were used to form the topic-unigram feature.

In order to obtain the frequencies of the extracted topical terms, a second DTM was created with a minTF of two and a minDF of ten. This DTM was used to count the occurrences of the extracted top 20 topical words for each author.

During the processing of the test and validation data similar DTMs were created without the restriction of minTF and minDF.

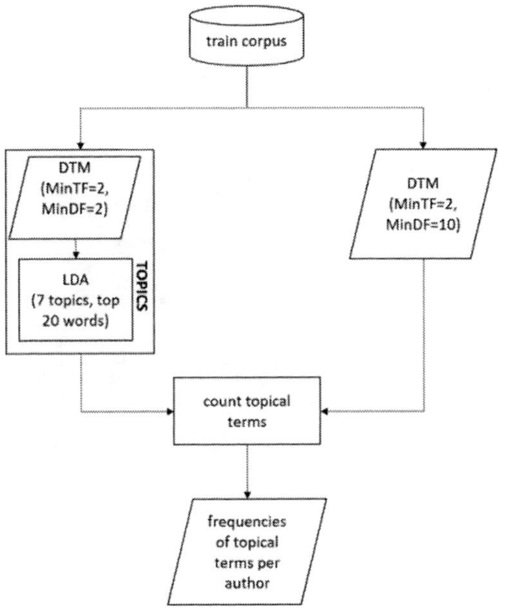

Fig. 2. Process of determining topical term frequency.

As shown in Figure 3 topics as features were very successful for differentiating both, bots and humans, as well as females and males. Bots turned out to be mostly talking about work, weather and news but also about advertising-related topics like gaming or YouTube. Human authors on the other hand were interested more in sports, politics, social networks, technology and free time activities.

Furthermore, it was observed, that female authors mostly wrote about topics like social networks and private events and male authors rather wrote about free time activities or politics.

The top 100 word bigrams were extracted from the data sets as a final feature. During this process, a document frequency minimum of 10 and a term frequency minimum of 2 was chosen to prevent overfitting [4] [11]. The extraction process was similar to the one of the topic-unigrams.

D. Feature-Evaluation

In order to evaluate the predictability of the different features an SVM was trained for each of them, using a ten-fold cross-validation after scaling the features. In Figure 3 the results of this evaluation are shown.

For both tasks the topic-unigrams and top 100 bigrams turned out to be the best features with accuracies of up to 100%. Generally, the single feature accuracies do not differ largely between the languages Spanish and English.

Retweet- and user mention count are, with accuracies of approximately 80%, also good features for differentiating between bots and humans. Ellipsis as a feature has the worst discrimination power for differentiating human and bots, yet it is the best surface-level feature for differentiating between females and males. Generally, surface-level feature have a slightly less discrimination power in the female/male differentiating task.

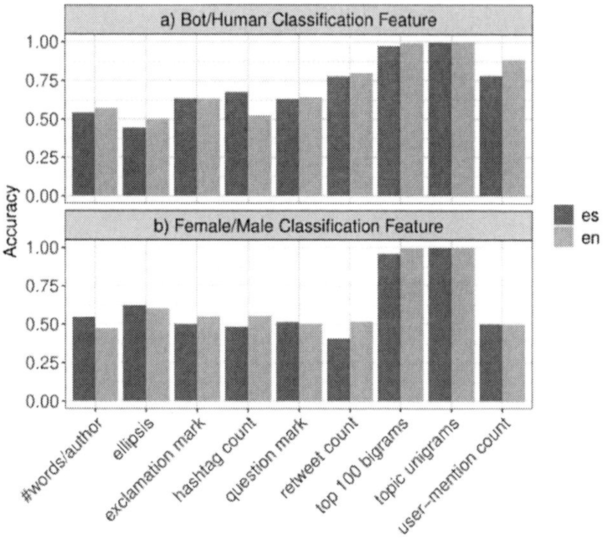

Fig. 3. Accuracy overview of the individual features of the Bot/Human classification in a) and of the Female/Male classification in b)

E. Experimental Design

In order to test the approach presented in this paper, four different feature sets were created. Firstly, a feature set that includes all of the discussed features (aF). Secondly, a feature set that only incorporates topic unigrams (U). Lastly, feature sets that are specific for each classification (Fk). These include for the Bot/Human classification a combination of document length, hashtag-, user-mention-, retweet-, and question mark count as well as topic-unigrams and top 100 bigrams and for the Female/Male classification a combination of document length, user-mention-, question mark-, exclamation mark- and ellipsis count as well as topic-unigrams and top 100 bigrams. For each of the classification tasks, a linear SVM was trained. Furthermore, for comparison, three baseline approaches were considered. For one baseline a Naive Bayes classifier (NB) was used and trained with the surface-level features hashtag-, user-mention count and document length. These surface-level features were chosen, since the accuracies on both, the Spanish and English data set, were very similar for each classification task (Figure 3). This baseline was used to set a minimal accuracy limit that definitely had to be surpassed and was not supposed to be especially challenging. It was utilized as an orientation what accuracy only few features can achieve. The other two baselines were taken from the literature.

[4] and [15] show the challenges that are supposed to be surpassed. The results in [4] serve as a baseline because the used approach is similar to the one used in this paper and, thus, is a good reference. Furthermore, [15] is the paper with the best accuracies for the given task. Thus, the goal in this paper was to surpass these accuracies.

V. Results and Discussion

A comparison of all three baselines and results of the classification with the given Test (TD) and Validation Data (VD) sets are presented in Table II. This Table shows results for all possible combinations of feature- and data sets. As explained in Subsection IV-E the feature sets are all of the discussed features (aF), only topic unigrams (U) and specific feature sets for the classification at hand (Fk). The table is also split into the languages Spanish and English, as well as the sub-problems Bot/Human (B\H) and Female/Male (F\M).

TABLE II
Final results in comparison to three baselines.

	Spanish		**English**	
	B\H	F\M	B\H	F\M
Baseline NB	0,713	0,5717	0,8677	0,5548
Baseline [4]	0,91	0,78	0,92	0,82
Baseline [15]	0,9333	0,8172	0,9360	0,8356
SVM+aF+TD	1	1	0,9992	1
SVM+Fk+TD	0,9978	1	1	1
SVM+U+TD	0,9967	1	1	1
SVM+aF+VD	0,985	0,9933	1	1
SVM+Fk+VD	0,9906	0,9922	0,9996	1
SVM+U+VD	0,9917	0,9922	0,9985	1

The most important result is that all baselines were surpassed by at least 7%. The difference between the accuracies reached with the naive bayes and all SVM results is especially great. This is a good result, since this baseline was supposed to be the lowest limit that had to be exceeded. Furthermore, the baselines by [4] and [15] were surpassed, too.

It can be noticed that the Female\Male differentiation of the English data is always at an accuracy of 100%. A reasonable cause for this outcome may be overfitting, even though precautions were taken to prevent this. Additionally the 100% accuracy of the Spanish TD concerning this task, may also be explained by overfitting.

Furthermore, there is only a minimal decline in the accuracies from the test to the validation data set. The results of the validation data set in comparison to the test data set dropped in no case more than 1.5%. This maximal loss in accuracy occurs in the Bot\Human differentiation of the Spanish data between the test and the validation data set using all features (aF). However, between the test and the validation data set the results even increased by 0.08%, in the case of Bot\Human differentiation of the English data. Nevertheless, the results are all in the same range at nearly 100% accuracy, which is a surprising outcome.

Moreover, it can be noticed, that the topic unigram feature is enough to enable a nearly perfect classification. The single feature accuracies (U) hardly differ from the results of the feature set (Fk) or the usage of all features (aF) in combination. Thus, the surface-level features and top 100 bigrams only minimally improve the accuracy in combination with the topic unigrams. With this knowledge the question arises, whether the given data sets are possibly obtained or filtered for one or more specific topics. That would make the obtained results using topic unigrams less surprising. Unfortunately, there is no information available regarding the creation process.

The reason for the similarities between languages can be caused by their similar statistic characteristics or that the used approach is indeed language independent.

VI. Conclusion and Future Work

In this paper, topics as a feature for the author profiling classification tasks of differentiating between Twitter users and bots, as well as females and males was tested on a PAN data set containing English and Spanish Twitter data and found to surpass the results of existing works. Topics as feature were not considered in previous work. Furthermore, the tweets were first classified into the categories human and bot and the latter then further divided into female and male.

In summary, it was established that for the given author profiling tasks the topic feature in combination with a linear SVM provides the best results with accuracies up to 100%. This feature outperforms all other considered features except of bigrams, which yields similar performance.

Nevertheless, some improvements can be made in future works.

A second validation using a new completely independent data set would be useful. This data set should be created for English and for Spanish tweets without any topic restrictions. With this new data set, the overfitting hypothesis could be validated.

References

[1] I. Zeifman, "Bot Traffic Report 2016," Jan. 2017, [Last Accessed: 06-26-2021]. [Online]. Available: https://www.imperva.com/blog/bot-traffic-report-2016/?redirect=Incapsula

[2] Z. Chu, S. Gianvecchio, H. Wang, and S. Jajodia, "Detecting Automation of Twitter Accounts: Are You a Human, Bot, or Cyborg?" *IEEE Transactions on Dependable and Secure Computing*, vol. 9, no. 6, pp. 811–824, 2012.

[3] S. Wojcik, S. Messing, A. Smith, L. Rainie, and P. Hitlin, "Bots in the Twittersphere," Apr. 2018, [Last Accessed: 05-16-2021]. [Online]. Available: https://www.pewresearch.org/internet/2018/04/09/bots-in-the-twittersphere/

[4] I. Vogel and P. Jiang, "Bot and Gender Identification in Twitter using Word and Character N-Grams," *Notebook for PAN at CLEF 2019*, 2019.

[5] A. Bessi and E. Ferrara, "Social bots distort the 2016 U.S. Presidential election online discussion," *First Monday*, vol. 21, no. 11, Nov. 2016. [Online]. Available: https://firstmonday.org/ojs/index.php/fm/article/view/7090

[6] K. Thomas, C. Grier, D. Song, and V. Paxson, "Suspended Accounts in Retrospect: An Analysis of Twitter Spam," in *Proceedings of the 2011 ACM SIGCOMM Conference on Internet Measurement Conference*, ser. IMC '11. New York, NY, USA: Association for Computing Machinery, 2011, p. 243–258. [Online]. Available: https://doi.org/10.1145/2068816.2068840

[7] E. Ferrara, O. Varol, C. Davis, F. Menczer, and A. Flammini, "The Rise of Social Bots," *Commun. ACM*, vol. 59, no. 7, p. 96–104, Jun. 2016. [Online]. Available: https://doi.org/10.1145/2818717

[8] F. Rangel, P. Rosso, M. Koppel, E. Stamatatos, and G. Inches, "Overview of the author profiling task at pan 2013," *CLEF Conference on Multilingual and Multimodal Information Access Evaluation*, pp. 352–365, 2013.

[9] PAN, "Offizielle PAN Aufgabenstellung: Bots and Gender Profiling 2019," [Last Accessed: 11-18-2020]. [Online]. Available: https://pan.webis.de/clef19/pan19-web/author-profiling.html

[10] O. Varol, E. Ferrara, C. Davis, F. Menczer, and A. Flammini, "Online Human-Bot Interactions: Detection, Estimation, and Characterization," *Proceedings of the International AAAI Conference on Web and Social Media*, vol. 11, no. 1, pp. 280–289, May 2017. [Online]. Available: https://ojs.aaai.org/index.php/ICWSM/article/view/14871

[11] M. Martinc, I. Škrjanec, K. Zupan, and S. Pollak, "PAN 2017: Author Profiling-Gender and Language Variety Prediction (Notebook for PAN at CLEF 2017, 2nd place)," *Notebook for PAN at CLEF 2017*, 02 2018.

[12] M. Martinc, B. Škrlj, and S. Pollak, "Fake or Not: Distinguishing Between Bots, Males and Females (Notebook for PAN at CLEF 2019)," *Notebook for PAN at CLEF 2019*, 2019.

[13] S. Qi, L. AlKulaib, and D. A. Broniatowski, "Detecting and Characterizing Bot-Like Behavior on Twitter," in *Social, Cultural, and Behavioral Modeling*, R. Thomson, C. Dancy, A. Hyder, and H. Bisgin, Eds. Cham: Springer International Publishing, 2018, pp. 228–232.

[14] A. Basile *et al.*, "N-GrAM: New Groningen Author-profiling Model," *Notebook for PAN at CLEF 2017*, 2017.

[15] J. Pizarro, "Using N-grams to detect Bots on Twitter," in *CLEF 2019 Labs and Workshops, Notebook Papers*, L. Cappellato, N. Ferro, D. Losada, and H. Müller, Eds. CEUR-WS.org, Sep. 2019. [Online]. Available: http://ceur-ws.org/Vol-2380/

[16] R. F. S. Dias and I. Paraboni, "Combined CNN+RNN Bot and Gender Profiling," *Notebook for PAN at CLEF 2019*, 2019.

[17] J. P. Dickerson, V. Kagan, and V. S. Subrahmanian, "Using sentiment to detect bots on Twitter: Are humans more opinionated than bots?" in *2014 IEEE/ACM International Conference on Advances in Social Networks Analysis and Mining (ASONAM 2014)*, 2014, pp. 620–627.

[18] M.-C. Yang and H.-C. Rim, "Identifying interesting Twitter contents using topical analysis," *Expert Systems with Applications*, vol. 41, no. 9, pp. 4330–4336, 2014. [Online]. Available: https://www.sciencedirect.com/science/article/pii/S0957417414000141

[19] K. H. Lim, S. Karunasekera, and A. Harwood, "ClusTop: A Clustering-based Topic Modelling Algorithm for Twitter using Word Networks," in *2017 IEEE International Conference on Big Data (BIGDATA)*, 12 2017, pp. 2009–2018.

[20] A. Mukherjee and B. Liu, "Improving Gender Classification of Blog Authors," in *Proceedings of the 2010 Conference on Empirical Methods in Natural Language Processing*. Cambridge, MA: Association for Computational Linguistics, Oct. 2010, pp. 207–217. [Online]. Available: https://www.aclweb.org/anthology/D10-1021

Evaluation of Filter Methods for Feature Selection by Using Real Manufacturing Data

Alexander Gerling
Business Informatics
Furtwangen University of Applied Science
Furtwangen, Germany
e-mail: alexander.gerlinghs-furtwangen.de

Holger Ziekow
Business Informatics
Furtwangen University of Applied Science
Furtwangen, Germany
e-mail: holger.ziekow@hs-furtwangen.de

Ulf Schreier
Business Informatics
Furtwangen University of Applied Science
Furtwangen, Germany
e-mail: ulf.schreier@hs-furtwangen.de

Christian Seiffer
Business Informatics
Furtwangen University of Applied Science
Furtwangen, Germany
e-mail: christian.seiffer@hs-furtwangen.de

Andreas Hess
Business Informatics
Furtwangen University of Applied Science
Furtwangen, Germany
e-mail: andreas.hess@hs-furtwangen.de

Djaffar Ould Abdeslam
IRIMAS Laboratory
Université de Haute-Alsace
Mulhouse, France
e-mail: djaffar.ould-abdeslam@uha.fr

***Abstract*— The importance of Machine Learning (ML) in the domain of manufacturing has been increasing in recent years. Especially, ML techniques are used to predict and explain errors in the production. One challenge of using ML in this domain is to deal with the often-high number of features in the datasets. However, a product defect can in many cases be traced back to a few relevant characteristics. In this paper, we investigate methods for finding reduced feature sets in the context of manufacturing. Here, the feature reduction promises two key advantages. One improvement is the prediction quality of the ML model. The second advantage concerns the explainability of a product error. With a reduction of features from the original dataset, we also reduce the search space for the product error origin. We investigate three different filter methods for feature selection based on 25 real manufacturing datasets, which are highly unbalanced. We describe the implementation of these and test them in three experimental approaches. Furthermore, we optimize the feature selection using a cost-based metric. Optimizing on the basis of the cost-based metric is shown to be in several cases more useful for reducing the number of features than well-established and frequently used classification metrics. In various experiments, we were able to improve the result and simultaneously reduce the number of features with our cost-based metric.**

Keywords: Filter-Based Feature Selection methods; Machine Learning; Cost based Metric; Production; Production data.

I. INTRODUCTION

Machine Learning (ML) has been increasingly used in the domain of manufacturing, particularly in the production line to predict corrupted product parts [1][2]. Data scientists and quality engineers are user roles in a company, which analyze malfunctions in the production to eliminate production errors. The task of these user roles is it to find the cause of a production error. Highly advanced production lines result in only few, but costly, errors. This is reflected in the data by just few errors to analyze, which result as a main challenge for this domain. A ML system can support data scientists and quality engineers, e.g., by creating prediction models and identifying relevant features in datasets from test stations. The evaluation methods for feature selection methods can be divided into five groups: embedded, hybrid, ensemble, wrapper and filter. In this paper we investigate the effect of filter selection methods. Filter methods have the advantage of better time performance in comparison to wrapper methods and are classifier independent [3]. Independence of classifier is particularly important for the flexibility to choose a different classifier regarding black box optimization. Another advantage of the filter-based methods is the ability to scale up to high-dimensional datasets [4]. This is particularly useful because a large number of measurements are recorded in a production line. Even a single test station in a production line can check numerous features, but not every feature is equally important for a classification. Unnecessary features in the dataset are features, which are not related to a specific error message. These features should be removed from the dataset to provide (1) a better result and (2) to support the explainability of resulting models. Such tasks could be solved automatically by using Automated Machine Learning (AutoML) tools. Different AutoML solutions emerged over the past few years

[5][6]. An AutoML tool can take over various steps of the data science pipeline and prepare data or ML models for users. Our work is part of the project PREFERML [7] that investigates challenges and holistic system solutions in this context. Within our project, we provide the user an optimized dataset including only selected features from the original dataset. The selection of features will help to reduce the error cause space and support targeted analyses. We will test three different forms of state-of-the-art filter methods on real manufacturing data.

The following research questions (Q) emerge from the above description:

- (Q1) Can state of the art filter methods provide a benefit in the given use case?
- (Q2) Which is the best filter method in our use case?
- (Q3) Can further feature reductions be achieved by using alternatives to standard metrics?
- (Q4) How long does the optimization of the model take and is there a fastest filter method?

The paper is organized as follows: Section 2 describes our use case and the challenges in this domain. In Section 3, we describe related work. The fundamentals for our experiments are described in Section 4; this includes the used metrics and the filter methods. In Section 5, we describe the filter selection algorithm. Our setup for the experiment and the different experiment approaches are described in Section 6. Section 7 is dedicated for the evaluation of the results. Section 8 summarizes the work of this paper.

II. USE CASE

In this section, we provide basic information about the manufacturing domain and describe our use case. Production lines can be equipped with different numbers of test stations. In a production line, many test stations can be arranged in sequence or in parallel. Various production errors can be detected at different test stations. While an error is detected at a specific station, measurements from preceding stations may contain clues about the error and thus it is possible to stop the production of corrupted parts earlier in the production process avoiding additional costs. To analyze this, it is important to link data from several test stations and trace back the individual products through the production line. A general description of a production line can be found in [8]. Within this scenario, we can use feature selection based on specific product errors to investigate their causes. The objective is to use machine learning on data from the test stations to predict and prevent production errors. However, the number of recorded test measurements is very high and only a fraction of the data is useful to explain specific errors. Surplus data can negatively impact the model performance. Therefore, it is important to reduce the number of features to train the ML model. Another reason to reduce the number of features is the explainability of correlations between errors and their underlying causes. After reduction, only a few features are left from the origin dataset. Thus, we also have reduced the search space for quality engineers that seek to understand error causes. A quality engineer often just has simple tools to investigate the data from the test stations. Without adjusted analyzing tools for this task, a quality engineer must search in a wide range of features for correlation with the product error. After the reduction of the dataset with a feature selection method, a quality engineer can analyze the product error with better focus on the relevant data and easier find the root cause. Another important point to be considered for ML training in our use case are the highly unbalanced datasets. These can severely impact the performance of a ML model, if not accounted for. This could be solved by using various sampling methods. Another method to tackle this challenge is to use weight parameters in learning models. In our experiments, we use weights and hyperparameter tuning to counteract the unbalanced dataset by adjusting the associated parameter with different ratios.

III. RELATED WORK

Zhang et al. [9] introduced a case study to optimize the process of a production by using feature selection methods was conducted. To do so, the authors used feature selection methods based on acceptance testing strategies. As a result, they show a reduction of 81% of inspection time while keeping the same accuracy with current industrial strategies to distinguish a non-qualified from a qualified product. An industrial strategy is e.g., acceptance sampling, which is commonly used as a statistical quality control method. The objective of the case study was to reduce the total testing time and optimize the production capability while still secure the accuracy of quality inspection for industrial products. Therefore, the reduction is not to meant to find an error cause, as in our use case. What is not considered in this reduction is that tests could be removed that would lead to the origin of a product error.

Liu et al. [10] show the problem of feature selection methods is investigated. They address the problem that standard feature selection methods do not take into account the imbalance of classes. During the selection process, the majority class is taken into account to a greater extent, which may lead to incorrectly selected features. To handle the problem, the F-measure metric was used for optimization, as it performs better on unbalanced data than accuracy does. For the investigation of the cost-sensitive classification, they generated and assigned various costs for the different classes based on a rigorous theory guidance. As result, they could reduce the number of features by optimizing with the F-measure metric. This work is similar to ours in terms of unbalanced data. [10] aim to reduce features in a cost-optimized way. Unlike the discussed work, we use a cost-based metric to optimize the results of real-world data and use further filter selection methods for our experiments.

The subject of cost-sensitive classifier and MetaCost is covered in [11]. Their approach uses a cost matrix with different costs for the errors. Afterwards, the classifier is adjusted based on this matrix. Due to the allocated costs of different errors, this approach is well suited for imbalanced datasets. A cost reduction can be accomplished with this approach compared to the cost-blind classifier. In this cost matrix the minority class was set to 0 and the majority class set to 1, based on a two-class (fail, no fail) classification. The error costs for the cost matrix was set to C(0,0) = C(1,1) = 0; C(0,1) = 1000; C(1,0) = 1000 *r*. In our approach the C(0,0) and C(0,1) cases are relevant, because they correspond to a corrupted product, that is predicted as such (factor C(0,0)) and a good product, that is predicted as bad product (factor C(0,1)).

Huang et al. [12] investigate the correlation and significance among labels for multi-label data. To handle this problem, they introduce label significance into cost-sensitive feature selection. Furthermore, they suggest a feature selection algorithm, which utilize test cost based on label significance. Three distributions (namely Uniform, Normal and Pareto distribution) with positive region generate a test cost matrix, which are combined with the suggest algorithm. Moreover, by analyzing the feature cost integrated in the positive region, they define a feature significance metric. As result, they could validate the efficiency of the algorithm with the influence of an additional parameter on various test costs in their experiments and analysis of the suggested method on four real datasets.

The subject of feature selection is a popular field in different applications or domains [13][14]. One of the important reasons to use feature selection is the reduction of high dimensional data. Another reason is to select only important features to explain a certain behavior or correlation. Also, in the domain of manufacturing feature selection is also an important aid [15][16]. Our work contributes to the case of manufacturing. We are using feature selection to reduce the original dataset, which helps us to identify the origin of error causes. We are doing so by optimizing with a cost-based metric. Further, we are using filter selection methods for our experiment and use case. By using filter selection methods, we can exchange the underlying algorithm without hesitation. This characteristic helps us in terms of AutoML. Regarding this, the related works do not provide specific insights in what optimization methods and metrics work best in the manufacturing domain.

Wrapper methods for feature selection evaluate a subset of all features using a specific machine learning algorithm. These have a pre-defined search strategy to check for the best possible result from the feature subsets [26]. Wrapper methods have a high computation time, especially for datasets with many features because it must search for the best subset of features. Our advantage compared to wrapper methods is that we use the filter methods to pre-sort the most important features. Therefore, we can always replace the learning algorithm (XGBoost) in the background with another one. Furthermore, we would also have a time advantage if, for example, only the n most important features should be taken. In addition, the ordered feature list can be used for further analyses. We also go through several subsets of the features, but these are already sorted by the feature importance.

Our work is inspired by the existing works and tests several approaches for handling feature selection and hyper parameter tuning with real world data. We thereby provide insights into the benefits of different optimization metrics and strategies under realistic conditions.

IV. FUNDAMENTALS

In this section, we describe fundamental concepts behind selection methods and metrics. We first introduce three different filter methods used in our experiments and afterwards two metrics.

ANalysis Of VAriance (ANOVA) is a statistical and state of the art approach to select features in datasets. ANOVA tests the statistical significance of mean differences among different groups of scores [17]. We chose SelectKBest [18] from scikit-learn as tool to implement ANOVA filter method for our experiments. The underlying feature scores are assigned by ANOVA F-Value [19], a metric which calculates linear dependencies between two variables. The advantage of ANOVA is that if there is little or no statistical significance, these features are considered late in the ordering and can often be excluded. A disadvantage of ANOVA is that it considers only one independent feature in relation to the prediction outcome.

Kendall's rank coefficient or also called Kendall's tau (τ) is a measure for the correlation between an observation of at least two ordinally scaled features x and y. The rank correlation shows the correlation between these variables, in which no hypothesis about the statistical distribution of the variables is made [20]. An advantage of Kendall's tau is the robustness against outliers. The disadvantage of this method is that some information of the original data can be lost, for example the true distribution function. We implemented the kendalltau function from the scipy.stats package for our experiments [21].

The permutation feature importance [22] is another method to select features from a dataset. The permutation feature importance for a classifier measures the impact of a feature on the performance of a model (e.g., the accuracy). In this procedure, the performance is measured with and without permuted values of the feature. The difference between the performance with and without permuted values is computed for each model and averaged to get the feature importance see e.g., [23]. A clear advantage of this is that it can handle different metrics. This leaves us a free space for our own metrics to use. A disadvantage of permutation feature importance is the higher computational cost, compared to ANOVA or Kendall's Rank. To calculate the permutation feature importance, we must execute first an independent algorithm.

To understand the metrics, we want to clarify the groups of the confusion matrix in the context of our use case. In our experiments, we focus on the minority class because product errors occur far less than good products in a production line. This fact should be considered when choosing the metrics. Firstly, a True Positive (TP) instance is a corrupted product, that is predicted as such. A False Positive (FP) instance is a good product, that is predicted as bad product. The next group is the False Negative (FN) instance, which represent a corrupted product, that is predicted as good product. The last group is the True Negative (TN) instance. This is a good product, which is predicted as such. The explained groups of the confusion matrix are used by the upcoming metrics, to calculate the performance of the ML model.

The first metric we want to describe is the Matthews Correlation Coefficient (MCC) [24]. The value of the MCC metric gets calculated by:

$$\mathrm{MCC} = \frac{\mathrm{TP} * \mathrm{TN} - \mathrm{FP} * \mathrm{FN}}{\sqrt{(\mathrm{TP}+\mathrm{FP})(\mathrm{TP}+\mathrm{FN})(\mathrm{TN}+\mathrm{FP})(TN+FN)}} \quad (1)$$

The MCC metric is a good solution for unbalanced datasets in terms of a binary classification. The MCC metric takes both classes into account and can therefore provide a good statement about the performance of the ML model. Moreover, the MCC metric has been increasingly used in the past years and is a state-of-the-art metric for a classification.

The following metric is our own cost-based metric, which is based on the cost formula of [11]. This metric is a calculation to predict the cost savings for all predictions. Symbol α represents the cost saving factor or ratio of savings of an identified error in relation to the costs of an instance incorrectly classified as an error. A quality engineer can adjust α for different products and can therefore decide product by product which ML configuration is the most suitable. Therefore, we want to use the Expected Benefit Rate (EBR) metric to maximise the possible savings for a company.

$$\text{Expected Benefit Rate} = \frac{\mathrm{TP} * \alpha - \mathrm{FP}}{\mathrm{TP}+\mathrm{FP}+\mathrm{TN}+\mathrm{FN}} \quad (2)$$

Within the EBR metric, the numerator represents the absolute savings or our expected benefit. We derive the formula from [11] and obtain the total costs by TP*C(0,0) + FP*C(0,1) + FN* C(1,0) + TN*C(1,1). Here the individual parts represent C(0,0) = α, C(0,1) = -1, C(1,0) = 0, C(1,1) = 0, which leads us to the numerator TP* α - FP. The denominator is used to normalize the savings by dividing the numerator by all instances. As result, we can show the expected benefit rate for all predictions. The EBR metric intends to demonstrate the benefits to use a ML system in production. Without a ML system, it is difficult to get hints on possible correlations in the data for the quality engineer. Without these hints on the origin of the error, we cannot save any costs, i.e., all instances must be classified as negative. Therefore, all error instances will belong to class FN. To describe a positive result, we use the terms of cost savings or benefit. Conversely, costs are negative savings or a negative benefit. By using a ML system, a previous FN could be turned into a TP, which increases savings in the production. To be precise, we would correctly predict a corrupted part that would otherwise proceed further in the production line. A FP would still produce costs but less than the savings of a TP, which we consider by α. By dividing the numerator by all predictions within the metric calculation, the result could be in the hundredths or thousandths range. The outcome result looks maybe like a small saving, but it is very profitable in mass production.

V. DESIGN OF FILTER SELECTION ALGORITHMS

This section is dedicated to the explanation of the implementation summarized as condensed pseudocode in Listing 1.

Listing 1: Pseudocode for feature selection

```
1.  Fselect(F, m, ≥r, p, T, V)
2.    S ← F, opt ← −∞
3.    Sort(F, ≥r)
4.    For i = 1 to |F|
5.      C ← {fk ∈F | k ≤ i}
6.      score ← m(C,p,T,V)
7.      If score > opt and lp < α
8.        opt ← score
9.        S ← C
10.   Return (S)
```

The pseudocode describes the core approach for all experiments. We subsequently discuss the pseudo code and the variations for the different experiment. Line 1 defines the parameters for the feature selection. In this representation, *F* is a set of features and *m(C,p,T,V)* is a metric that evaluates a prediction mechanism *p* that is trained over data *T* and evaluated on validation data *V*. The symbol $\geq_r$ is an ordering relation over features according to some importance measure, with (f1, f2) ∈ $\geq_r$ if f1 is more important than f2.

At the start, we define list *S* with F (all features), in the case that there will be no better result and a variable *opt* that we define as negative infinity in Line 2. A for-loop to iterate over the number of the features |*F*| is defined in Line 4. This is to implement a version of a sequential feature selection filter method. In Line 5 we select a current subset of features *C* within the for-loop, with the features f_k from the passed ordering relation over the features $\geq_r$. For every iteration, the next feature from F ordered by $\geq_r$ is added to *C*. In Line 6 we calculate the *score* based on the passed metric *m(C,p,T,V)* to optimize. Note, that m wraps the training process for the predictor p and is an important design choice. One may make compromises concerning the implementation for the sake of reducing computation time, e.g., implement m with or without hyperparameter optimization.

The calculation of *score* is followed by a check if the calculated *score* is greater than the *opt* variable and that *lp* is smaller than α. The *lp* variable represents the p-value from the two-sided dependent T-test [25] and α is set to 0.05. The p-value is calculated for the baseline model, which represent the model with all features trained and the current model within an iteration of the for-loop, to make sure that our current model is significantly better than the original model. If this condition is met, we update *opt* with the *score* value *in Line 8* and set *C* as *S in Line 9*. At the end, we return the feature list *S* in Line 10.

VI. EXPERIMENTS

We ran several experiments based on the approach that we introduced in the previous section. These experiments differ (1) in the way hyperparameter tuning is integrated and (2) in the implementations for the ordering relation $\geq r$.

We integrate hyperparameter tuning in three different ways. The basic approach (A) does not include any hyperparameter tuning. The predictor with default parameters is trained and used on data projected on the selected features. Experiment approach (B) adds hyperparameter tuning as subsequent step to approach (A). After returning *S* at the end of Listing 1, we reduce the original dataset to the selected features and optimize a new model with the parameters from TABLE 3. For the optimization via hyperparameter tuning, we went through all possible combinations of the parameters from TABLE 3, i.e., we implemented a grid search strategy. With this new optimized model, we create the final results. The third experiment approach (C) integrates hyperparameter tuning into the basic experiment (A) by optimizing the parameters of every single model during the training of mechanism m in line 5. At the end of the function, we return the best result and the selected features.

We consider three alternative methods in order to create the ordering $\geq r$. As a first case (a), features are ordered according to measurements based on ANOVA. An alternative sorting (b) is provided by Kendall's rank coefficient. As third method (c) we chose permutation feature importance. This procedure requires an additional ML model in advance to calculate the importance of each feature. Based on this, we create the ordered feature list using a certain metric, which was EBR or MCC, depending on the optimization.

We ran experiments with all possible settings of hyperparameter tuning. These include three variations with respect to the feature ranking $\geq r$, yielding a number of 18 sets of experiments in total (Optimizing according to EBR and MCC). To optimize the model, we used the training set for training and test set to evaluate the model. We continue to perform a final 10-fold cross validation with a T-test on the optimization metric based on the best model. Therefore, we ensure that the final model is not worse than the baseline model based on the training set. If so, we use the baseline model instead of the optimized model.

A. Test Setup

For our experiments, we used a machine with Windows 10 64Bit. The test system has an Intel(R) Xeon(R) W-2133(12x 3.60 GHz) processor and 32 GB RAM. We used the Anaconda Distribution with Numpy Version: 1.18.1, Pandas Version: 1.0.1, Scikit-learn Version: 0.22.1 and Python 3.7.6. All shown experiments were executed on the CPU. For the experiments, we used the well-known XGBoost algorithm with the version 0.90. XGBoost is a state-of-the-art algorithm to predict product quality [27]. Furthermore, the comprehensibility of the results is an important criterion for quality engineers, which is most likely to be fulfilled by decision trees [8].

TABLE 3: XGBOOST OPTIMIZATION PARAMETER

Hyperparameter	
n_estimators	50, 100, 150
max_depth	3, 6, 9
learning_rate	0.1, 0.3
class_weight	({0:1, 1:1}, ({0:1, 1:10}), ({0:1, 1:int(M)}), (M = (sum(negative instances) / sum(positive instances))

All optimizations for the experiment approaches B and C have been calculated using the parameter search space from TABLE 3.

B. Data Preparation for Training

To prepare the datasets for classification, we used a sequential split. The data is ordered by time. We set the split for the training set to first 67% of the total amount of errors in the data. Therefore, we have always 33% of the total amount of errors in the test set to validate the quality of the ML model.

C. Datasets

For our experiments, we used 25 highly unbalanced datasets from six different production lines. Within these production lines, we took the measurements from various sequential test stations and addressed various error messages. TABLE 2 shows the ratio between good and corrupted product parts.

TABLE 2: DATASETS

Dataset	Class 0	Class 1	Instances	Features	IR (Class 1 / Class 0)
A	57499	530	58029	64	0.009218
B	7127	73	7200	17	0.010243
C	88928	553	89481	23	0.006219
D	67065	1885	68950	133	0.028107
E	55204	1570	56776	29	0.028440
F	42894	1187	44081	33	0.027673
G	59321	245	59566	30	0.004130
H	43373	182	43555	90	0.004196
I	58345	799	59144	103	0.013694
J	55473	139	55612	64	0.002506
K	58585	1747	60332	19	0.029820
L	194318	614	194932	22	0.003160
M	6867	33	6900	34	0.004806
N	86664	388	87052	99	0.004477
O	6939	129	7068	38	0.018591
P	189809	233	190042	53	0.001228
Q	87292	388	87680	34	0.004445
R	43356	199	43555	90	0.004590
S	6854	33	6887	96	0.004815
T	11228	123	11351	22	0.010955
U	11349	48	11397	54	0.004229
V	13029	212	13241	30	0.016271
W	10604	117	10721	102	0.011034
X	89204	687	89891	17	0.007701
Y	190183	400	190583	20	0.002103

Class 0 represents a good and Class 1 represents a corrupted product part. The imbalance of the two classes is shown by the column IR. Dataset K has the highest IR value with 0.02982 and dataset P the lowest with 0.001228. This fact stresses the importance of considering imbalance in the domain of manufacturing, in particular for highly optimized production lines. For our experiments we use numerical and categorical data. Numerical values are measurements from one or several combined test stations.

A further point is the number of features of the datasets. Especially interesting are the datasets D, H, I, N, R, S, W because of the high number of features (90+). The effect of the feature reduction should be seen clearly on these.

VII. EVALUATION

In this section, we present the results from the executed experiments. We used all three presented feature ranking methods for each optimization approach. The objective was to find out, which combination of ranking and optimization approach is the most suitable regarding the prediction quality and execution time. To evaluate the results with one key figure we used the EBR metric. Even if we optimize according to MCC we calculate the EBR value to compare. We set $\alpha=10$ in our experiments. According to our project partner, this is a reasonable assumption for α in many cases. However, the specific values may vary greatly throughout the production lines and error types. Yet, we keep a fixed number to make the results on different experiments comparable. For the analysis, we first compared the EBR value and the number of necessary features.

InTABLE 3, we show the baseline results of the test without any optimization, filter methods or the use of the Fselect function. These results are our baseline to compare later results and were created with the standard settings from the XGBoost algorithm. For the baseline results, we do not consider the imbalance of the classes. There are several aspects to point out inTABLE 3. First, some datasets have a high number of features. The next point is the EBR value. If an EBR value is 0, this does not mean that the model did not find a relation in the data, but the predicted error probabilities are too low for making an economically reasonable error prediction (i.e., the cost for false positives would outweigh the savings through true positives and hence TP = 0, FP = 0). These results do not provide a meaningful prediction, but they show a possible hint to the quality engineer regarding the error causes. A further point is the negative EBR value. In this case, the model estimated the confidence in error prediction too high, resulting in higher cost through false positive predictions than savings through true positive results.

TABLE 4 shows the results of the experiment approach A. To highlight the best results (best EBR, using the number of features as tie-breaker) for a dataset in TABLE 4 and following tables, these lines are colored with a green background color. If there is no green background color in a

TABLE 3: BASELINE RESULTS
(MODELL TRAINED WITH ALL FEATURES)

Dataset	Features	EBR Value	Dataset	Features	EBR Value
A	64	0.00042199	N	99	-0.000073042462
B	17	0.03246753	O	38	-0.003707627
C	23	0.00050081	P	53	0
D	133	0.21394069	Q	34	-0.000193916
E	29	0.00270392	R	90	0.074146982
F	33	0.00084728	S	96	0
G	30	0	T	22	0
H	90	-0.00040975	U	54	0
I	103	0.00157487	V	30	0.001569859
J	64	0	W	102	0.002081165
K	19	0	X	17	0.001777727
L	22	0	Y	20	0
M	34	-0.00021906			

TABLE 4: EXPERIMENT APPROACH A

Dataset Name	ANOVA				Kendall's rank coefficient				Permutation Feature Importance			
	Optimized according to EBR		Optimized according to MCC		Optimized according to EBR		Optimized according to MCC		Optimized according to EBR		Optimized according to MCC	
	Features	EBR Value	Features	EBR Value	Features	EBR Value	Features	EBR Value	Features	EBR Value	Features	EBR Value
A	64	0.000421987	64	0.000421987	64	0.000421987	64	0.000421987	64	0.000421987	64	0.000421987
B	17	0.032467532	17	0.032467532	17	0.032467532	17	0.032467532	17	0.032467533	17	0.032467533
C	23	0.000500814	17	0.00109553	23	0.000500814	23	0.000500814	23	0.000500814	23	0.000500814
D	2	0.213996855	2	0.213996855	1	0.213996855	1	0.213996855	133	0.213940688	133	0.213940688
E	2	0.000600871	2	0.000600871	7	0.000600871	7	0.000600871	2	0.00135196	3	0.00135196
F	33	0.000847278	33	0.000847278	33	0.000847278	33	0.000847278	33	0.000847278	4	0.00021182
G	1	0	30	0	1	0	30	0	1	0	30	0
H	1	0	1	0	1	0	1	0	1	0	1	0
I	1	0	89	0.00157487	1	0	103	0.00157487	1	0.001532306	1	0.001532306
J	64	0	64	0	64	0	64	0	64	0	64	0
K	1	0	1	0	1	0	1	0	1	0	1	0
L	22	0	22	0	22	0	22	0	22	0	22	0
M	34	-0.000219058	34	-0.000219058	34	-0.000219058	34	-0.000219058	34	-0.000219058	34	-0.000219058
N	1	0	2	-0.032576938	1	0	1	0	99	-0.000073042462	99	-0.000073042462
O	38	-0.003707627	38	-0.003707627	38	-0.003707627	38	-0.003707627	38	-0.003707627	38	-0.003707627
P	53	0	53	0	53	0	53	0	53	0	53	0
Q	1	0	2	-0.034856381	1	0	1	0	34	-0.000193916	34	-0.000193916
R	4	0.067585302	9	0.067585302	4	0.067585302	1	0.077427822	5	0.077755906	5	0.077755906
S	96	0	31	0	74	0	25	0	16	0	18	0
T	22	0	5	0	22	0	22	0	22	0	16	0
U	54	0	54	0	54	0	54	0	54	0	54	0
V	30	0.001569859	30	0.001569859	30	0.001569859	2	0.001098901	30	0.001569859	30	0.001569859
W	102	0.002081165	102	0.002081165	102	0.002081165	102	0.002081165	102	0.002081166	6	0.004682622
X	3	0.002599687	2	0.002007111	3	0.002599687	2	0.002007111	1	0.001835073	1	0.001835073
Y	20	0	20	0	20	0	20	0	20	0	20	0

TABLE 5: EXPERIMENT APPROACH B

Dataset Name	ANOVA				Kendall's rank coefficient				Permutation Feature Importance			
	Optimized according to EBR		Optimized according to MCC		Optimized according to EBR		Optimized according to MCC		Optimized according to EBR		Optimized according to MCC	
	Features	EBR Value	Features	EBR Value	Features	EBR Value	Features	EBR Value	Features	EBR Value	Features	EBR Value
A	64	-0.014659475	64	-0.000990753	64	-0.014659475	64	-0.000990753	64	-0.014659475	64	-0.000990753
B	17	0.032467532	17	0.032467532	17	0.032467532	17	0.032467532	17	0.032467533	17	0.032467533
C	23	0.000500814	17	0.019531739	23	0.000500814	23	0.019531739	23	0.000500814	23	0.019531739
D	2	0.213996855	2	0.213996855	1	0.213996855	1	0.213996855	133	0.213940688	133	0.213940688
E	2	0.029968454	2	0.000600871	7	0.031320415	7	0.004206099	2	0.000225327	3	0.00135196
F	33	0.000847278	33	0.008825814	33	0.000847278	33	0.008825814	33	0.000847278	4	0.018428299
G	1	0	30	0	1	0	30	0	1	0	30	0
H	1	0	1	-0.233302602	1	0	1	0	1	0	1	-0.233302602
I	1	0	89	0.000595897	1	0	103	0.00157487	1	0.001532306	1	-0.632459351
J	64	0	64	-0.3219757	64	0	64	-0.3219757	64	0	64	-0.3219757
K	1	0	1	-0.21820103	1	0	1	-0.356447849	1	0	1	-0.119182847
L	22	0	22	0	22	0	22	0	22	0	22	0
M	34	-0.000219058	34	-0.000219058	34	-0.000219058	34	-0.000219058	34	-0.000219058	34	-0.000219058
N	1	-0.001436502	2	-0.651952668	1	0	1	-0.965450915	99	-0.151806584	99	-0.151806584
O	38	-0.003707627	38	-0.003707627	38	-0.003707627	38	-0.003707627	38	-0.003707627	38	-0.003707627
P	53	0	53	0	53	0	53	0	53	0	53	0
Q	1	0	2	-0.965604169	1	0	1	-0.163955884	34	-0.000193916	34	-0.05189674
R	4	0.125	9	0.074146982	4	0.125	1	0.163385827	5	0.130249344	5	0.077755906
S	96	0	31	0	74	0	25	0	16	0	18	0
T	22	0	5	0	22	0	22	0	22	0	16	0
U	54	0	54	0	54	0	54	0	54	0	54	0
V	30	0.001569859	30	0.006279435	30	0.001569859	2	-0.001098901	30	0.001569859	30	0.006279435
W	102	0.012747138	102	0.004162331	102	0.012747138	102	0.004162331	102	0.012747138	6	0.002341311
X	3	0.01062813	2	0.010226708	3	0.01062813	2	0.010226708	1	0.009137134	1	0.009997324
Y	20	0	20	-0.066429903	20	0	20	-0.066429903	20	0	20	-0.066429903

line, there are only identical results and therefore no winner. For this experiment we also used the standard parameters for the algorithm and did not consider the unbalanced dataset. Compared to Table 3 we improved the result in 16 out of 75 experiments based on the EBR optimization. However, this is contrasted by eight deteriorations compared to the baseline. One of the possible reasons for the deterioration of results is a concept drift in the data. During the training, a model was found that performed better on the training set but afterward worse based on the test set. This is because the production processes are subject to constant change. With these results, we can show that our safety mechanism based on the T-test is working. That is, we avoid significant deterioration through failed optimization while gaining benefits when the optimization works. We can already notice an improvement in approach A compared to the baseline results. We were able to reduce dataset X to 3 out of 17 features with ANOVA. Dataset D could be reduced from 133 to 1 feature using

TABLE 6: EXPERIMENT APPROACH C

Dataset Name	ANOVA				Kendall's rank coefficient				Permutation Feature Importance			
	Optimized according to EBR		Optimized according to MCC		Optimized according to EBR		Optimized according to MCC		Optimized according to EBR		Optimized according to MCC	
	Features	EBR Value	Features	EBR Value	Features	EBR Value	Features	EBR Value	Features	EBR Value	Features	EBR Value
A	30	-0.124339498	64	0.000421987	44	-0.095901218	47	-0.056032585	19	-0.005082196	29	0.002843828
B	2	0.037962038	17	0.032467532	3	0.061938062	17	0.032467532	2	0.058941059	14	0.044955045
C	5	0.019093527	23	0.000500814	5	0.019093527	5	0.019250031	1	0.013334168	1	0.0134593715
D	2	0.213996855	133	0.213940687	2	0.213996855	2	0.213996855	133	0.213940688	133	0.213940688
E	3	0.027264534	29	0.002703921	7	0.031320415	7	0.002103049	5	0.031921286	6	0.003530119
F	25	0.003177293	33	0.000847278	30	0.005154275	30	0.005154275	14	0.014333122	12	0.014756761
G	1	0	30	0	1	0	16	-0.045876679	1	0	2	-0.069512535
H	1	0	90	-0.000409752	1	0	3	-0.214146691	1	0	29	-0.020692481
I	1	0	103	0.00157487	23	0.001234358	23	0.002085639	1	0.001532306	1	-0.632459351
J	64	0	64	0	64	0	24	-0.102042613	64	0	3	-0.387920409
K	1	0	19	0	1	0	6	-0.226214062	1	0	1	-0.119182847
L	22	0	22	0	22	0	22	0	22	0	2	-0.367024358
M	34	-0.000219058	34	-0.000219058	34	-0.000219058	34	-0.000219058	34	-0.000219058	2	-0.120920044
N	1	-0.001436502	99	-0.000073042462	1	0	1	-0.965450915	61	-0.239652318	10	-0.350311648
O	4	-0.094632768	38	-0.003707627	1	-0.01059322	20	-0.000706215	9	-0.002295198	8	-0.000176554
P	53	0	53	0	53	0	53	0	53	0	53	0
Q	2	-0.128663192	34	-0.000193916	1	0	1	-0.163955884	34	-0.000193916	34	-0.05189674
R	2	0.107611549	90	0.074146982	2	0.107611549	4	0.125	2	0.107611549	9	0.144685039
S	40	0.002192982	96	0	29	0	6	-0.000877193	14	0	14	0
T	5	0	22	0	22	0	5	0	22	0	1	-0.235951417
U	54	0	54	0	54	0	10	0.000895255	54	0	12	-0.002088929
V	2	-0.00266876	30	0.001569859	3	-0.000784929	2	-0.000941915	1	0.003296703	30	0.006279435
W	29	0.010665973	102	0.002081165	8	0.014308012	6	0.008584807	6	0.020031218	15	0.00364204
X	3	0.01062813	17	0.001777727	3	0.01062813	3	0.01062813	1	0.009137134	1	0.009997324
Y	20	0	20	0	20	0	7	-0.044448366	20	0	6	-0.075010754

TABLE 7: EXECUTION TIME COMPARISON

Dataset Name	Experiment Approach A			Experiment Approach B			Experiment Approach C		
	ANOVA Execution Time	Kendall's rank coefficient Execution Time	Permutation Feature Importance Execution Time	ANOVA Execution Time	Kendall's rank coefficient Execution Time	Permutation Feature Importance Execution Time	ANOVA Execution Time	Kendall's rank coefficient Execution Time	Permutation Feature Importance Execution Time
A	0:00:48	0:00:48	0:00:47	0:02:54	0:02:54	0:02:55	1:25:45	1:33:30	1:26:19
B	0:00:09	0:00:09	0:00:07	0:00:51	0:00:51	0:00:49	0:09:33	0:10:44	0:09:36
C	0:01:17	0:01:16	0:01:16	0:09:36	0:09:18	0:09:16	2:01:46	2:13:55	2:01:46
D	0:21:54	0:22:51	0:25:27	0:23:27	0:23:37	1:03:34	41:04:49	47:06:54	47:58:57
E	0:01:16	0:01:21	0:01:11	0:02:51	0:04:24	0:02:36	2:24:09	2:40:13	2:14:30
F	0:01:12	0:01:11	0:01:05	0:07:19	0:07:09	0:06:59	2:10:01	2:24:19	1:59:42
G	0:01:04	0:01:00	0:01:04	0:02:10	0:02:03	0:02:11	2:01:41	2:05:21	2:01:08
H	0:04:36	0:04:35	0:04:45	0:05:24	0:05:04	0:05:40	8:35:13	9:13:34	8:53:49
I	0:17:07	0:15:38	0:15:30	0:18:19	0:16:36	0:16:38	32:33:45	33:00:00	29:47:19
J	0:05:26	0:05:21	0:05:25	0:20:25	0:20:25	0:20:24	9:20:57	9:54:35	9:17:51
K	0:00:37	0:00:38	0:00:39	0:01:25	0:01:14	0:01:49	1:02:49	1:08:30	1:11:56
L	0:03:05	0:03:05	0:02:58	0:25:21	0:25:18	0:25:08	5:04:10	5:33:01	4:50:34
M	0:00:08	0:00:09	0:00:09	0:00:41	0:00:42	0:00:42	0:14:31	0:16:18	0:14:33
N	0:10:26	0:10:19	0:10:55	0:11:45	0:11:04	0:31:19	17:56:08	19:27:29	18:37:31
O	0:00:08	0:00:09	0:00:08	0:00:43	0:00:43	0:00:43	0:17:39	0:19:18	0:17:51
P	0:12:02	0:12:03	0:12:07	0:53:41	0:53:13	0:53:56	21:01:48	22:33:36	21:19:08
Q	0:01:40	0:01:39	0:01:51	0:03:03	0:02:26	0:10:06	2:51:35	3:04:39	3:00:01
R	0:07:39	0:07:35	0:07:19	0:09:11	0:09:03	0:09:11	10:48:54	11:48:45	10:27:05
S	0:00:45	0:00:44	0:00:47	0:01:46	0:01:38	0:01:13	1:04:45	1:11:51	1:06:39
T	0:00:09	0:00:09	0:00:10	0:01:13	0:01:13	0:01:13	0:16:26	0:18:17	0:16:57
U	0:00:43	0:00:44	0:00:44	0:02:32	0:02:34	0:02:34	1:06:24	1:12:42	1:07:40
V	0:00:19	0:00:19	0:00:20	0:01:55	0:01:55	0:01:55	0:35:19	0:38:05	0:35:08
W	0:02:07	0:02:03	0:02:05	0:05:20	0:05:16	0:05:21	3:28:33	3:41:16	3:27:00
X	0:00:31	0:00:32	0:00:31	0:02:13	0:02:13	0:01:41	0:55:23	1:00:46	0:55:43
Y	0:02:06	0:02:07	0:02:06	0:18:11	0:19:31	0:18:11	3:18:35	3:34:56	3:16:28

Kendall's rank. For dataset I, we reduced the number of features from 103 to 1 using Permutation Feature Importance. In TABLE 4, we show that the ANOVA selection method was the best for approach A. In TABLE 5, we show the results of experiment approach B. For Dataset X (ANOVA), parameter optimization improved the result from 0.002599687 to 0.01062813 for the same number of features. However, some results are already optimized by a reduction to the most important features e.g., dataset D with Kendall's rank or dataset I with permutation feature importance. In this approach we could provide 21 out of 75 better and nine worse results based on the EBR optimization compared to TABLE 3. Therefore, we show a benefit to adjust the parameter of the algorithm to provide better results with this approach. With approach B we improved 11 out of 75 results and six out of 75 got worse based on the EBR optimization compared to approach A. For approach B the Kendall's rank provided the best method for the feature selection if we consider the results from the EBR and MCC optimization.

In TABLE 6, we visualized the results from approach C. Within this table we can show the most changes in the number of features and the difference between the optimization metric. First, we provide 16 out of 25 best results based on the EBR and MCC optimization with the Kendall's rank selection method in this approach. We also could reduce in 21 out of 75 cases the number of features and improve the result by optimizing with the EBR metric. In contrast, we only could reduce and improve the results twice by optimizing with the MCC metric. Here, we can clearly show the benefit to use our cost-based metric. Compared to approach B we improve 20

TABLE 8: RESULT OVERVIEW

	Number of tests where BEST results is with EBR	Number of tests where BEST results is with MCC	Number of tests where BEST results is with EBR and Features reduced	Number of tests where BEST results is with MCC and Features reduced	Number of tests where optimizing with EBR is BETTER than baseline	Number of tests where optimizing with MCC is BETTER than baseline	Number of tests where optimizing with EBR is WORSE than baseline	Number of tests where optimizing with MCC is WORSE than baseline
Approach A, ANOVA	3	2	2	1	5	4	3	4
Approach A, Kendall	2	2	0	1	2	3	3	2
Approach A, Permutation	1	1	0	1	5	3	2	3
Approach B, ANOVA	10	5	3	1	7	4	3	9
Approach B, Kendall	9	5	0	1	5	7	1	7
Approach B, Permutation	8	6	0	1	5	6	4	9
Approach C, ANOVA	10	6	9	0	9	0	6	0
Approach C, Kendall	12	6	1	1	8	9	4	11
Approach C, Permutation	15	7	4	2	10	10	3	12

results and got worse in 15 cases based on the EBR result. As mentioned before, the deterioration of the results may be due to a concept drift in the data.

In TABLE 7, we compare the computation time needed for each experiment approach for different datasets. We colored the best time results with different colors for each approach. For the experiment approach A the permutation feature importance selection method achieved in 11 out of 25 cases the best results. At experiment approach B the Kendall's rank selection method achieved in 13 out of 25 cases the best time results. For experiment approach C, the ANOVA selection method achieved in 15 out of 25 datasets the best time result.

When comparing experiment approach A and C in terms of the EBR result and required time, we can point out that the use of hyperparameter tuning does show a significant enhancing effect in most of our experiments. However, the calculation time for 19 datasets was demanding in terms of time (over one hour needed), especially in dataset D. With the experiment approach A and the benefit of EBR metric, we can demonstrate a significant advantage towards the baseline. Nevertheless, the experiment approach C could be used to obtain the best possible result. We summarize all experiments and results in a brief overview in TABLE 8. In this table we can show that an optimization according to MCC achieves better results than the baseline, but also often worsens especially in Approach C Kendall's rank and permutation feature importance. Therefore, we recommend optimization according to EBR.

VIII. CONCLUSION

In this paper, we showed three filter methods and used adapted cost-based metric EBR, to reduce features in real manufacturing datasets. Regarding the research questions from the introduction, we demonstrate benefits in a real-world use case, which answers Q1. We showed a benefit by using different filter methods and optimizing the XGBoost algorithm with the EBR metric. However, the different filter methods overall yield similar results. We obtain most of the best results with experiment approach C. Experiment approach B is favorable with respect to computation time. These findings provide insights on Q2. Overall, most of the best results for the experiment approaches were achieved by using the permutation feature importance selection method based on TABLE 8. Moreover, we have shown that more features of the dataset can be reduced when using the EBR metric compared to the MCC metric. This answers our question Q3. The answer for question Q4 depends on the experiment approach. The time difference between experiment approaches A and B is tolerable for better results. The training duration of a model is especially important to consider as soon as many models must be trained in parallel for different products. Especially because there are only limited computing resources. However, the Kendall's rank selection method could be used in combination with experiment approach B as fastest method regarding the best possible results. To summarize our contributions in this paper, we state the following:

First, we showed benefits of feature reduction in our use case with highly unbalanced real-world data. Second, using our EBR metric reduces the number of features in comparison to the MCC in our experiments. Third, the experiment approach B indicates the best improvement compared to the baseline regarding the computation time.

ACKNOWLEDGEMENTS

This project was funded by the German Federal Ministry of Education and Research, funding line "Forschung an Fachhochschulen mit Unternehmen (FHProfUnt) ", contract number 13FH249PX6. The responsibility for the content of this publication lies with the authors. Also, we want to thank the company SICK AG for the cooperation and partial funding.

REFERENCES

[1] Z. Li, Z. Zhang, J. Shi, and D. Wu, "Prediction of surface roughness in extrusion-based additive manufacturing with machine learning," Robotics and Computer-Integrated Manufacturing, vol. 57, pp. 488-495, 2019 doi:10.1016/j.rcim.2019.01.004.

[2] V. Hirsch, P. Reimann, and B. Mitschang, "Data-Driven Fault Diagnosis in End-of-Line Testing of Complex Products," 2019 IEEE International Conference on Data Science and Advanced Analytics (DSAA), 2019, doi:10.1109/dsaa.2019.00064.

[3] J. C. Ang, A. Mirzal, H. Haron, and H. N. A. Hamed, "Supervised, unsupervised, and semi-supervised feature selection: a review on gene selection," IEEE/ACM transactions on computational biology and bioinformatics, vol. 13, no. 5, pp. 971-989, 2015.

[4] Y. Peng, Z. Wu, and J. Jiang, "A novel feature selection approach for biomedical data classification," Journal of Biomedical Informatics, vol. 43, no. 1, pp. 15-23, 2010.

[5] L. Kotthoff, C. Thornton, H. H. Hoos, F. Hutter, and K. Leyton-Brown, "Auto-WEKA: Automatic Model Selection and Hyperparameter Optimization in WEKA," Automated Machine Learning The Springer Series on Challenges in Machine Learning, pp. 81-95, 2019, doi:10.1007/978-3-030-05318-5_4.

[6] E. LeDell and S. Poirier, "H2o automl: Scalable automatic machine learning," In Proceedings of the AutoML Workshop at ICML vol. 2020, 2020.

[7] H. Ziekow et al., "Proactive Error Prevention in Manufacturing Based on an Adaptable Machine Learning Environment," From Research to Application, vol. 113, 2019.

[8] A. Gerling et al., "A Reference Process Model for Machine Learning Aided Production Quality Management," Proceedings of the 22nd International Conference on Enterprise Information Systems, 2020, doi:10.5220/0009379705150523.

[9] Y. Zhang, E. Tochev, S. Ratchev, and C. German, "Production process optimization using feature selection methods," Procedia CIRP, vol. 88, pp. 554-559, 2020.

[10] M. Liu et al., "Cost-sensitive feature selection by optimizing F-measures," IEEE Transactions on Image Processing, vol. 27m no. 3, pp. 1323-1335, 2017.

[11] P. Domingos, "MetaCost: A General Method for Making Classifiers Cost-Sensitive," Proceedings of the Fifth ACM SIGKDD International Conference on Knowledge Discovery and Data Mining - KDD '99, 1999, doi:10.1145/312129.312220.

[12] J. Huang, W. Qian, B. Wu, and Y. Wang, "Cost-Sensitive Feature Selection Based on Label Significance and Positive Region," In 2019 International Conference on Machine Learning and Cybernetics (ICMLC), pp. 1-7, 2019.

[13] M. Ali and T. Aittokallio, "Machine learning and feature selection for drug response prediction in precision oncology applications," Biophysical reviews, vol. 11, no. 1, pp. 31-39, 2019.

[14] Y. Liu, J. W. Bi, and Z. P. Fan, "Multi-class sentiment classification: The experimental comparisons of feature selection and machine learning algorithms," Expert Systems with Applications, vol. 80, pp. 323-339, 2017.

[15] H. Liu, M. Zhou, and Q. Liu, "An embedded feature selection method for imbalanced data classification," IEEE/CAA Journal of Automatica Sinica, vol. 6, no. 3, pp. 703-715, 2019.

[16] F. Feng, K. C. Li, J. Shen, Q. Zhou, and X. Yang, "Using cost-sensitive learning and feature selection algorithms to improve the performance of imbalanced classification," IEEE Access, vol. 8, pp. 69979-69996, 2020.

[17] B. G. Tabachnick and L. S. Fidell, "Experimental designs using" ANOVA, Belmont, CA: Thomson/Brooks/Cole, pp. 724, 2007.

[18] SelectKBest, Sklearn.feature_selection.SelectKBest, from https://scikit-learn.org/stable/modules/generated/sklearn.feature_selection.SelectKBest.html, (n.d.). Retrieved October 01, 2020

[19] F_classif, Sklearn.feature_selection.f_classif, from https://scikit-learn.org/stable/modules/generated/sklearn.feature_selection.f_classif.html, (n.d.). Retrieved October 05, 2020.

[20] K. Siebertz and D. van Bebber, Statistische versuchsplanung. T. Hochkirchen (Ed.). Springer Berlin Heidelberg, 2010.

[21] Kendalltau, Scipy.stats.kendalltau, from https://docs.scipy.org/doc/scipy-0.15.1/reference/generated/scipy.stats.kendalltau.html, (n.d.). Retrieved October 05, 2020.

[22] A. Altmann, L. Toloşi, O. Sander, and T. Lengauer, "Permutation importance: a corrected feature importance measure," Bioinformatics, vol. 26, no 10, pp. 1340-1347, 2010.

[23] G. Casalicchio, C. Molnar, and B. Bischl, "Visualizing the feature importance for black box models," In Joint European Conference on Machine Learning and Knowledge Discovery in Databases, Springer, Cham, pp. 655-670, September 2018.

[24] B.W. Matthews, "Comparison of the Predicted and Observed Secondary Structure of T4 Phage Lysozyme," Biochimica Et Biophysica Acta (BBA) - Protein Structure, vol. 405, no. 2, pp. 442–51, 1975, https://doi.org/10.1016/0005-2795(75)90109-9.

[25] SciPy.org, scipy.stats.ttest_ind - SciPy v1.6.3 Reference Guide. (n.d.). https://docs.scipy.org/doc/scipy/reference/generated/scipy.stats.ttest_ind.html, May 2021.

[26] Y. B. Wah, N. Ibrahim, H. A. Hamid, S. Abdul-Rahman, and S. Fong, "Feature Selection Methods: Case of Filter and Wrapper Approaches for Maximising Classification Accuracy," Pertanika Journal of Science & Technology, vol. 26, no. 1, 2018.

[27] N. Zhou, Q. Ren, and J. Zhou, "Identification of Critical-to-quality Characteristics Based on Improved XGBoost," In Proceedings of the 3rd International Conference on Data Science and Information Technology, pp. 205-209, July 2020.

Modelling the Consistency between Customer Opinion and Online Rating with VADER Sentiment and Bayesian Networks

Alexandros Bousdekis
Department of Business Administration
School of Business, Athens University of Economics and Business
Athens, Greece
e-mail: albous@mail.ntua.gr

Dimitris Kardaras
Department of Business Administration
School of Business, Athens University of Economics and Business
Athens, Greece
e-mail: dkkardaras@yahoo.co.uk

Stavroula Barbounaki
Merchant Marine Academy of Aspropyrgos
Aspropyrgos, Greece
e-mail: sbarbounaki@yahoo.gr

***Abstract*— Customers have access to different sources of information, and generate their own content and share their views and experiences which are expressed through online review comments and ratings about products and services. However, the increasing amount of data has reached a level that makes manual processing impossible, requiring data-driven approaches. Sentiment analysis is rapidly emerging as an automated process of examining semantic relationships and meaning in reviews. Despite the large amount of research works dealing with sentiment analysis, the consistency between the customer opinions expressed in review comments and the rating that they provide has not been explored. In this paper, we propose an approach incorporating the Valence Aware Dictionary for Sentiment Reasoning (VADER) algorithm for extracting the polarity of the review comments and Bayesian Networks for revealing the relationships between the aforementioned sentiment scores and the online rating. The proposed approach was validated in the tourism domain using a dataset with hotel reviews, extracted from the TripAdvisor.**

Keywords—sentiment analysis; probabilistic model; machine learning; data analytics; hotel review; tourism management; opinion mining.

I. Introduction

Customers have access to different sources of information, and generate their own content and share their views and experiences which are expressed through online review comments and ratings about products and services. However, the increasing amount of data has reached a level that makes manual processing impossible, requiring data-driven approaches. Sentiment analysis is rapidly emerging as an automated process of examining semantic relationships and meaning in reviews. Analyzing the sentiment tendency of consumer evaluation can not only provide a reference for other consumers but also help businesses on e-commerce platforms to improve service quality and consumer satisfaction [1].

E-commerce platforms use ratings in order to quantify customer's preferences and satisfaction on products and services. Several techniques like clustering, nearest-neighbour methods, matrix manipulations, point-of interest modelling have been used to model user interest patterns so as to maximize purchase satisfaction [2]. However, these ratings are biased by certain hidden factors like brand adherence and product-prejudice [2]. On the other hand, review comments is a valuable source of data related to customers' opinions. However, different people use different ways of expressing themselves, leading to variations in the sentiment scores. In addition, the customers select some main points to be mentioned in the review comments. However, there are various aspects that affect their level of satisfaction and their preferences that are not mentioned at all and remain at their own mind. In this sense, there may be review comments with similar content and sentiment but different ratings. These facts lead to inconsistencies between the customer opinions expressed in review comments and the rating that they provide.

Despite the large amount of research works dealing with sentiment analysis, the consistency between the customer opinions expressed in review comments and the rating that they provide has not been explored. In this paper, we propose an approach incorporating the Valence Aware Dictionary for Sentiment Reasoning (VADER) algorithm for extracting the polarity of the review comments and Bayesian Networks for revealing the relationships between the aforementioned sentiment scores and the online rating. The proposed approach was validated in the tourism domain using a dataset with hotel reviews, extracted from the TripAdvisor.

The rest of the paper is organized as follows: Section II describes the related work with a focus on sentiment classification of review comments and analysis of review rating. Section III presents the proposed approach for modelling the consistency between customer opinion and online rating. Section III presents and discusses the results of the application of the proposed approach to the e-tourism domain. Section IV concludes the paper and outlines our plans for future work.

II. Related Work

Sentiment analysis uses algorithms to extract and analyse opinions from text (e.g., customers online reviews), as well as to identify positive, neutral and negative opinions to measure a customer's attitude toward an issue [3]. In other words, sentiment analysis aims at identifying the polarity of text by extracting sentiments, opinions and emotions [4][5]. There is a wide range of applications, from customer satisfaction to political opinions [5], or even diagnosis of health care related problems identified by the patients themselves [6]. Sentiment analysis does not correspond to one single problem but it may incorporate several different objectives, such as: sentiment classification (e.g., polarity determination, vagueness resolution), subjectivity classification, and opinion spam detection [2][3][7].

A. *Sentiment Classification of Review Comments*

Sentiment classification is a widely explored research area with a variety of methods and techniques that have been proposed in the literature. There are three main categories of approaches [7][8]: (i) lexicon dictionary-based methods; (ii) machine learning-based methods; and, (iii) hybrid methods.

Lexicon dictionary-based methods deal with creating a sentiment lexicon, i.e., words carrying a sentiment orientation [9][10]. These methods can create the dictionary from initial seed words, corpus words (related to a specific domain) or combining the two. Frequently, the dictionary is fed with synonyms and antonyms [8]. One of the most well-known dictionary-based algorithms is VADER [11]. The increasing amounts of data generated by commercial platforms in which the customers are able to rate and comment on products and services has fostered the emergence of various data-driven approaches for sentiment analysis [12]. However, the machine learning approach requires an already labelled dataset to learn from, and it is not certain that knowledge learned in one domain is transferable to another domain [5]. Such approaches usually require human intervention to obtain the sentiment category of the input text. Traditional machine learning methods commonly used include Naive Bayes [13][14], Support Vector Machine [13][15], K-Nearest Neighbor [16], maximum entropy [17], logistic regression [18], Random Forest [19] and conditional random fields model [1].

B. *Analysis of Review Ratings*

Several research works propose approaches, methods and algorithms that also incorporate the review ratings provided directly by the customer. Chua and Banerjee [20] examined review helpfulness as a function of reviewer reputation, review rating, and review depth. Chen et al. [21] introduced an attention mechanism to explore the usefulness of reviews, and proposed a Neural Attentional Regression model with Review-level Explanations (NARRE) for recommendation. Hassan and Shoaib [22] presented a Gated-Recurrent-Unit (GRU) based Recurrent Neural Network (RNN) architecture for multi-class review rating classification problem. Their model incorporates domain-specific word embeddings and does not depend on the reviewer's information. Ahmed and Ghabayen [23] proposed a review rating prediction framework using deep learning. Seo et al. [24] proposed to model user preferences and item properties using Convolutional Neural Networks (CNNs) with dual local and global attention, motivated by the superiority of CNNs to extract complex features. By using aggregated review texts from a user and aggregated review text for an item, their model can learn the unique features (embedding) of each user and each item. Songpan [25] proposed the analysis and prediction rating from customer reviews who commented as open opinion using probability's classifier model. Overall, the embodiment of review ratings along with the review comments shows a potential to further enhance the algorithms in providing predictions but also extracting useful insights on the performance of products and services. However, they pose additional challenges to their modelling capabilities due to the inconsistencies existing between the review text and the review rating.

III. The Proposed Approach for Modelling the Relationship between Customer Sentiment and Online Rating

In this section, we present our proposed approach for modelling the consistency between customer opinion and online rating. Customer opinions may be explicitly mentioned with the use of ratings and binary feedback, implicitly mentioned through online review comments, and not mentioned at all by not expressing their preferences, satisfaction or dissatisfaction for specific aspects. This classification is depicted in Figure 1. Most of the time, there are combinations of opinion's expression.

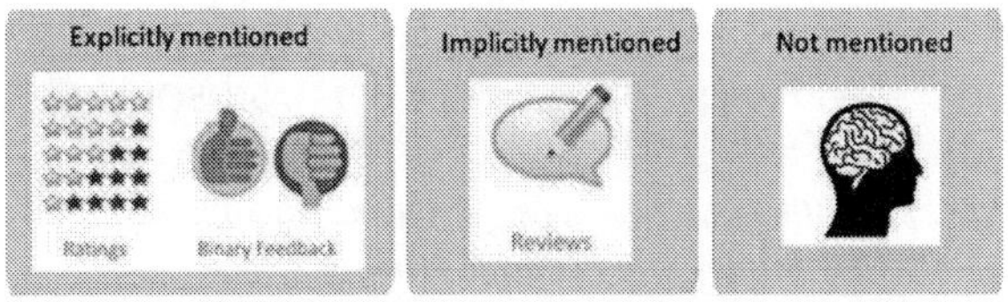

Figure 1. The steps of the proposed approach.

The proposed approach consists of five steps that are described in the following sections: (A) Data Acquisition; (B) Extraction of Sentiment Scores with the VADER Algorithm; (C) Assignment of Sentiment Scores to a Discrete Scale; (D) Modelling the Relationships between Sentiment and Review Rating with Bayesian Networks; and, (E) Evaluating the Consistency between Customer Opinion and Online Rating.

A. *Data Acquistion*

In this step, the data are acquired from the database storing the review comments and the online rating about the product or service, provided by the customer. Then, they are pre-processed by being subject to cleaning in order to remove records that do not include either the review comment or the review rating. Finally, the acquired data are structured so that they feed into the next steps for further processing.

B. *Extraction of Sentiment Scores with the VADER Algorithm*

In this step, the online review comments are processed in order to extract their sentiment scores with the use of the VADER algorithm for sentiment analysis, an algorithm that has been proved to outperform several other sentiment analysis lexicons [11]. VADER sentiment is a lexical sentiment classifier and it is used to do initial sentiment labelling of each review comment [11]. A sentiment lexicon is a lexicon where the words have been annotated with semantic scores, often between -1 and 1. VADER sentiment can also aggregate sentiment scores from individual words into sentence scores. The support for sentence sentiment also takes into account booster words (e.g., "very" in "very happy") and negation words (e.g., "not" in "not happy") [5].

VADER uses a combination of qualitative and quantitative methods in order to produce a sentiment lexicon that is especially attuned to microblog-like contexts. These lexical features take into account generalizable rules that embody grammatical and syntactical conventions that humans use when expressing or emphasizing sentiment intensity [11]. VADER is applicable to various domains, such as social media text as well as product and service reviews.

C. *Assignment of Sentiment Scores to a Discrete Scale*

In this step, the sentiment scores extracted from the previous step are assigned to a discrete scale consisting of ranges of sentiment score values. The number of the scale items should be the same with the respective scale of the review rating so that they are directly comparable. For example, if the review rating takes values between 1 and 5 (which is the most common case), the sentiment scores are classified to a respective discrete scale:

- [-1, -0.6] is assigned to "DISASTER"
- (-0.6, -0.2] is assigned to "MANY THINGS NEED TO BE IMPROVED"
- (-0.2, +0.2] is assigned to "FAIR ENOUGH"

- (+0.2, +0.6] is assigned to "PERFECT"
- (+0.6, +1] is assigned to "ABSOLUTELY PERFECT"

D. *Modelling the Relationships between Sentiment and Review Rating with Bayesian Networks*

In this step, the relationships between the sentiment discrete scale created in the previous step and the review rating of the customer are modelled in a probabilistic model with the use of Bayesian Networks. A Bayesian Network (BN) is a powerful tool for knowledge representation and reasoning under conditions of uncertainty and visually presents the probabilistic relationships among a set of variables [26]. A BN has many advantages such as combination of different sources of knowledge, explicit treatment of uncertainty and support for decision analysis, and fast responses.

More formally, BNs are directed acyclic graphs whose nodes represent random variables from the domain of interest, in the Bayesian sense. Therefore, a BN is defined as a pair $B = (G, \Theta)$. $G = (V, E)$ is a Directed Acyclic Graph (DAG) where $V = \{v_1, \ldots, v_n\}$ is a collection of n nodes, $E \subset V \times V$ a collection of edges and a set of parameters Θ containing all the Conditional Probabilities (CP) of the network.

Each node $v \in V$ of the graph represents a random variable X_V with a state space $\boldsymbol{X_V}$ which can be either discrete or continuous. An edge $(v_i, v_j) \in E$ represents the conditional dependence between two nodes $v_i, v_j \in V$ where v_i is the parent of child v_j. If two nodes are not connected by an edge, they are conditional independent. Because a node can have more than one parent, let π_v the set of parents for a node $v \in V$.

Therefore, each random variable is independent of all nodes $V \setminus \pi_v$. For each node, a Conditional Probability Table (CPT) contains the CP distribution with parameters $\theta_{xi|\pi i} := P(x_i|\pi_i) \in \Theta$ for each realization x_i of X_i conditioned on π_i. The joint probability distribution over V is visualized by the BN and can be defined as

$$P(X_1, \ldots, X_n) = \prod_{i=1}^{n} P(X_i|\pi_i) \quad (1)$$

E. *Evaluating the Consistency between Customer Opinion and Online Rating*

In the last step of the proposed approach, the consistency between the customer opinion and the provided rating is evaluated in order to identify the customer behaviour. Moreover, these results may reveal the level of satisfaction of the customer when this is not explicitly evident from the review comments. For example, a customer may not mention some aspects, although they affect their opinion and thus, the online rating.

IV. APPLICATION IN HOTEL ONLINE REVIEWS FROM THE TRIPADVISOR

In this section, we present the application of the proposed approach in the tourism and hospitality industry. More specifically, we used a dataset of hotel online reviews and ratings from the TripAdvisor in order to evaluate the proposed approach for modelling the inconsistency between the review comments and the review rating. Finally, the implemented model is validated as a predictor and a learning mechanism for the adoption of future records.

A. *The Tourism and Hospitality Industry*

Recently, data available online related to tourism is increasing exponentially [27]. Sentiment analysis can effectively aid decision making in tourism, by improving the understanding of tourist experience [8]. Sentiment analysis of hotel guests' online reviews has undergone major developments in recent years [28]. These online reviews in the e-tourism era, in the format of both textual reviews (comments) and ratings, generate an electronic Word Of Mouth (eWOM) effect, which influences future customer demand and hotels' financial performance [29].

Online customer ratings play a key role in the hospitality industry [29]. Online hotel reviews also provide comparative and benchmarking insights about customer satisfaction [29][30]. Although, overall customer ratings are provided in these websites, there is a need to understand how far these ratings are consistent with the actual customer sentiments expressed through the reviews [31]. To this end, modelling the complex dynamics of online hotel review data in order to derive meaningful insights is of outmost importance [32].

B. *The TripAdvisor Dataset*

TripAdvisor is an American travel website company providing reviews from travellers about their experiences in hotels, restaurants, and monuments [8].

TABLE I. DATA SAMPLE FROM THE TRIPADVISOR

ID	***Review Title***	***Full Review***	***Rating***
1	Great location, comfortable. Neo-classical boutique hotel	Nice. Brilliant location opposite the cathedral. Bed and linen ideal for a good night's sleep. Good combination of design in neo-classical building. Quiet. The roof terrace is currently very trendy for an early evening drink. Great view. The "8 hours before sunrise" cocktail is, incidentally, fun and delicious. Breakfast has a good choice and is good quality. Staff professional and friendly. We will definitely want to revisit.	5 of 5 bubbles
2	Fairly nice hotel, not much amenities	If you want a hotel walking distance from town but don't want to be in the center of town, then this place is good. Not much on amenities and while they tell you not to drink/brush your teeth with the water, they will provide bottled water-at a fee! That just didn't feel right. The staff was friendly and the breakfast was fine-nothing out of the ordinary.	3 of 5 bubbles
3	Not worth it!!	We stayed 4 nights. We had arranged with the hotel shuttle to pick up us. It was confirmed twice. After 45 min of no show we finally took a taxi and paid 20 Euros!! The room was a little dirty. The worse part was the bathroom, towels, and the pillows they have as headboards!! We thought we will be able to walk to the town. It was impossible, there are no side walk, and the road is just dirt and not safe to walk on the street. The hotel free shuttle into the Town (which leaves every 2 hours) was good. This was the only way into town because of the hotel's location and a small number of taxis on the island. The breakfast buffet was very good and the staff here was very friendly.	2 of 5 bubbles

Tourists can read the accumulated opinions of millions of everyday tourists. Linked to this is the bubble rating (user rating), a 1–5 scale. Together with this rating, users include their opinions, which can cover the performance of a restaurant, hotel, or tourist spot. The dataset under consideration consists of 10,276 online reviews from the TripAdvisor. A sample of 3 records is shown in Table I. After pre-processing, each record includes the review title, the full review, and the rating.

C. *Implementation*

The implementation of the proposed approach was performed using the Python programming language. The VADER algorithm that extracts the sentiment scores out of the review comments was implemented with the use of the Natural Language ToolKit (NLTK) library (version 3.6.2) [33]. NLTK provides easy-to-use interfaces to over 50 corpora and lexical resources such as WordNet, along with a suite of text processing libraries for classification, tokenization, stemming, tagging, parsing, and semantic reasoning.

The Bayesian Network that models the relationships between the extracted sentiments and the review rating was implemented with the use of the PyBBN library and PyMC3 library. The former incorporates the junction tree algorithm or Probability Propagation in Trees of Clusters. PPTC is applied to BNs with all discrete variables. When dealing with a BBN with all Gaussian variables, exact inference is conducted through an incremental algorithm manipulating the means and covariance matrix. The latter performs Bayesian estimation, particularly using Markov Chain Monte Carlo (MCMC).

D. *Results*

The VADER algorithm extracts the sentiment score for each record. The sentiment scores are assigned to 5 discrete classes as it was described in Section III.C. The output of the algorithm provides a dataset with all the record IDs along with the Rating (R) ("bubbles"), each one assigned to a sentiment score (ranging from -1 to +1), and an associated class of the Discrete Scale (DS) ("DISASTER", "MANY THINGS NEED TO BE IMPROVED", "FAIR ENOUGH", "PERFECT", "ABSOLUTELY PERFECT"). Table II presents a sample output based on the records presented in the data sample of Table I.

It can be noticed that the rating does not always match to the discrete scale as derived from the sentiment scores. For instance, the comments with IDs 2,3, and 5 are assigned to "ABSOLUTELY PERFECT", since their sentiment scores are far above +0.6; however, all of these three comments are accompanied with a different rating provided by the customer. Such inconsistencies between the rating provided by the customer and the discrete scale as derived from the sentiment score exist in the whole dataset. In order to model those relationships and reveal the inconsistencies, the aforementioned output of all the records feeds into the Bayesian Network.

More specifically, the Bayesian Network consists of two layers. The upper layer includes the parent nodes with the values of the discrete scale that has been derived from the sentiment scores. The lower level includes the child nodes with the values of the online rating. Therefore, it is possible to estimate the probability of receiving a specific rating given the discrete scale. The structure of the Bayesian Network is depicted in Figure 2. Every parent node is linked to every child node. Based upon this structure, the Conditional Probabilities Table (CPT) is calculated for each node.

TABLE II. SAMPLE OUTPUT FROM THE VADER ALGORITHM

ID	*Rating*	*Sentiment Score*	*Discrete Scale*
1	5 of 5 bubbles	0.987	ABSOLUTELY PERFECT
2	3 of 5 bubbles	0.8504	ABSOLUTELY PERFECT
3	2 of 5 bubbles	-0.5471	MANY THINGS NEED TO BE IMPROVED

Based upon this structure, the parameters of the Bayesian Network are learned. Table III presents the resulting conditional probabilities of receiving a specific rating (R) given a specific discrete scale (DS) that has been derived from the sentiment score. In this way, the consistency between the customer opinion and the provided rating is evaluated in order to identify the customer behaviour. Moreover, these results may reveal the level of satisfaction of the customer when this is not explicitly evident from the review comments.

TABLE III. CONDITIONAL PROBABILITIES OF RATING GIVEN THE DISCRETE SCALE

		Discrete Scale (DS)				
	P(R|DS)	***DISASTER***	***MANY THINGS NEED TO BE IMPROVED***	***FAIR ENOUGH***	***PERFECT***	***ABSOLUTELY PERFECT***
Review Rating (R)	***1 of 5 bubbles***	45.27%	22.69%	17.99%	9.56%	1.14%
	2 of 5 bubbles	27.90%	21.85%	19.05%	14.67%	2.17%
	3 of 5 bubbles	19.97%	34.87%	33.33%	32.89%	9.04%
	4 of 5 bubbles	5.34%	11.76%	19.05%	25.56%	28.07%
	5 of 5 bubbles	1.52%	8.82%	10.58%	17.33%	59.57%

E. *Discussion*

The diagonal cells of Table III indicate the percentages of the exact consistency between the discrete scale as derived from the sentiment scores and the review rating as indicated by the customer. Based on the results, the highest consistencies exist in the extreme values, i.e. P(R = *1 of 5 bubbles* | *DS* = *"DISASTER"*) = 45.27% and P(*R* = *5 of 5 bubbles* | *DS* = *"ABSOLUTELY PERFECT"*) = 59.57%.

Interestingly, for the rest of the review ratings, the highest percentages do not belong to the diagonal cells indicating a higher level of inconsistency between the customer opinion and the review rating. The greatest difference exists in the review rating of 2 bubbles, since P(*R* = *2 of 5 bubbles* | *DS* = *"DISASTER"*) = 27.90%. The cases of 3 and 4 bubbles have a lower difference with the respective diagonal cells, i.e. P(*R* = *3 of 5 bubbles* | *DS* = *"MANY THINGS NEED TO BE IMPROVED"*) = 34.87%, and P(*R* = *4 of 5 bubbles* | *DS* = *"ABSOLUTELY PERFECT"*) = 28.07%.

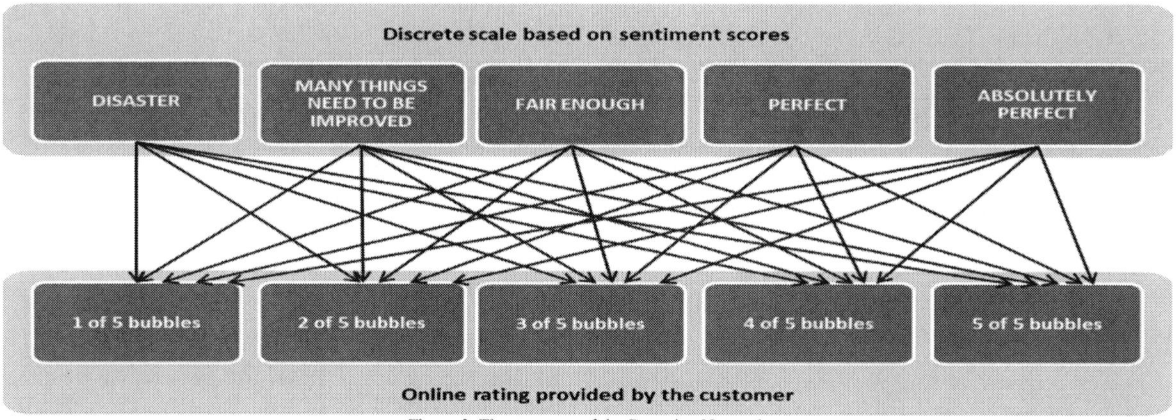

Figure 2. The structure of the Bayesian Network.

The results also show the trend that the ratings of 2 and 3 bubbles tend to be higher than the discrete values derived from the sentiment score. On the other hand, the trend of the rating with 4 bubbles tends to be lower than the discrete values derived from the sentiment score. It should be noted that the nature of the discrete scale does not allow distinguishing the values that are close to the value that indicates a scale change. For example, the value -0.61 is assigned to the "DISASTER" scale, but there is a high uncertainty about whether it belongs to that scale or to the next one, i.e. "MANY THINGS NEED TO BE IMPROVED". This limitation will be addressed in our future work. However, even in this case, it can be noticed that a significant percentage of online review comments are not consistent with the provided rating. This is evident by the fact that the percentages belonging to cells that are not near the diagonal are relatively high.

These results validate the statement that there are usually inconsistencies between the review comments and the review ratings. As already mentioned, this fact occurs for two main reasons. First, different people use different ways of expressing themselves. For example, the phrase "very good" may reflect a different level of satisfaction among different customers. Therefore, there are variations in the sentiment scores extracted from the review comments. Second, the customers select some main points to be mentioned in the review comments. However, there are various aspects that affect their level of satisfaction and their preferences that are not mentioned at all and remain at their own mind. In this sense, there may be review comments with similar content and sentiment but different ratings.

The application of the proposed approach in the e-tourism domain reveals such kind of inconsistencies. From the business perspective, the proposed approach can support product and service managers to look beyond the ratings into the sentiments of the customers. Human language can express emotions which quantitative ratings cannot capture. On the other hand, customers can choose from services that brings them desired satisfaction. The proposed approach enables customers to look beyond online customer ratings while selecting products and services. It brings forth experiences of previous customers in a qualitative and interpretable manner, so that new customers can make informed decisions.

Going through several thousands of comments present online could be a tedious task. The proposed approach summarizes the underlying sentiments of the comments for customers to easily comprehend and decide. Sometimes, fake ratings can distort the actual image of the hotels for the customers. Our study presents a framework for relating ratings with reviews, which can be used for validation.

V. CONCLUSION

Customers have access to different sources of information, and generate their own content and share their views and experiences, which are expressed through online review comments and ratings about products and services. However, the increasing amount of data has reached a level that makes manual processing impossible, requiring data-driven approaches.

Despite the large amount of research works dealing with sentiment analysis, the consistency between the customer opinions expressed in review comments and the rating that they provide has not been explored. In this paper, we propose an approach incorporating the VADER algorithm for extracting the polarity of the review comments and Bayesian Networks for revealing the relationships between the aforementioned sentiment scores and the online rating.

The proposed approach was validated in the tourism domain using a dataset with hotel reviews, extracted from the TripAdvisor. The proposed approach is able to model effectively the aforementioned relationships in order to derive the consistency between the review comments and the online rating. The results showed there are usually inconsistencies between the review comments and the review ratings, because different people use different ways of expressing themselves, while the customers select some main points to be mentioned in the review comments.

However, there are various aspects that affect their level of satisfaction and their preferences that are not mentioned at all. From the business perspective, the proposed approach can support product and service managers to look beyond the ratings into the sentiments of the customers. On the other hand, customers can choose from services that brings them desired satisfaction.

Our future work will move towards the following directions: First, we will implement fuzzy logic approaches in order to address the issues related to the fact that different people use different ways of expressing themselves leading to variations in sentiment scores. Second, we will apply probabilistic and fuzzy approaches in order to relax the discrete scale derived from the sentiment scores in order to tackle with sentiments that are close to the borders between two discrete values. Third, we will examine how different aspects of the review comments (e.g., different services of the hotels) affect the overall sentiment and rating.

REFERENCES

[1] L. Yang, Y. Li, J. Wang, and R. S. Sherratt, "Sentiment analysis for E-commerce product reviews in Chinese based on sentiment lexicon and deep learning," IEEE Acc., vol. 8, no. 1, pp. 23522-23530, 2020.

[2] S. Hu, A. Kumar, F. Al-Turjman, S. Gupta, and S. Seth, "Reviewer credibility and sentiment analysis based user profile modelling for online product recommendation," IEEE Acc., vol. 8, no. 1, pp. 26172-26189, 2020.

[3] E. Ma, M. Cheng, and A. Hsiao, "Sentiment analysis–a review and agenda for future research in hospitality contexts," Int. J. of Contemp. Hosp. Man., 2018.

[4] R. S. Jagdale, V. S. Shirsat, and S. N. Deshmukh, "Sentiment analysis on product reviews using machine learning techniques," in Cognitive Informatics and Soft Computing. pp. 639-647, Springer, Singapore, 2019.

[5] A. Borg and M. Boldt, "Using VADER sentiment and SVM for predicting customer response sentiment," Exp. Sys. with App., vol. 162, no. 1, pp. 113746, 2020.

[6] M. T. Khan and S. Khalid, "Sentiment analysis for health care", in Big Data: Concepts, Methodologies, Tools, and Applications, pp. 676-689, IGI Global, 2016.

[7] K. Ravi, and V. Ravi, "A survey on opinion mining and sentiment analysis: tasks, approaches and applications," Knowl. Sys., vol. 89, no. 1, pp. 14-46, 2015.

[8] A. Valdivia, M. V. Luzón, and F. Herrera, "Sentiment analysis in tripadvisor," IEEE Intel. Sys., vol. 32, no. 4, pp. 72-77, 2017.

[9] M. Taboada, J. Brooke, M. Tofiloski, K. Voll, and M. Stede, "Lexicon-based methods for sentiment analysis," Comp. Ling., vol. 37, no. 2, pp. 267-307, 2011.

[10] C. S. Khoo and S. B. Johnkhan, " Lexicon-based sentiment analysis: Comparative evaluation of six sentiment lexicons," J. Inform. Sc., vol. 44, no. 4, pp. 491-511, 2018.

[11] C. Hutto and E. Gilbert, "Vader: A parsimonious rule-based model for sentiment analysis of social media text," in Proceedings of the International AAAI Conference on Web and Social Media, vol. 8, no. 1, 2014.

[12] S. Anis, S. Saad, and M. Aref, "Sentiment Analysis of Hotel Reviews Using Machine Learning Techniques," in International Conference on Advanced Intelligent Systems and Informatics, pp. 227-234, Springer, Cham, 2020.

[13] V. Kharde and P. Sonawane, "Sentiment analysis of twitter data: a survey of techniques," arXiv preprint arXiv:1601.06971, 2016.

[14] V. S. Shirsat, R. S. Jagdale, and S. N. Deshmukh, "Sentence level sentiment identification and calculation from news articles using machine learning techniques," in Computing, Communication and Signal Processing, pp. 371-376, Springer, Singapore, 2019.

[15] N. Nandal, R. Tanwar, and J. Pruthi, "Machine learning based aspect level sentiment analysis for Amazon products," Spatial Information Research, vol. 28, no. 5, pp. 601-607, 2020.

[16] R. M. Duwairi and I. Qarqaz, "Arabic sentiment analysis using supervised classification," in 2014 International Conference on Future Internet of Things and Cloud, pp. 579-583, IEEE, 2014.

[17] R. Xia, C. Zong, and S. Li, "Ensemble of feature sets and classification algorithms for sentiment classification," Inf. Sc., vol. 181, no. 6, pp. 1138-1152, 2011.

[18] A. Prabhat and V. Khullar, "Sentiment classification on big data using Naïve Bayes and logistic regression," in 2017 International Conference on Computer Communication and Informatics (ICCCI), pp. 1-5, IEEE, 2017.

[19] B. K. Bhavitha, A. P. Rodrigues, and N. N. Chiplunkar, "Comparative study of machine learning techniques in sentimental analysis.," in 2017 International conference on inventive communication and computational technologies (ICICCT), pp. 216-221, IEEE, 2017.

[20] A. Y. Chua and S. Banerjee, "Understanding review helpfulness as a function of reviewer reputation, review rating, and review depth," J. of the Assoc. for Inf. Sc. and Tech., vol. 66, no. 2, pp. 354-362, 2015.

[21] C. Chen, M. Zhang, Y. Liu, and S. Ma, "Neural attentional rating regression with review-level explanations," in Proceedings of the 2018 World Wide Web Conference, pp. 1583-1592, 2018.

[22] J. Hassan and U. Shoaib, "Multi-class review rating classification using deep recurrent neural network," Neur. Proc. Let., vol. 51, no. 1, pp. 1031-1048, 2020.

[23] B. H., Ahmed and A. S. Ghabayen, "Review rating prediction framework using deep learning," J. of Amb. Intel. and Hum. Comp., vol.1, no. 1, pp. 1-10, 2020.

[24] S. Seo, J. Huang, H. Yang, and Y. Liu, "Interpretable convolutional neural networks with dual local and global attention for review rating prediction," in Proceedings of the eleventh ACM conference on recommender systems, pp. 297-305, 2017.

[25] W. Songpan, " The analysis and prediction of customer review rating using opinion mining," in 2017 IEEE 15th International Conference on Software Engineering Research, Management and Applications (SERA), pp. 71-77, IEEE, 2017.

[26] J. Cheng, R. Greiner, J. Kelly, D. Bell and W. Liu, "Learning Bayesian networks from data: an information-theory based approach," Artif. Intell. Vol. 137, no. 1–2, pp. 43–90, 2002.

[27] A. R. Alaei, S. Becken, and B. Stantic, "Sentiment analysis in tourism: capitalizing on big data," J. of Trav. Res., vol. 58, no. 2, pp. 175-191, 2019.

[28] J. Luo, S. Huang, and R. Wang, "A fine-grained sentiment analysis of online guest reviews of economy hotels in China," J. of Hosp. Mark. & Manag., vol. 30, no. 1, pp. 71-95, 2021.

[29] K. L. Xie, Z. Zhang, and Z. Zhang, "The business value of online consumer reviews and management response to hotel performance," Int. J. of Hosp. Manag., vol. 43, no. 1, pp. 1-12, 2014.

[30] A. G. Mauri and R. Minazzi, "Web reviews influence on expectations and purchasing intentions of hotel potential customers," Int. J. of Hosp. Manag., vol. 34, no. 1, pp. 99-107, 2013.

[31] M. Geetha, P. Singha, and S. Sinha, "Relationship between customer sentiment and online customer ratings for hotels-An empirical analysis," Tour. Manag., vol. 61, pp. 43-54, 2017.

[32] A. Bousdekis, and D. Kardaras, "Hotel Quality Evaluation from Online Reviews Using Fuzzy Pattern Matching and Fuzzy Cognitive Maps," in The Ninth International Conference on Data Analytics (DATA ANALYTICS), 2020.

[33] S. Bird, E. Klein, and E. Loper, "Natural language processing with Python: analyzing text with the natural language toolkit," O'Reilly Media, Inc., 2009.

[34] J. Salvatier, T. V. Wiecki, and C. Fonnesbeck, "Probabilistic programming in Python using PyMC3," PeerJ Computer Science, 2, 2016.